THE CARAVAN
MANUAL

A GUIDE TO MAINTENANCE, REPAIRS AND IMPROVEMENTS

JOHN WICKERSHAM

Haynes

"There you are!" cried the Toad, straddling and expanding himself. "There's real life for you, ... here today, up and off to somewhere else tomorrow! Travel, change, interest, excitement! The whole world before you, and a horizon that's always changing! ... Come inside and look at the arrangements. Planned 'em all myself, I did!"

Mr Toad proudly shows off his caravan. From **Wind in the Willows**, by Kenneth Grahame, first published 1908.

© John Wickersham 1993

First published in 1993.
Reprinted 1993 & 1994.

Published by:
Haynes Publishing
Sparkford, Nr Yeovil, Somerset
BA22 7JJ, England

A catalogue record for this book is available from the British Library

ISBN 1 85010 894 3

Printed in Great Britain by
J. H. Haynes & Co. Ltd.

While every effort is taken to ensure the accuracy of the information given in this book, no liability can be accepted by the author or publishers for any loss, damage or injury caused by errors in, or omissions from, the information given.

Gas Regulations
Gas Regulations and the way in which appliance manufacturers interpret them regarding the installation of their products are subject to continuing change. It is ***strongly recommended*** that anyone contemplating the installation of a gas appliance should consult the applicance manufacturer's customer service department before undertaking any work themselves. This may reveal different recommendations from those stated here, in which it is suggested that a competent amateur could consider tackling the preliminary carpentry, and fitting work in accordance with the installation instructions. However, it is suggested in the Chapters concerned with gas systems and appliances, that work on the gas connection(s), flues and the final testing of an installation should always be entrusted to a competent gas engineer.

Contents

Acknowledgements

Two things have always puzzled me. Why are there so many people who share my enthusiasm for caravanning, and why are there so few books to help us enjoy our hobby?

The first question is left for reflection; the second is one I am now able to answer. It has taken five years for this book to reach completion and dozens of people have helped to make this possible; and that was just to prepare the text and to take the photographs! Before that, there were thirty five years spent learning about caravans, experiences which started as a child around the time when a British expedition first conquered Everest.

To be invited to write a practical manual was an honour; fulfilling the task was worse than conquering a mountain. A manual concerned with caravans is inevitably going to touch on a diverse array of technical subjects. This was particularly daunting In spite of having built a caravan from scratch and repaired many more, there was always the worry that a technical error would creep into the text.

In the quest for accuracy, I decided to consult countless people whose skills and qualifications cover many areas. I also made sure that certain key chapters were carefully checked by experts in particular fields. These helpers are owed a great debt of gratitude and receive my sincere thanks. Then there are others, too, who passed on valuable advice, lent equipment to test, and permitted me to reproduce their own photographs and drawings.

Even now, there's undoubtedly an error or two which missed our scrutiny, or perhaps a new widget or whatever is about to revolutionise caravanning comfort and has been accidentally overlooked. Suffice it to say, this is an attempt to fill a desperate gap in the caravanning literature; but of course, it couldn't include everything.

The aim to achieve technical accuracy was helped by the following people:

Chapters One and Two General information on matters of caravans and towing were checked by Barry Williams, Editor of *Caravan* magazine. Barry has been closely involved with the industry for many years, he is a judge in the Towcar of the Year competition, and as a break from editing the longest running caravan journal in Britain, spends his holidays caravanning.

Chapter Three A number of specialists were associated with this chapter, some of whom were able to check certain sections. I am grateful to Brendan Witter, Rodney Witter and Keith Colder of Witter Towing Brackets. In addition, Ray Jordan, who is responsible for Bulldog products, and David Williamson formerly of Scott Halleys, both of whom were valued advisers.

Chapter Four The information on caravan chassis received extremely close scrutiny from Richard Miller-Mead, Tony Robinson and Tim Hammond of

Al-Ko Kober Ltd. (formerly Al-Ko B&B Ltd). Their technical knowledge is enviable. I am especially grateful to Mr P.M. Lelliott, Managing Director for permission to use illustrations, and to Iain Stanford, Marketing Manager who accepted me on to an Al-Ko Kober Service engineer's course

Chapter Five Successfully completing a further service engineers' course in body repairs at Compass Caravans was also invaluable. In this respect I am indebted to Raymond Cook, Managing Director of Compass Caravans together with Eric Hepplewhite and John Clarke. I am also grateful to Steve Trossell and the staff of CI Caravans for showing me, the production techniques at the Newmarket Factory. Many of my photographs showing construction in progress were taken during visits to Compass and CI factories.

Chapter Six Help in many caravan building and refurbishment schemes has been given by John Turpin of Caralux Upholstery Ltd. Soft furnishings and upholstery are crucial for comfort.

Chapters Seven and Eight The accuracy of both chapters dealing with electricity was verified by John Chamberlain, Managing Director of Plug-in Systems Ltd. At an earlier stage, technical staff from Hawkins Electrical also checked the accuracy of some of the drafts.

Chapter Nine A.G. 'Lucky' Moore is one of the industry's best-known experts in water pumping systems. Having checked the chapter, 'Lucky' also arranged for it to be proof-read by Nigel Eves, Chief Executive of Munster Simms Engineering Ltd. The visit to the 'Whale' factory in Northern Ireland was most helpful, too. John Corbett of Carver (Engineers) Ltd also checked the accuracy of information relating to the Crystal Water system.

Chapters Ten and Eleven The chapters on gas and gas appliances were the hardest to write and took the longest time to complete. I was especially indebted to the proof reading carried out by a major company in Britain which has a long association with LPG. Their request, not to be mentioned by name, is honoured. Their acute concern about safety is shared, and the view, that the installation of LPG gas equipment must not be undertaken by do-it-yourselfers, is reiterated in the text. I am also grateful to Charles Moran and John Corbett of Carver (Engineers) Ltd who, with similar misgivings, checked the accuracy of information regarding Carver appliances and gas installation in general. The recommendations received from David Whitehead, Assistant Technical Officer of the National Caravan Council also led to additional cautionary notes being added to the text. In addition, Ron Dodd has been especially helpful regarding appliances distributed by Gimeg Rondo.

Chapter Twelve The accuracy of the chapter on refrigeration was achieved with the help of Michael Leete, Manager of Electrolux Leisure. With the assistance of Mike Green, Hugh Lamberton and Doug South, every detail was checked with great care.

Chapter Thirteen A number of people assisted with this chapter. In particular I am especially grateful to Barry Hogarth formerly of Optimus UK.

Chapter Fourteen I am grateful to the manufacturers and distributors of the products reviewed, fitted and illustrated in this chapter. The reports exemplify the kind of things an owner might fit, but in no way is it implied that other products might not be equally suitable for installation.

In addition to those who checked or were involved with specific chapters, thanks are also expressed to the following people whose contribution was appreciated:

Michael Angerson (Trylon Ltd)
Wim Batiste (Powerpart, BCA Leisure Ltd)
Alan Baxter (formerly of Fiamma UK)
Tony Bradford (Former Editor, *Caravan* magazine)
David Bridle (Editor, *Caravan, Motor Caravan & Camping Mart*)
Jacki Buist (Editor, *Practical Caravan*)
Stuart Craig (*Caravan Life*)
Richard Ford-Glazebrook Grade (UK) Ltd
Peter Frost (Editor, *Camping and Caravanning*)
Dorothy Gatiss (Compass Caravans Ltd)
Paul Gregg (LabCraft Ltd)
Gordon Hawkins (Hawkins Electrical)
Jim Hewitt (Shurflo, Leisure Accessories Ltd)
Janella Horne (Automotive Products)
Rex Howells (H. Burden Ltd)
'Lachie' McCleod (Traffic Dept, Strathclyde Police)
Peter Miller (CI Caravans, formerly of Thetford Ltd)
Les Siddle (Lam-Plas (Durham) Ltd)
Graham Westerby (Plug-in Systems Ltd)

Finally, it was a privilege to learn that Mr Edward Marriott, formerly Press and Publicity Officer of The Caravan Club put my name forward to Haynes Publishing Group when the idea of producing this manual was first discussed.

John Wickersham

Chapter 1

INTRODUCTION AND OVERVIEW

Practical matters

Information published in 1992 by the National Caravan Council (NCC) reported that an estimated 560,000 touring caravans were in use the previous year in the United Kingdom. Today, it is almost certain that the number of owners is even higher.

Amongst this high number, there are many practical people. This is hardly surprising because on a caravanning holiday there

are gas cylinders to change, batteries to charge and towing electrics to check. Some owners relish this side of caravanning and tackle their own repairs back at home; others upgrade their caravan's fixtures and fittings. Taking this into account, it is surprising, therefore, that no-one has recently published a manual guiding owners how to service, repair or improve their caravan. Until now.

Appropriately, this much needed book is joining a formidable list of titles in the Haynes Manual series. Many readers will have bought a Haynes Manual for a car they've owned. Invariably some of the pages will have greasy finger marks showing that the book has guided its owner through a successful repair job.

This book is about caravans rather than cars, but it will be a

Left, top: Caravan holidays at home are extremely popular and the National Caravan Council reports that over 600,000 people in the United Kingdom are caravan owners.

Left, below: A large proportion of caravan owners tour abroad; but wherever the venue, the caravan needs to be in good working order.

Caravanners are often practical people. There are tasks to carry out on holiday and equally important tasks to perform when you've returned home.

mark of failure if its pages remain clean. The aim is to encourage caravanners to carry out jobs themselves using the guidance given in words and pictures. Other Haynes Manuals like those on car body repairs and car electrics are helpful too, and these receive mention in the text.

Inevitably there are many subjects to cover. Accordingly a large part of the material has been drawn up with guidance from experts associated with the caravan industry. The final chapters were also checked carefully by specialists in different fields. Key chapters covering things like chassis construction, refrigeration, pumps, or gas appliances were all verified by qualified people working in these particular fields.

From the outset it was acknowledged that there wouldn't be enough space to include everything about caravanning. In consequence it was decided not to include material on motor caravans, even though much of the

This manual looks at caravans from a wide age range. There are thousands of elderly models giving good service like this 1972 Lynton Javelin.

content has an undoubted relevance. Similarly, the focus is on touring caravans rather than static holiday homes.

As regards the scope, it must also be acknowledged that some jobs are **not** appropriate for amateurs to tackle. For example in the chapter dealing with gas appliances, some jobs are described as straightforward whereas in other matters the reader is clearly instructed to seek the services of a qualified gas engineer.

In addition, some items of equipment described in this manual are not 'user serviceable'. For example items like inoperable heavy duty flasher relays or electronic circuitry in a fluorescent light fitting should be replaced rather than repaired.

Background information
In a National Caravan Council and National Opinion Poll survey conducted in 1981, it was found that the 'useful life' of a touring caravan is approximately fourteen years. However, there are still many 1970s second-hand caravans being advertised for sale and a substantial number of elderly models provide their owners with good service.

Accordingly, this manual

covers models from a wide age band. There would be little point devoting most space to the latest products. Moreover, the life of any caravan is lengthened if it receives regular maintenance. It can also be upgraded by fitting appliances like a new refrigerator, or new service items such as an electric water pump. The notion of a fourteen year 'useful working life' can be disregarded if an owner is prepared to spend time looking after a caravan.

The life of any caravan is lengthened if it receives regular maintenance. Cleaning is just one of the routine jobs.

Taking age into account, the manual often prefaces a section with historical notes on a particular topic. One reason for this is to help an owner identify the age of a second-hand caravan which he or she is planning to purchase. Unlike cars, caravans have no DVLA registration document. Whilst there may have been a stamped metal label attached to the drawbar, these have often been detached or defaced. Hence our descriptions of changing designs helps you to pin down the age or the origin of a

caravan. In particular, chapter 5, which deals with caravan structure, discusses important changes in constructional technique which provide invaluable clues to the true age of a model. Needless to say, *some* second-hand 'bargains' are claimed to be younger than they really are.

Handbook help
Until recently, many new caravans were not sold with detailed handbooks. There have even been instances where fundamental information like recommended tyre pressures has been accidentally omitted.

But things have improved and technical information must be included in a caravan handbook in order to meet British Standards (BS). If this is omitted, a caravan does not meet the requirements for receiving a BS badge of approval – a scheme which is administered by the National Caravan Council. Noting the paucity of documentation previously provided, this strict approach is fully justified. A customer who has spent many thousands of pounds on a new model deserves a detailed 'owners' handbook.

With regard to a secondhand caravan purchased without a handbook, much of the data contained in this manual will provide the appropriate guidance. In addition, Owners' Associations can often provide information about a particular model.

Contents of the manual
Early chapters consider the towcar and adaptations that have to be made. The exterior of caravans is covered next, looking at both the body and the chassis. Moving inside, general issues are covered such as the structure of furniture followed by matters relating to soft furnishings.

Chapters are also devoted to the main services: low voltage provision, mains voltage, water services and gas supply. Specific appliances are covered too, like refrigerators and space heating systems. Finally some ideas are given for upgrading and renovating a caravan. Some of the projects carried out on the author's own caravans are reported and everything discussed has been tried and tested.

British Standards, EEC Directive and NCC Certification
In most cases, caravans manufactured in this country fulfil British Standards' specifications. Some imported products similarly comply, although in a few cases this compliance is a result of adaptations made by the importer to meet BS criteria. However, this is not the case for all foreign imports.

Caravans must also be equipped with systems mentioned in the current Road Vehicles (Construction and Use) Regulations and EEC Directive 71/320 (ECE13). Meantime, any number plate displayed on a caravan must comply with BS AU145a and be marked accordingly.

In general, this manual avoids making repeated reference to prescriptions laid down in the EEC Directive and British Standards' publications. However, in this introduction, it is appropriate to explain that for several years, the British Standards governing touring caravans has been BS 4626. This is presently undergoing revision and the replacement standard, BS 6765 will derive much of its content from International Standards. For instance, BS 6765 Part 3: 1989 which deals with specification requirements for 12v DC electrical installations was based on ISO 8818. At the time of writing, much of Parts 1 and 2 of BS 6765 will be drawn from ISO 7422 which deals with Leisure Accommodation Vehicles; habitation requirements. This includes elements such as the design and construction of caravans. It is anticipated that by the time this manual is published, manufacturers will be complying with all three parts of British Standards 6765.

Legislation
Caravans are rigidly covered by legislation, and like British Standards' criteria, this is ever-changing as well. For this reason, the legal elements currently in force are only mentioned briefly with an accompanying cautionary comment to check the latest position. Requirements in force some years ago such as the display of a 50 mph plate and the display of Kerbside Weight on the drawbar are two of many elements which have changed.

Inevitably, legislation is often complex and some points are only of interest to the caravan manufacturer. But issues like speed limits *are* important. When towing a touring caravan, the maximum speed limits in the UK (current in July 1993), are 60 mph on motorways and dual carriageways. On other roads, the limit is 50 mph. In both cases these limits only apply if there is not a lower limit in force.

Another issue of importance is the fact that when towing, you are not permitted to use the outside lane of a three-, four- or five-lane motorway. Moreover, the driver must also have a full driving licence; a provisional licence is not acceptable.

Matters on legislation issues are often contained in literature available from the caravanning clubs. The reader must keep up-to-date on this matter, particularly with regard to changes which inevitably occur as a result of developing partnerships with our European neighbours.

Chapter 2

TOWING MATTERS

The majority of caravanners tow with a saloon or hatchback car. Indeed it is most fortunate that you don't need to purchase a heavy duty vehicle like a Range Rover for the job. Nevertheless, certain guidelines have to be followed when pairing a car and caravan and the aim of this chapter is to deal with the issues involved.

Car manufacturers

In recent years, an increasing number of motor manufacturers have recognised that motorists often use their vehicles for towing. For instance Citroen, Ford, Vauxhall and Volvo have produced literature on the subject and accessories like extension mirrors, tow brackets, and electrical conversion kits appear in their lists of optional extras.

In addition, the annual 'Towcar of the Year Award' has helped reinforce this need. Before the Award's inauguration in 1978, car manufacturers often paid no attention to the fact that there were many people who wanted to tow a caravan. But attitudes have changed. Market

analysis has shown manufacturers that many owners buy a car on account of its merits as a towing vehicle; they have little interest in the number of seconds it takes to accelerate from 0 – 60 mph.

With caravans hitched, the Towcar contest is held on a test track where a team of judges assesses features like traction, hillclimbing ability, ride, suspension, handling, stability, acceleration, braking, general performance and so on. The outcome is reported in the caravanning press and there have been vehicles with front-wheel-drive, rear-wheel-drive and four-wheel-drive. Moreover, models from nine different manufacturers have won the award. Since 1978, winners have been:

1978 Rover 3500
1979 Renault 20TS
1980 Peugeot 505
1981 Toyota Crown Super
1982 BMW 528i
1983 Volkswagen Santana
1984 Citroen BX 16TRS
1985 Volvo 360 GLEi
1986 Ford Sierra XR4x4

1987 Renault 21GTS
1988 Vauxhall Senator 3.0i CD
1989 Vauxhall Cavalier SRi 2.0i
1990 Vauxhall Cavalier 4x4 2.0i
1991 Rover 416 GTi
1992 Volvo 940 SE Turbo
1993 Vauxhall Calibra
        Turbo 4 x 4

These are the outright winners, but the contest also includes class winners from different price groups. Since 1991, special class awards are given for diesel cars and 'all terrain' vehicles as well.

More manuacturers realise that cars are sometimes needed for towing, and vehicle specifications give the maximum weight which can be handled. However, this sometimes differs from recommendations given by the caravanning clubs or the National Caravan Council. Some car manufacturers overstate performance potential and use engine pulling power as the key criterion. But weight ratios, mentioned in the Car and Caravan weight ratios Section also have to be considered.

The majority of caravanners tow with a saloon or a hatchback car.

Whilst four wheel drive 'off road' vehicles make excellent towcars, you don't need to own a model like this to tow a typical touring caravan.

Courses in towing techniques arranged by The Caravan Club enable beginners to acquire skill and confidence at private venues before setting out on the roads.

(courtesy Caravan Club)

Caravanning clubs

Towing guidance is available from the caravan and camping clubs. There are Owners' Clubs representing particular makes of caravan and groups such as the Retired Caravanners' Association, the Services Caravan Club, and caravanning clubs connected to Church denominations.

However, the two largest clubs are the Caravan Club whose Head Office is at East Grinstead and the Camping and Caravanning Club whose Central Office is at Coventry. Their combined memberships approach half a million and advice on many topics is available. For instance the Caravan Club produces Information Leaflets on subjects like *'Choice of Towcar'* and *'Choice of Trailer Caravan'*. They also sell instructional video programmes such as *'Confident Caravanning'*. Towing techniques and manoeuvrability skills can also be learned on courses run by The Caravan Club which are based at old airfields or similar venues.

Towing guides

A further source of towing information is the Caravan Club Handbook, entitled, *'Your Practical Guide to Caravanning'*. This, however, is only available for members.

Another helpful publication is called, *'The Caravan Towing Code'*. This is jointly compiled by the Tourer Marketing Group of the National Caravan Council, The Caravan Writers' Guild, The Caravan Club, The Camping & Caravanning Club and the Department of Transport. This costs £2.00 and can be obtained either from a caravan dealer or direct from the National Caravan Council (NCC). The address appears in the Appendix.

Finally, promotional launches by the NCC have included the 'Caravanning: Get up and Go' campaign. This has been supported by a free booklet entitled *'Everything you need to know about caravans'*. This first appeared in 1990 and to meet demand, a further edition was published in March 1991.

National journals

In addition to members' magazines circulated by the two main national clubs, the caravanning press is another important source of information. Journals appear every month and contain valuable advice on towing, purchasing, product reviews, practical features and so on. In addition, there are useful data listings on towcar capacities, caravan weights, dimensions, and prices. Editorial policy also includes clear recommendations about weight relationships between the towcar and its caravan.

Car and caravan weight ratios

A fully laden caravan can be surprisingly heavy and this has two implications. Firstly, the power of its towcar must be adequate, with power in hand to complete overtaking manoeuvres and to cope with hill starts. Secondly, the relative weight of a caravan and its towcar must be checked to ensure that there is no likelihood of instability.

Several terms are used when dealing with weight differentials and the explanations below are important to understand:

1. Car Kerbside Weight (KW): The car's weight, including tow bracket, a full tank of petrol, a normal load including toolkit, standard equipment like a spare wheel, but excluding the driver and other occupants.

2. Maximum Laden Weight (MLW): The permitted total weight of a fully loaded caravan as stated by the caravan manufacturer.

3. Delivered Weight (DW): The weight of an empty caravan as it leaves the works.

4. Actual Laden Weight (ALW): The weight of a caravan when packed and ready for the road.

5. Loading Margin (LM): The maximum weight of the load you can carry, established after subtracting DW from MLW.

6. Nose Weight (NW): The maximum noseweight which can be placed on the towball of the towing vehicle.

The permitted noseweight often varies, and you may find different maximum limits given by the car manufacturer and the manufacturer of a towing bracket. Sometimes a limit is stamped on the top of a caravan coupling head as well. For obvious reasons, the lowest limit is the one which must not be exceeded. In the event, some vehicles can take an unusually high noseweight and the upper limit for a 1991 Citroen XM is 100 kg (220 lb). However, this is not relevant for a caravanner whose coupling head is likely to be rated with a much lower figure.

The typical loading on a caravan towing coupling is 50 – 75 kg (110 – 165 lb). Some manufacturers specify the lower figure of 50 kg but this may not be the same for all models in the range. For example, in a listing of Ford vehicles appearing in *'What will your car tow?'* (Published 1990, Link House Publishers as a supplement to *'Caravan Magazine'*), the maximum noseweight for a 1990 Sierra is reported as 50 kg; the figure for the smaller Escort is 75 kg.

Also important is the relationship of the KW of the towcar and the ALW of the caravan. In general, the heavier the towcar the better and caravanners are strongly recommended not to tow a caravan if its Actual Laden Weight exceeds 85% of the towcar's Kerbside Weight. This recommendation is in the interests of stability and helps avoid the risk of 'snaking' described in Chapter Three.

When contemplating the purchase of a new car, readers often write to magazines asking which vehicles will achieve the 85% weight recommendation needed for their caravan. To find an answer, the first step is to establish the caravan's actual laden weight (ALW) by loading it up with holiday gear and taking it to a public weighbridge. The ALW must then be multiplied by 1.2 to arrive at the minimum kerbside weight needed by the tow car.

Notwithstanding the wisdom behind the 85% caravan/car weight ratio, a driver with long experience of towing may be able to exceed this loading recommendation. Even so, when towing with a conventional saloon, hatchback, coupe, estate or convertible car, it is most important *never* to allow the weight of the caravan to *exceed* the weight of the towing vehicle. In a few exceptional cases, it is accepted that certain commercial vehicles and Land Rovers are able to tow trailers whose weight actually exceeds their own weight. But this is an exceptional situation and even the most experienced driver would have to exercise particular vigilance.

Engine power and gearing
The power of a vehicle's engine is also important. When providing towing data, some car manufacturers base their recommendations on a vehicle's capability to restart on a 12% gradient, i.e. around 1 in 8. This introduces the subject of torque, or 'turning power'.

If the phrase 'horses for courses' implies that a Grand National Winner may prove a poor performer towing a heavy cart, the converse also applies. A cart horse offers no contest on a race track. In the automotive context, highly tuned sports saloons may be wholly unsatisfactory performers when saddled with a caravan. This is because their engines are built to produce maximum torque at high engine speed. However, a good towcar needs an engine which has generous torque at *low* engine speeds.

A vehicle whose engine has good 'low-end torque' might not be one which achieves high top speeds. But this is unlikely to concern the caravanner, especially when taking into account the maximum speed limits currently enforced in Britain.

Good low-end torque is also important to note regarding vehicles with a fifth gear. When towing at the legal limit on a motorway in this country (60 mph), fifth gear will mean that engine speed is notably slow. Moreover, if an engine achieves its best torque at high rpm, towing in fifth gear may be disappointingly sluggish, particularly if this top gear is markedly higher than the normal 1:1 ratio of fourth gear. It is particularly annoying if you have to keep dropping down to fourth gear to avoid a labouring engine. Further guidance on this can frequently be found in the literature published by the Caravan Clubs.

Questions are also regularly raised regarding automatic transmission. At one time, the caravanner was advised not to purchase a car with an automatic gearbox. This was because the transmission oil could overheat when towing, with disastrous results. This can be overcome by fitting a special oil cooler. Nowadays, however, an oil cooling system is a standard feature, and this has led to a complete reversal in recommendations.

The modern four-speed automatic is often a good performer without the disappointing economy of earlier three speed transmission systems. You can also over-ride the automatic 'drive' mode if a gradient causes the vehicle to keep changing up and down on account of the road speed. This facility of being able to lock into a low gear is also invaluable when manoeuvring a caravan on a muddy site.

Bearing in mind that there is no clutch on a vehicle with automatic transmission, this gives another clear advantage when towing in slow moving conditions. In traffic jams, clutch wear and overheating is one of the problems on a manually operated gearbox. Not surprisingly, the automatic gearbox is now regarded as having particular merit for a towcar.

Drive, suspension and fuel
Other issues include the front versus rear-wheel-drive argument. Generally a towcar with front-wheel-drive is inclined to lose some of its traction when towing, though it isn't usually a serious problem. Rear-wheel-drive is normally better. However, the best traction is achieved with a 4x4 model and driving such a car is most impressive.

In addition, the suspension is inclined to be soft on some cars although there are towing aids to produce a firmer system. Connected to this is the length of rear overhang as well. Obviously it is better to have a tow ball situated as close to the rear axle as possible; if a car has a boot which projects a long way rearwards of the back axle, a heavy noseweight is more detrimental to the suspension system.

Lastly, there's a growing support for diesel cars. With the benefit of a turbo charger, the performance is enhanced greatly, sufficient to impress the devotees of petrol engined vehicles who have hitherto dismissed diesels as sluggish.

Together with growing interest in lead-free petrol, the

fuel issue is something else to consider when buying a towcar.

Caravan choice
When purchasing a caravan, many people make their choice on the basis of an interior layout or the colour of the upholstery. These points are important, but towing matters shouldn't be forgotten, particularly the length of a caravan.

A newcomer to caravanning is certainly unwise to start with a long 'van. Generous living space is attractive, but buying an awning might be a better option. There's no doubt that some of the longer caravans currently available are unsuited to winding country lanes.

It is also important to understand the merits and demerits of double axle caravans. On a site or when manoeuvring onto a garden storage spot, friction from the close coupled wheels makes it hard to turn the 'van. It is easier and you are less likely to cause a back injury if you use the B & H 'Handy Hitch' manufactured by H.C. Holifield. But it is still far harder than dealing with a single axle caravan and many owners of twin axle caravans simply keep them coupled up and develop their skill at reversing.

Another idea to facilitate manual manoeuvring was introduced by Lunar in 1991. The Company's hydraulic axle elevation system was an optional feature costing around £800.00. However, it's not seen very often.

Other disadvantages of twin axle models include elements like the greater cost and additional weight of the running gear. There are also claims that a twin axle caravan imposes additional stresses on a tow bracket.

Notwithstanding these disadvantages, a double axle caravan is impressively stable on the road. This becomes particularly apparent if there's a strong side wind or turbulence created by overtaking lorries. If a puncture occurs, it may also be possible to limp slowly and cautiously to a source of help.

Without question they have their devotees, and for a number of years, all Bessacar models have employed the twin axle system. However, the treble axle caravan which is often seen in the United States and Australia has yet to be introduced to Britain.

To summarise, there are a several issues relating to the compatibility of towcars and caravans. Care should be exercised when selecting suitable partners for this all-important marriage and if further advice is needed, technical literature published by the Caravan Clubs is especially helpful.

To manoeuvre a caravan by hand, the B & H Handy Hitch makes the task far easier – and less of a strain on your back.

Being able to reverse may take a little practice at first. But if you own a twin axle model which is harder to manhandle, it's a skill which is particularly valuable.

To facilitate manoeuvring a twin axle caravan when you want to park it by hand, Lunar has introduced a lifting axle system.

Chapter 3

ADAPTATIONS TO THE TOWCAR

All trailers have to display road lights which can be switched into operation by the driver of the towcar. Moreover, when towing a caravan from site to site, there is also a need to maintain the operation of a refrigerator if it is packed with perishable foodstuffs. In both cases, this means that a vehicle used for towing has to be suitably wired up to provide the power.

Some of the procedures discussed in this chapter are related to matters discussed in Chapter 7 (Low Voltage Supply System) and Chapter 12 (Refrigerators). Where appropriate, cross references are made to these other sections.

In addition, there are mechanical matters to consider and this chapter deals with subjects like the installation of a towing bracket, rear spring assisters and stabilising devices.

Operating the road lights
For more than twenty years, the means of linking the road lights on a towing vehicle to the road lights on a trailer has been via a seven pin plug and socket. The

connection components are referred to as the 12N plug and the 12N socket, where 'N' stands for 'normal'. An alternative five pin plug and socket system was discontinued a long time ago.

A full complement of road lights is required on caravans and other trailers, though you are not legally required to have a rear fog lamp for a trailed vehicle constructed before October 1979. On the other hand, many owners sensibly add a rear fog lamp for safety reasons.

It was legislation regarding fog lamps which prompted a change in the plug and socket provisions. Prior to October 1979, all facilities were fed via a single seven core cable. The seven feeds were allocated as follows:

The ruling on fog lamps prompted revisions, but so, too, did the fact that caravans were being built with many more 12v interior appliances. The present allocation is shown in the following table.

Serving interior 12v appliances
When legislation required trailers manufactured **after** 1st

October 1979 to have a rear fog lamp, it was decided that Pin 2, hitherto used for caravan interior lighting, would now provide the electrical feed. In any case, the use of a single

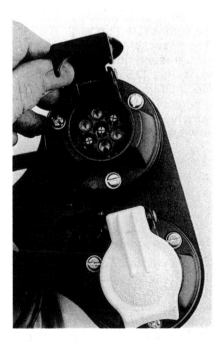

A 12N socket for road lights is black, whereas a 12S socket for caravan interior appliances has either a white or grey cover flap.

supply for caravan appliances was proving inadequate; many caravanners needed a special 12v feed for a refrigerator. Inboard batteries were also becoming more popular and these needed charging when travelling between sites.

In conseqence, it was decided that caravans, or any other type of trailer with interior appliances, would require a completely new supply route. The outcome was the introduction of the 12S (i.e. 'Supplementary') plug and socket leaving the 12N system to deal exclusively with road lights.

To prevent wrong connection, the centre brass tube of the 12S plug/socket is reversed. This means you cannot insert a 12S plug into a 12N socket and vice versa. In addition, 12S units are distinctively coloured in white, though you may find a plug in grey plastic instead. The feed cable, too, is not only thicker in girth on account of the demands of the fridge and charging facility; it is also covered in a grey sheath instead of the black insulation used for the multicore cable connected up to a 12N plug or socket.

At present, not all the seven feeds on a 12S circuit are allocated and most caravanners only use four connections, namely Pins 2, 3, 4 and 6. However, allocation is as follows:

The allocation of pins on a 12N and 12S socket usually adopts this pattern. This follows the National Caravan Council recommendation in which Pin 2 on the 12S socket is assigned to charging an auxiliary battery using an ignition controlled feed from the towcar.

(courtesy of Indespension)

Notwithstanding the allocations shown here, there is an alternative connection procedure for charging an auxiliary battery. (Shown here as Pin 2 above). This is discussed in the section called *Alternative wiring for battery charging*.

When considering the advent of the twin socket arrangement, it must not be forgotten that there are many caravans in use which were manufactured before October 1979 (i.e. without rear fog lights). With only 12v lights in the 'van, it is understandable that their owners are content to continue with a single plug and socket system. Owners of trailers are similarly content with a single 12N arrangement. But this provision is inappropriate for modern caravans.

Switchable sockets

A variation on the standard 12N socket is a version which incorporates a switching arrangement for the tow vehicle's rear fog lamp. As soon as the 12N plug is inserted, the feed to the trailer is connected whereas the feed to the towcar is switched off. This switching arrangement means that when you are towing in fog, distracting light from the car's fog lamp is not reflected from the front of the caravan.

Another point is that the increased load of fog lamps on both car and caravan might cause a fuse to blow on the towing vehicle. This could be overcome by fitting a fuse with an increased amp rating, although this means that the circuit is now 'over-fused'

Allocation for the 12S System

Pin 1 Yellow wire for reversing lights or for a catch on an inertia brake
Pin 2 Blue wire for auxiliary battery charging
Pin 3 White wire for earth (i.e. negative return)
Pin 4 Green wire to provide a permanent power supply from the car battery
Pin 5 Brown wire for a sensing device
Pin 6 Red wire for a refrigerator
Pin 7 Black wire but with no allocation

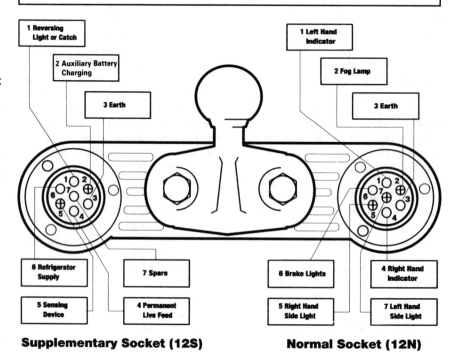

Supplementary Socket (12S)   **Normal Socket (12N)**

Allocation for the 12N System

Pin 1 (sometimes marked L) - Yellow wire for left indicator
Pin 2 (sometimes marked 54G) - Blue wire for rear fog lighting
(Prior to October 1979 this was used for caravan interior
lights)
Pin 3 (sometimes marked 31) - White wire for earth i.e. negative
return
Pin 4 (sometimes marked R) - Green wire for right indicator
Pin 5 (sometimes marked 58R) - Brown wire for right-hand tail light
Pin 6 (sometimes marked 54) - Red wire for brake lights
Pin 7 (sometimes marked 58L) - Black wire for left-hand tail lights
and number plate light

This unit is simple to fit, but you will need a length of *eight* core cable as well as the 12N switchable socket. In addition to the usual plain coloured wires, this eight core flex includes a bi-coloured wire with red and brown insulation. When wiring up the system, you have to modify the wiring at the rear of the towing vehicle.

To fit a switchable fog lamp system, you must first find out which feed wire in the car serves the fog lamp or lamps. You can do this using a wiring diagram for the vehicle or by consulting the appropriate Haynes Owners Workshop Manual. Alternatively you can switch on the fog lamp and then carry out tests on the wires in the boot or hatchback part of the car using one of the voltage checkers mentioned later in the Section called *Fitting a 12N socket*.

Once the fog lamp wire has been located, disconnect the vehicle battery and then cut the fog lamp feed with pliers. You then take the end of the severed wire coming from car's fog lamp switch and connect it to the blue wire in the eight core cable. This in turn should be wired up to pin 2 in the 12N socket. Then you must turn attention to the bi-coloured red and brown

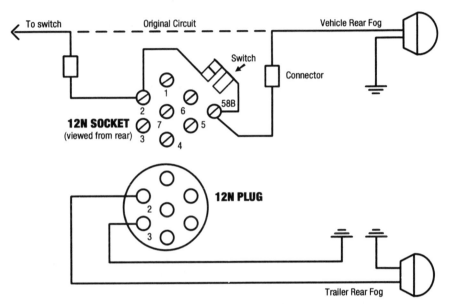

Diagram enclosed with Hella electrical kit showing the principle of a rear fog lamp cut out socket and circuit.
(courtesy of Hella)

whenever the caravan isn't in tow. A better answer is to fit a switchable 12N socket.

Good electrical contact can be maintained if the plugs and sockets are sprayed with a water repellent like Tri-Flow.

cable. One end of this must be connected to the special eighth pin in the socket – marked 58B, whereas the other end must be connected up to the car's foglamp.

The modification means that whenever the car's foglamp is switched into action when driving solo, the current will be taken to the lamp *via* the 12N socket. However, as soon as you hitch up and insert the 12N plug of a caravan or trailer into the socket, it forces two electrical contacts apart, thereby severing the continuity of the feed back up the red and brown wire to the vehicle's foglamp. Instead, current passes down the multicore cable to the rear foglamp on the 'van or trailer.

Sockets like this are manufactured by Hella and they should be protected from road dirt and damp because the feed to the car's foglamp is now permanently re-routed via the 12N socket. It is a good idea to spray the contacts in the socket with a water repellent product such as Tri-Flow; this penetrant lubricant is available in spray cans from any well-stocked caravan dealership. Furthermore if you find that the 12N socket gets accidentally knocked on a kerbstone or on rough terrain, check immediately that the operation of the vehicle's rear foglamp has not been affected.

Fitting a 12N socket
Until recently, you could fit and connect up a 12N socket to any vehicle without much difficulty. In fact the amateur should be able to carry out the tasks described here on most older vehicles. However, an increasing number of cars are now being equipped with electronic monitoring panels which advise the driver when a bulb has failed.

These electronic check systems are fitted on many executive saloons, and dashboard warnings indicate

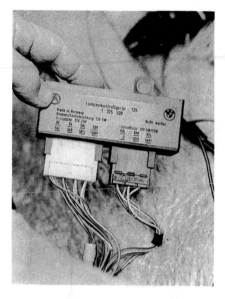

In cars with fascia monitoring panels which warn of bulb failure, the sensing unit must be located when fitting towcar wiring. In some BMW vehicles, the unit is under the rear seat squab.

when a stop lamp or a side lamp has ceased to operate. Monitoring systems are unquestionably useful, but they require that towing connections for stop lamps and side lamps are made on the *input* side of the central sensing units. In other words you cannot adopt the usual practice of connecting up 12N socket feeds directly to the wires entering the rear light clusters.

If your car has a bulb failure monitor, you will probably need to purchase a special electrical towing kit from a main dealer. Moreover, its installation may also be quite involved and recognising that electronic components can be damaged by incorrect wiring, it is the kind of job that might be better left to a main dealer.

If your car does not have one of these devices, most connections are merely taken from the wiring loom near the rear light clusters. As regards tools, you would be well advised to purchase a small circuit tester

which looks rather like an electrical screwdriver with a clear handle; there is also a wire terminated by a crocodile clip attached to the top of this handle. These are modestly priced and can be purchased from DIY automotive suppliers. When the crocodile clip is attached to the negative terminal of a battery and the point of the tester touched on the positive terminal, the light in the handle illuminates.

This tester is very useful for identifying the different feed wires supplying the rear lamp cluster. With the appropriate rear lamp switched on at the dashboard and the crocodile clip attached to a bared contact on the bodywork, the probe is simply touched on each lamp terminal in turn until the handle illuminates. If the terminals are obscured, the sharp point of the probe can be used to penetrate the sheathing of the car's wires thereby touching the core filaments. However, this should be done with caution and puncture points in the sheathing should be covered later with insulation tape, even if the point of penetration is little more than a pin prick.

When mounting 12N and 12S sockets, choose positions well clear of the ground. There are several types of mounting plates to suit the British type of bracket, including models like the Sto Stop. This incorporates an over-run plate which can prevent the trailer coupling head from accidentally hitting the boot of the tow car during the hitching-up process.

Swan neck Continental-type towing ball and bracket designs are less versatile and usually have socket mounting plates welded on the sides of the central tube.

Purpose-made seven core cable should be used to connect up with the 12N socket. Alternatively, an eight core 12N cable is needed if you decide to fit a socket with the facility for switching off the car fog lamp whenever a trailer is in tow. Both versions are covered with a black insulation sheath to distinguish them from the more sturdy 12S grey multicored cable.

Looking at individual wires in the black 12N cable, the white earth wire has a cross sectional area of 2.0 mm square to yield a continuous current rating of 17.5 amps. Its core is made up of 28 filaments which makes it noticeably larger than the other coloured wires which are made from 14 strands. These are 1.5 mm square in cross sectional area and yield a continuous current rating of 8.75 amps. Wire of this rating is needed for efficient operation of the road lights.

Other items needed are a protective rubber cover to prevent road dirt entering the rear of the socket and bolts to hold the socket to its mounting plate. These are standard items stocked at caravan accessory shops.

Components can be purchased separately, although

A rubber cover around the rear of sockets should project beyond the mounting plate and firmly enclose the cable.

complete packages like Hella installation kits include items such as a heavy duty flasher unit. Moreover, sockets in Hella's kit are already pre-wired and pre-mounted on to a socket plate which is a useful time saver. Connecting wires into a socket needs a small electrical screwdriver, a wire stripper and plenty of patience.

After connecting to the 12N socket, the multicore cable must then be routed neatly into the boot or hatchback compartment of the vehicle, remembering that any hole which has to be drilled in the rear body skirt or floor of the boot must be protected with a rubber grommet. The negative lead from the car battery should now be disconnected.

Once inside the back of the car, you will have to remove some of the black outer sheath from the multicore cable. Trim panels in the boot must also be removed to uncover the wiring loom and rear light clusters.

On most cars, it is then easy to make the connections once you know the functions of the different wires. You will notice that the tail lights on the caravan are served separately via pin 5 (off-side) and pin 7 (near-side). This separation is especially useful if the car has parking light switching. However, it means

that wires from the multicore cable will usually have to split up and head either to the right- or the left-hand side of the tow car. It will be the same, too, with the direction indicator feed wires.

As regards the white earth wire from the seven core cable, it is essential that this is fixed to a dependable earth point on the body of the car. Often you can use an existing earthing point by attaching a crimp fit metal eye to the white earth return wire in the 12N multicore cable.

All the other connections will need to be made to the wires which serve the car's road lights. A common method of connecting 12N wires to the vehicle's feed wires uses snap-on connectors. 'Scotchlocks', as they are sometimes called, are placed around the pick-up wire in the vehicle, making sure it locates in a moulded groove in the plastic casing. The new wire from the multicore cable is placed in an adjacent groove.

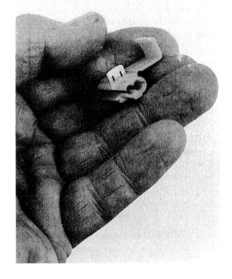

For a number of years, coupling up the wires in a multicore cable to the towcar has been done using snap-on or 'Scotchlock' connectors.

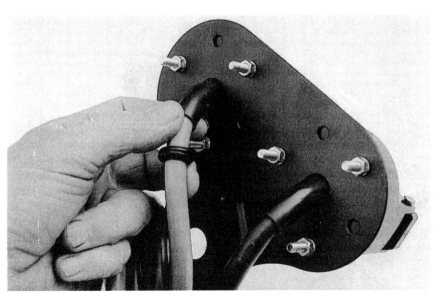

The plastic assembly is then closed, thereby encasing both wires. You next use a pair of pliers to squeeze a metal tag on the connector so that it cuts through the insulation of both wires. The tag penetrates to the copper filaments, thus forming an electrical coupling. Lastly a hinged plastic flap on the connector is clicked into place so that it covers the exposed part of the tag.

Snap on connectors are quick to use, but many auto electricians prefer to make connections with crimp connectors. This usually means fitting a double socket connector into one of the wires feeding the vehicle's road lights. Then a male bullet connector is crimped to the end of the appropriate receiving wire in the 12N cable for insertion into the socket. Arguably this system creates better connections and is more consistent with electrical procedure in automotive work.

When all connections are complete, it is easy to carry out a check if you own a trailer lighting board which can be plugged in and laid by the driver's door. Alternatively you can use the circuit tester described earlier. This involves holding the socket's spring-loaded cover flap open, and clipping the crocodile clip to the earth connector which is in the 5 o'clock position. Then you go round each of the pins in turn with the appropriate lights switched on; however, a helper is needed to check the brake light.

An inexpensive circuit tester is ideal for checking wiring to multipin plugs and sockets.

Heavy duty flasher unit and dashboard warning light

Another task to carry out is to fix a replacement heavy duty flasher unit and warning light. The light is a legal requirement and will notify the driver if a direction indicator on the trailer is inoperative.

There are two types of device which fulfil this objective. The first is a heavy duty flasher unit which is specific to your particular vehicle and which is a **replacement** for the original item. You must get the correct type and then need to find where the original unit has been mounted. Look under the facia,

around the steering column, as well as checking in the engine compartment.

A different approach is to fit an electronic component which you connect up to your existing system. An example is the Lucas Karaflash 5 Electronic Flasher Relay which is supplied complete with mounting panel, warning light, connectors and instructions. This is connected up between the vehicle's power

Some Hella heavy duty replacement flasher kits are purpose-made for particular cars and come complete with a mini-wiring loom.

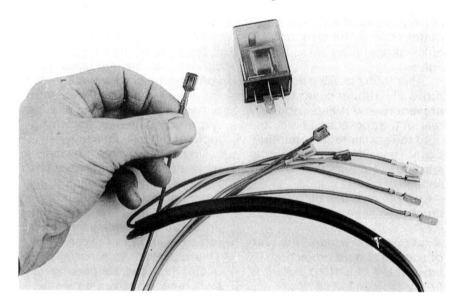

supply and original flasher circuit.

Electronic units are popular although cheap examples can be unreliable. For example if direction indicators start to operate incorrectly, the fault can often be traced back to this component. Blistering on the casing is not unusual and shows that the unit has burnt out.

It is also a legal requirement to have a warning to inform the driver if one of the caravan direction indicators isn't working. Audible warning systems are rarely used, and a dashboard lamp is usually preferred. Some cars already have this pre-built into the facia lights and you merely have to connect it up. Instructions accompanying a replacement flasher relay explain how one part of the warning lamp must be earthed whereas the other connection is made to a terminal on the relay.

Fitting a 12S socket
The reasons for needing a 12S supplementary socket are explained in the section called *Servicing interior 12v appliances.* At present, the facilities in most modern caravans only call for 4 connections:

Pin 2 Blue wire for auxiliary charging
Pin 3 White wire for earth (i.e. negative return)
Pin 4 Green wire to provide a permanent power supply from the car battery
Pin 6 Red wire for a refrigerator

Note: Sometimes an alternative method is used for charging a car battery as described in the Section called *Alternative wiring for battery charging.*

Whereas the supply from Pin 4 is always live, the supplies from Pins 2 and 6 are wired through a relay so that they are only activated when the car ignition is switched on.

Like the 12N socket discussed earlier, a 12S socket is mounted alongside the tow bracket on a support plate and its grey multicore cable is routed into the car in the same manner. This cable is thicker than its 12N black counterpart on account of the demands of the fridge and charging facilities. For example the white earth wire is made up of 36 strands to produce a cross sectional area of 2.5 mm square and a continuous current rating around 21.5 amps. The other coloured wires have 21 strands to produce a 1.5 mm square cable and a continuous current rating around 13 amps.

The white earth wire should be connected up to the body work of the towcar, and an existing earth point can be used. The green wire must then be taken through to a permanent live supply which usually means removing trim and carpet so that the supply can be hidden.

Normally the green wire needs extending and you should purchase automotive wire of at least 1.5 mm square. This is usually made up of 14 copper filaments to give a continuous rating of 13 amps. The best source is the car battery, fitting an in-line 10 amp fuse as close to the battery as possible. Do not be tempted to connect up to a clock feed or the feed to the boot light. Although these are permanently live, they are usually served by wire in the car loom which is not rated high enough to operate additional items such as a caravan TV, water pump or additional lights.

Once connected, you must remember that Pin 4 in the 12S socket on your car is permanently live and pins should be protected with a moisture repellent like Tri-Flow; this was mentioned in the section called *Switchable Sockets.*

Unlike the green wire connected to Pin 4, the refrigerator supply via Pin 6

should not be permanently live. The high current consumption of a refrigerator (minimum 8 amps) would quickly discharge a battery and so a supply should only be given when the engine is running and the alternator is charging. The same is applicable to the charge supply for a caravan battery via Pin 2.

On the subject of caravan battery charging, Chapter 7 explains more about trickle charging. Boost charging is explained in the Section called *Battery Boxes* and should be consulted in conjunction with the points made here.

Meantime, the supply to Pins 2 and 6 needs a switching system to ensure that a 12v supply sent to the fridge and inboard battery will be arrested as soon as the car engine is switched off. The device which achieves this is called a 'relay'.

The need for a relay to disconnect a caravan battery is slightly different from the need for a relay to control current feeding a fridge. If you merely connected up the caravan battery directly to the vehicle 12v system, this second battery would not only be a receiver of current; it could also become a provider. In other words, electrical equipment in the tow car such as a starter motor could **draw** current from the caravan battery. Hence the purpose of introducing a relay into the feed to pin 2 is to ensure that there is only 'one way current'.

If their purpose is different, the relays which serve supplies on Pins 2 and 6 are usually identical. In essence they are switches operated by an electro-magnet which is activated whenever you switch on the ignition.

Any caravan or trailer specialist supplies relays which are made specifically for these tasks and products from Trend, Lucas and Hella are well known. Both double and single units are available and wiring diagrams

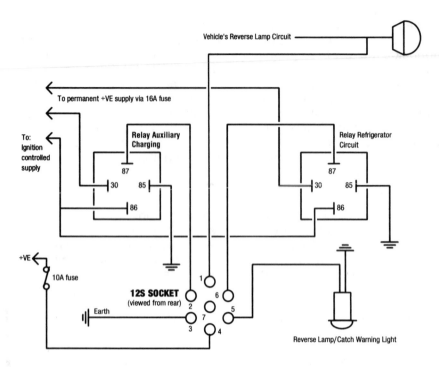

Vehicle's Reverse Lamp Circuit

To permanent +VE supply via 16A fuse

To:
Ignition
controlled
supply

Relay Auxiliary
Charging

87
30   85
86

Relay Refrigerator
Circuit

87
30   85
86

+VE
10A fuse

12S SOCKET
(viewed from rear)

Earth

1
6
2   5
7
3   4

Reverse Lamp/Catch Warning Light

The wiring diagram supplied with a Hella relay kit shows clearly how to couple up with the tow car and the 12S socket.
(courtesy of Hella)

are easy to follow. The products are intended for cars with a negative earth i.e. the negative battery terminal is connected to the vehicle bodywork.

Normally a relay is fitted in the engine compartment as near to the battery as possible. Fitting procedures for a Hella relay are as follows:

i) Disconnect vehicle battery.
ii) Install relay and connect the appropriate terminal to the car body as described in the instructions.
iii) Connect terminal marked to the vehicle battery; include the in-line fuse holder containing a 16 amp fuse provided in the kit.
iv) Connect the final terminal to the vehicle ignition circuit.

The ignition connection is usually made using a Scotchlock attached to the supply coming from terminals WL or IND on the alternator. However, it is equally acceptable to connect up to any

other accessory feed in the car which becomes live when the ignition is switched on.

The wire from the relays to the 12S socket must be of substantial gauge. In the installation instructions for Electrolux refrigerators, a wire of at least 2 mm square (17.5 amps continuous current rating) is specified. A wire of similar rating is needed for battery charging, too. In the case of Hella kits, you are supplied with 36 strand auto wire which is 2.5 mm square in cross sectional area; this has a continuous current rating of 21 amp – well within the Electrolux recommendation. With regard to the Lucas relay, you are advised to fit even sturdier cable – notably 4.5 mm square and with a continuous current rating of 35 amps. You can again check this by counting up the filaments in the core – normally 65 strands of 0.33 mm copper.

The thicker the wire, the lower the resistance and the better the flow of current. However, it is unfortunate that when the feed in the car reaches the red wire in the grey sheathed multicore 12S cable, it will then couple up with

a 1.5 mm square/13 amp wire. Herein is one of the weaknesses in present caravan practice since this size of wire doesn't meet the minimum laid down by Electrolux for a refrigerator being operated on a 12v supply. This point is picked up in Chapter 12 in the Section called *Modes of operation* with reference to fridge installations and Electrolux recommendations are given in this later Chapter about restrictions on the length of 12S grey multicore cable which is used. Towcar charging of an auxiliary battery fitted in a caravan is less efficient for the same reason, a procedure appropriately referred to as 'trickle charging'.

Notwithstanding the 'weak link' in the electrical 'chain', you should still fit supply wires from the relays in the tow vehicle which are at least 2.5 mm square (21 amp). Moreover, if you can lift your caravan battery into the boot of the towcar for charging, you effectively shorten the run of wire. The shortening is achieved by connecting the battery negative terminal to an earth point on the car bodywork, whereas the positive terminal is connected up directly into a branch wire taken from the relay controlled supply. This improves the charge rate significantly and is referred to as 'boost charging'.

Alternative wiring for battery charging
Throughout this chapter, the provision for battery charging is based on the recommendations of the National Caravan Council, a procedure which is widely followed. This allocates Pin 2 in the 12S plug and socket for charging, via a relay. However, this arrangement has a weakness.

When the auxiliary battery is connected up in a caravan, it will be wired up, as described, via Pin 2 on the 12S plug and socket. This means that it receives a trickle charge when the 'van is being towed and the car engine is running. However, when you disconnect the 12S plug on arrival at a site, Pin 2 in the caravan plug remains live because it remains connected to the positive terminal of the inboard caravan battery. If rainwater were to get into the socket, this might lead to problems.

A solution is to fit an in-line 10 amp fuse in the Pin 2 charging wire somewhere near the caravan battery; this gives protection in the event of a short circuit.

But in spite of being able to take this precautionary measure, an alternative arrangement is sometimes recommended in which only three pins are allocated in the 12S socket. These are:

Pin 3 (White) Common return, negative earth
Pin 4 (Green) Permanent live feed **and** charging route
Pin 6 (Red) Relay switched supply to refrigerator

The revised allocation is an International Standard for 12v Electrical Installations which has been accepted in the UK and which will be introduced in due course into the relevant British Standard relating to touring caravans.

The alteration is based on the fact that many modern caravans incorporate a 12v switching panel which allows the owner to have control over the functions being served by the Pin 4 connection. On one hand you can operate a switch so that current is **drawn** from the car battery in order to power your caravan low voltage electrical system. On the other hand you can operate a **different** switch which enables the same Pin 4 route to be used as a means for **charging** the inboard caravan battery. When the system operates in this mode, a relay isn't needed in the tow car since

the circuitry within the caravan control panel now takes over the function of preventing a reverse flow of current. In other words the vehicle cannot steal power from the auxiliary caravan battery e.g. when the starter motor is being used.

Even though this new standard has the advantage of needing three rather than four 12S connections, it has several disadvantages. To begin with, it presumes that a caravan is equipped with a control panel offering the switch selection facilities described above. It also means that the total length of wire going to the auxiliary battery from the tow car will now need to be much longer, since it has to be routed via the control unit. This in turn will further reduce the charge rate to the auxiliary battery when it is left in the caravan. But even more important is the need placed on the owner to ensure that the correct switching has been selected for the towing situation and the on-site situation respectively.

A caravanner who relies solely on trickle charging for replenishing an auxiliary battery and who has a caravan with the appropriate type of electronic control panel, may prefer the wiring arrangement which uses three connections. Furthermore, this system means that a relay is no longer needed in the tow car. On the other hand this is not true if you also want to rig up a system in which the caravan battery is transferred to the boot of the car for boost charging. This was described in the section called *Fitting a 12N socket* and a relay forms an essential part of this supply arrangement. But the cost of a relay is modest and the advantage of boost charging is clear.

Weighing up the advantages of the National Caravan Council recommendation, coupled with the fact that many readers of

this manual may not own one of the latest models with panel selection facilities, the preference for allocating Pin 2 specifically for charging is understandable. At the same time, if readers come across literature which suggests that only 3 pins need allocation in the 12S socket, this alternative approach will now be understood.

Towing brackets

Compared with wiring up a vehicle for towing, fitting a tow bracket is usually much more straightforward. This presumes that you purchase a reputable product with clear installation instructions.

Modern vehicles are much lighter than older models and contain accident crumple zones. In consequence there are only a few points of suitable integrity for the attachment of a tow bar. It is for this reason that the car owner should **never** attempt to make up his own bracket.

Today, prototype brackets are put through rigorous test programmes before a new design is manufactured. However, the integrity of a bracket is of little merit if the key points of attachment on an older towcar are starting to deteriorate. Sound fitting points are essential.

In recent years, car manufacturers have paid more attention to the towing public and brackets for their vehicles are often marketed. However, brackets from independent manufacturers are usually exceedingly well made and may be as much as six times less expensive. This is currently a matter of considerable discussion in the caravan press.

If you decide to fit a bracket yourself, it is important to purchase a reputable product from a long established manufacturer, and to follow all the fitting instructions.

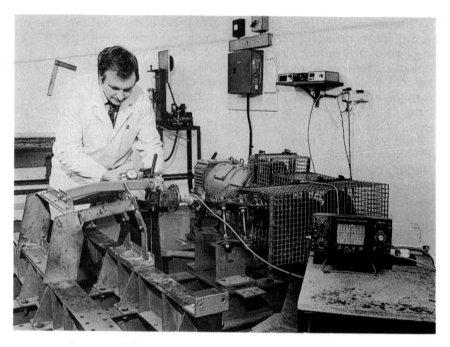

Each prototype Witter tow bracket is subjected to the most rigorous tests on a special rig.
(courtesy of C. P. Witter)

Fitting a towing bracket

A bracket is normally only finished with a cellulose undercoat. You should therefore start by adding a top coat; rusting brackets underneath a tow car are neither safe nor sightly. This can be done using a spray can of cellulose paint or by applying Hammerite paint. As regards access under the car, all usual safety precautions must be strictly observed.

In many installations you will need to remove the rear bumper and skirts for access. Thereafter, details of the work vary from car to car, but in some instances there are models where captive nuts are already mounted in situ. However, it is nearly always necessary to drill some additional attachment holes and you will need a centre punch to produce a small dent in the metal. This prevents the drill bit from skating around on the surface. It is also wise to start by making a small pilot hole e.g. 3 mm ($^1/_8$ in) before using a larger drill bit. This is inclined to centre rather better and makes later progress more easy.

In some installations, a few holes need to be enlarged quite substantially in order to insert a bush. This is a piece of steel tubing which will act as a spacer when inserted into a box section. Without this, the box section might collapse when you tighten up the securing bolt later.

To increase the size of holes, a cone shaped enlarging drill is useful such as the 'High Speed Steel Conecut' manufactured by G & J Hall Ltd of Sheffield. These are available in several sizes e.g. Size CC1 will enlarge holes from 6 to 20 mm ($^1/_4$ – $^{13}/_{16}$ in). Alternatively you can fit a rotary file in your electric drill such as the 'Wolfcraft Super Drill Saw, Part no 2512'. Wolfcraft accessories are available from tool specialists and many DIY outlets.

When the holes are formed in the vehicle, you will be able to attach the sections which form the bracket. Initially the bolts should be left loose but they must be methodically tightened when the assembly is finally completed.

Sequence photographs – Six photographs showing the installation of a Witter bracket to a BMW 7 Series car.

i) A good tow bracket kit will provide all necessary components together with clear installation instructions.

ii) Since brackets are only finished in undercoat, it is wise to add a good coating of auto enamel or Hammerite prior to installation.

iii) On many modern cars, the rear bumper and skirts need to be removed before the bracket can be fitted.

iv) On some cars, attachment points are already pre-drilled; on this installation, only one hole had to be made.

v) When the bracket sections are assembled, everything should be bolted loosely, offered up to the car and then finally tightened.

vi) When the tow ball is fitted and the bumper reinstated, there's no evidence of the bracket sections which would spoil the appearance of the car.

Notwithstanding the bolt-on possibilities of a British tow ball, you should not use this mounting point to carry an array of accessories.

The alternative Continental type of towball is known as a swan neck design and usually forms part of the bracket assembly. Removable versions are also available. Unfortunately the swan neck tow ball is less suitable if you want to fit a socket mounting plate. Whereas there are adaptors to provide stabiliser mounting points, some are not as secure as the types intended for bolt-on balls.

Removable tow balls are comparatively expensive. This type is held in place by tightening a retaining collar; steel balls then locate in the neck of the central tube.

Tow balls

On a British-style bracket, the 50 mm tow ball is a separate item which is attached using a pair of high tensile bolts. You must pay particular attention when tightening these. An advantage of this arrangement is the opportunity to attach additional components such as a stabiliser mounting, and a plate for mounting the electrical sockets.

Even though tow brackets are manufactured to produce a standard towing height, a drop plate is easy to fit if you have the British-type of tow ball. (British Standard height is 350 – 420 mm (13.8 – 16.6 in) from the centre of the towball to the ground when the vehicle is laden to maximum weight.) But whereas a drop plate is permissible to lower ball height for a caravan with an unusually low coupling, these plates must **never** be used to **raise** the height of the ball.

Adaptor plates like this model from Scott Halleys permit a blade type stabiliser to be fitted to a swan neck tow ball.

Stabilisers – their purpose

Stabilisers are another important part of modern towing equipment. Even the most careful caravanner cannot anticipate bad road surfaces or the effect of high sided vehicles overtaking at speed. Both cause temporary instability and a stabiliser is a safe way of checking unwanted movements initiated by external causes. At the same time, a stabiliser should never be used to cure a badly matched outfit, a badly loaded caravan or a 'van with a twisted chassis.

Instability occurs in two separate planes, vertical and horizontal. The former is referred to as pitching; the latter is usually called snaking. Pitching is the sudden up and down movement created when a caravan passes over a bad pothole whereas snaking is the effect caused by side winds or overtaking vehicles. Either way, these unwanted movements can be dangerous.

Some stabilisers, such as devices which dampen movements at the tow ball, usually only attenuate snaking rather than pitching movements. In the event, this is the potentially more dangerous form of instability, but other products, like spring blade stabilisers, dampen vertical pitching as well. Either way, most products are easy to install yourself.

To fit a ball acting stabiliser, the original coupling head must be removed.

Fitting an Al-Ko AKS 2000 or a Westfalia SSK stabiliser

Owners of modern caravans with a pressed steel coupling mounted on a tubular draw bar can replace the unit with a stabiliser. Both the Al-Ko and Westfalia units use the original bolting points and both include packing collars if the tubing has a narrow cross sectional diameter.

Fitting instructions provide a detailed account of installation, but the job adds up to little more than unbolting the original coupling head and replacing it with the stabiliser coupling. New high tensile nuts and bolts are provided.

Recognising that some caravans have a spring-loaded damper held within the drawbar tube by the original bolts, the Al-Ko unit includes temporary inserts. These are driven through the tube to push out the original bolts, but keeping the damper in place. When the stabiliser is in position, you then knock through the temporary inserts with the new bolts which replace them.

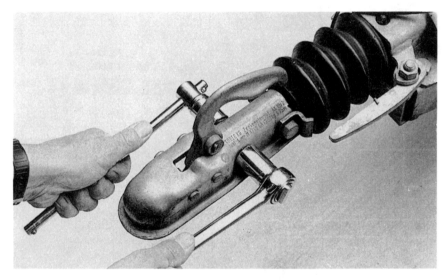

Packing collars are supplied by Westfalia and Al-Ko Kober to suit towing tubes with different diameters.

When needed, a collar is placed on the towing tube before the stabiliser is fitted.

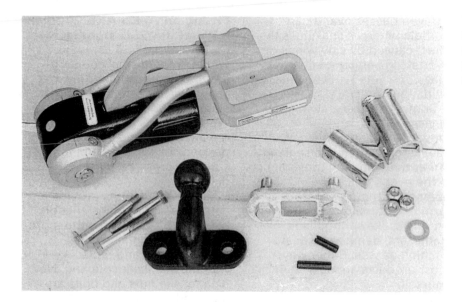

To suit brackets with bolt on towballs, the AKS 2000 is supplied with a replacement towball which projects slightly more than the standard type.

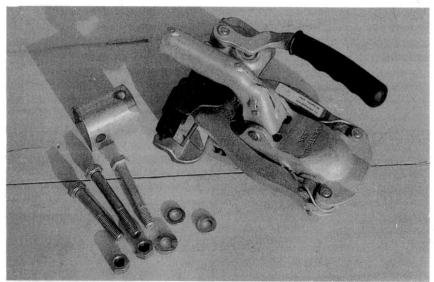

The latest MkII Westfalia stabiliser comes complete with high tensile bolts and an adaptor collar.

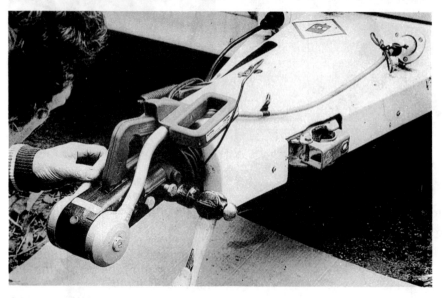

When the AKS 2000 is fitted, its attachment bolts are tapped through the tube, knocking out the temporary inserts supplied; these ensure the damper in the tube is held in place.

These stabilisers cannot be fitted to caravans built on the older type of chassis like the Peak or the B & B products. They may also require spacer plates behind a British towball; the Al-Ko AKS 2000 needs a replacement ball which is provided in the kit.

Convenience is one of the chief attractions of this kind of stabiliser because there are no separate items to store away.

The SSK Mk I is finally tightened on to the drawbar tube using the new high tensile bolts supplied with the kit.

The AKS 2000 is one of the easiest stabiliser units to couple up and includes a red/green button to confirm the unit is correctly engaged on the towball.

Operating a ball acting stabiliser

Contrary to usual practice, it is important to keep a tow ball grease-free when using this type of stabiliser. The principle behind its operation is that friction pads are clamped tightly against the ball surface. Although normal articulation of car and caravan is possible, freedom of movement is reduced so that any tendency to snake is met by resistance.

Obviously the friction bearing surfaces should be checked periodically and replacement inserts are obtainable. When coupling up the caravan, a hinged gas piston on the Westfalia SSK has to be clamped in place, and this presses Teflon coated pads against the sides of the ball. The Al-Ko APS 2000 is quicker to operate and includes a useful safety button which gives visual confirmation that coupling is complete.

Blade type stabilisers

When the Scott stabiliser was first developed in Aberdeen in the early 1960s, its designers could scarcely have realised that the product would eventually sell more than 200,000 units in the years which followed. Today there are a number of Scott models listed in recognition of variations in the types of towing brackets. This is necessary since part of the device is attached to the tow car.

Whilst the Scott Halleys stabiliser range continues to remain in prominence, other products have appeared which adopt the same operating principles. Blade type stabilisers are now made by other manufacturers, carrying trade names like Bulldog, Mowbray, Bumper to Bumper, and Staymount.

Stabilisers built to this pattern comprise three main

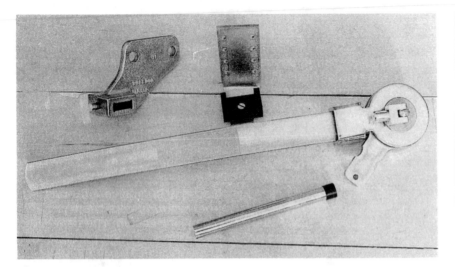

Blade-type stabilisers like the Bulldog 2000 comprise a car plate, the chassis 'L' bracket and a single leaf spring fitted on a friction-damped turntable.

components. Firstly there is a mounting plate which has to be fitted to the bracket on the tow vehicle. This is often called the 'car plate'. Secondly there is a single leaf spring which is attached at one end to a friction-damped turntable. Thirdly there is a trailer chassis bracket which receives the spring blade at the opposite end. On account of its shape, this is often called the 'L' bracket.

When the stabiliser is coupled up to car and trailer, side-to-side movements are conveyed to the blade which pivots around a turntable. Sandwiched inside the turntable are friction plates and it is important that sufficient tension is set on the central pin of the turntable to hold these in

close register to the metal surfaces bearing against each surface. Scott Halleys recommends that when a lateral resistance is applied at the end of the blade, rotation around the turntable should not occur until the load reaches 27 kgs (60 lbs). A spring balance is available so that the arm can be set correctly; a make-shift alternative is to push the blade against the platform of some bathroom scales.

The control of up and down pitching is achieved on account of the blade itself. In effect this operates like a single leaf spring and its attachment at both car and caravan provides a resistance in the vertical plane. In addition, it is claimed that the downward pressure of the blade where it is held within the L bracket of the caravan draw bar, creates a corresponding uplift to the boot of the car. This provides a small measure of

Scott Halleys recommends that the turntable on the Scott stabiliser is tightened to resist a load of 27 kg (60 lb) at the end of the blade.

compensation to the loading on the tow car.

One small problem with this type of stabiliser is the fact that it takes a certain amount of strength to locate the blade in the L bracket when the caravan is being coupled up. The blade has to be lifted to reach the height of the bracket as well as needing to be turned against the 27 kg sideways resistance. Several manufacturers have produced extension levers which make it easier to move the blade. However, more recent models feature quick release turntable mechanisms.

If you own a standard type of stabiliser, you may be able to convert it by fitting the quick release mechanism. Conversion kits are available from manufacturers like Bulldog and the QS package will fit Scott and Mowbray stabilisers whereas the LC/QB package fits their own

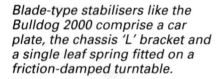

The Bulldog quick release kits allow many different makes of blade stabiliser to be converted, from a bolt arrangement, including the manufacturer's own earlier models.

Bulldog Major 200. The mechanism has a nut tightening facility for fine-tuning the turntable resistance, as well as a lever control which is used for unclamping or clamping-up the assembly when coupling up. This lever can be removed and stowed when coupling is completed.

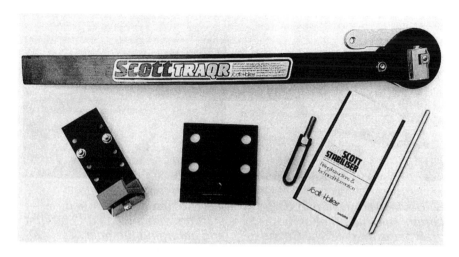

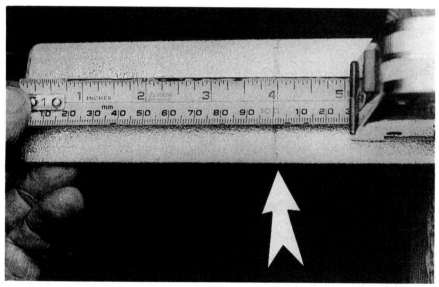

i) The kit comprises three components – the main unit, the 'L' bracket, and the car plate.

ii) A pencil line should be marked 100 mm (4 in) from the end of the blade.

Installing a blade stabiliser

The accompanying photo sequence shows how to install a Scott stabiliser and the principles would be much the same for fitting other makes as well. The job involves fitting the car plate to the towing vehicle and fitting the L bracket to the trailer or caravan draw bar.

On a British type of tow bracket, the car plate is easily fitted. This is mounted between the tow ball and the bracket mounting point, though longer tow ball bolts may be needed. Owners of Saab and Volvo tow cars may need a different type of mounting unit to suit the less conventional types of bracket usually fitted to these vehicles.

Similarly you will need a special collar bracket if your towcar has a tubular swan neck type of towball. For instance the Scott Halleys TC plate is especially positive in its method of location on a tubular neck. Where other variations exist, manufacturers like Bulldog and Scott Halleys usually have car plates to suit unusual tow bars.

Sequence photographs – Eight photographs showing the installation of a Scott blade-type of stabiliser.

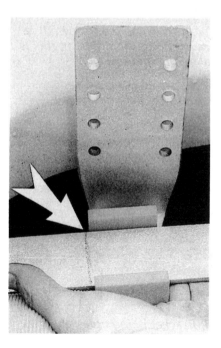

iii) With the L bracket cradling the blade, its position on the caravan drawbar is verified by the marked line.

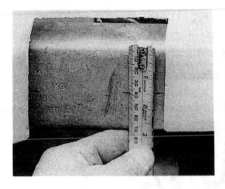

iv) Having removed part of the fairing, the mid point of the drawbar is marked. NB. On the latest chassis, drilling is not permissible and a clamp-on bracket is needed instead.

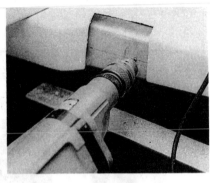

vii) The first hole is drilled, starting with a small drill bit first and enlarging the hole progressively.

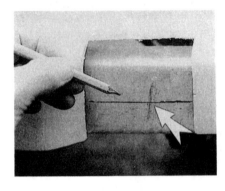

v) A horizontal line (arrowed) is drawn along the drawbar; this is called the 'neutral axis'.

viii) The L bracket is bolted in place, selecting a pair of holes which allows the blade to pass unheeded below the drawbar when turning tight corners.

vi) Bracket fixing holes are marked on the neutral axis line; the drilling points will then be marked precisely with a centre punch.

Once the car plate has been fitted, the car and caravan should be hitched up and parked on level ground. The stabiliser can then be located on the vehicle and aligned alongside the offside edge of the drawbar on the caravan 'A' frame. On certain older models, the jockey wheel is mounted on this side, in which case the installation has to be reversed. A Scott model can easily be mounted on the nearside drawbar instead; it involves dismantling the friction turntable, turning over the central locating bar and reassembling it. However, the design of a Bulldog stabiliser

allows you to attach the unit either side without alteration, though its reversible car plate will need to be mounted the other way round.

A further modification may be needed when a caravan drawbar is enclosed by a decorative cover. These are usually manufactured in glass reinforced plastic (i.e. GRP or fibre glass). Removing a small section to expose the metal draw bar is not a difficult job and a small cut-out can be formed with a hacksaw, a wood rasp and some glasspaper.

It is important that the L bracket is fitted correctly and this is done by temporarily offering it up so that 100 mm (4 in) of the blade extends beyond its rearward edge. To be certain of getting the position correct, it is useful to take this measurement and to make a pencil mark on the face of the blade.

The blade should now be elevated and propped up on some wooden blocks so that the L bracket can be positioned on the side of the trailer drawbar. The next photographs show holes being drilled and the bracket being attached. However, a warning should be made about this method of fixing because drilling is **not** permissible on an Al-Ko lightweight chassis manufactured in 1991 or later; if you disregard this matter, the chassis guarantee will be rendered invalid. Owners of 1990s caravans must therefore purchase an alternative clamping system in order to mount the L bracket.

The issue of drilling chassis should be fully understood and receives further mention in the following chapter. On older caravans made in the 1960s and 1970s, the chassis was made of heavy steel; examples like B & B and Peak chassis were especially popular. Caravans manufactured by CI, such as the well-known

Sprite models, were also constructed on the Company's own heavy chassis. Prior to the arrival of lighweight chassis, the L bracket for a stabiliser had two holes, one above the other in **vertical** alignment. The bracket was thus fitted to the heavy steel draw bar after holes of the appropriate size had been drilled.

When lightweight chassis appeared in the 1970s, indiscriminate drilling was immediately declared to be unacceptable. However, it was permissible to drill a pair of holes to accept a stabiliser L bracket as long as they were in a **horizontal** plane and along the neutral axis of the drawbar. The term, 'neutral axis', refers to the mid-point of the drawbar. To meet this requirement, stabiliser manufacturers now introduced L brackets with pairs of holes situated in horizontal alignment.

In 1991, the matter was reviewed again and Al-Ko then declared that **no** drilling should be undertaken on any subsequent chassis produced by the company. In consequence, the only way to fit a stabiliser L bracket is to employ a clamping system. This, too, has now been introduced by manufacturers like Bulldog and Scott Halleys.

With this in mind, if you acquire a second-hand stabiliser with the intention of fitting it to a modern caravan, it is **essential** that this bracket is replaced. If your caravan is built on a lightweight chassis made in the 1980s, you will need a bracket in which the drill holes are situated in a **horizontal** plane. Most stabiliser manufacturers sell these as separate items and Bulldog will supply a standard bracket (No. LC5) or an extended version (No. LC5E).

Alternatively if you own a caravan built in the 1990s, manufacturers like Bulldog and Scott Halleys can supply alternative clamping plates so that the 'L' bracket can be

Recognising the latest instruction that new chassis must not be drilled, the latest Scott stabiliser is supplied automatically with a clamp-on 'L' bracket as standard.

mounted without drilling any holes at all. The Bulldog LC7 clamp-on angle bracket, for example, is designed to fit most types of chassis whether new or old.

Similar cautionary notes are necessary if you have a caravan with an aluminium rather than a steel chassis. Lunar and

To avoid chassis drilling, the Bulldog universal clamping plate has been available for some time. Now there are specially made saddles to suit all makes of caravan.

Buccaneer caravans are examples. When fixing a steel L bracket to an aluminium chassis, you must use the special neoprene spacer washers supplied, fitting them between the draw bar and the bracket. Without them, the different metals would come into contact and the ingress of rainwater then causes an electrolytic action to take place. In effect this is the principle behind the operation of a battery and the metals in contact can corrode rapidly.

Overall, the blade type stabiliser is deservedly popular. However, its successful operation is dependent on the condition of the pads on its friction turntable, together with its setting. When you purchase a new stabiliser, it will invariably need re-tightening after eight or nine hundred miles. This is because the friction pads are bedding-in.

Many miles later, they may even need replacement but pads are usually quite easy to purchase. Manufacturers like Bulldog, Mowbray and Scott Halleys supply repair kits for their products, and the instructions show how to dismantle the friction assembly to replace the pads. In keeping with modern practice, these are usually asbestos free items.

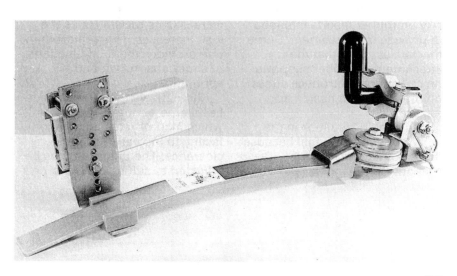

Spring assisters

Another matter to consider is the towcar suspension. Depending on the laden weight of a caravan, the National Caravan Council suggests that noseweight falls somewhere between 50 to 90 kgs (110 to 198 lbs); towbracket manufacturers, however, may specify a maximum nearer the lower end of this range.

A few cars, like models from Citroen, have load sensitive suspension systems with ride height compensation, but this is an exception. Other vehicles fare differently with some sustaining too much tail-end sag when a 'van is in tow.

When looking for an answer, some owners wrongly attribute the problem to the vehicle's shock absorbers. However, a shock absorber is simply a damping device to prevent the vehicle bouncing along on its springs; most shock absorbers contribute little, if anything, to the firmness of the suspension system. It is the springing system which needs firming up.

A number of products are designed to 'beef up' a vehicle's springs although it is advisable to obtain advice from a main dealer before buying accessories from a caravan accessory shop. A franchise dealer may suggest that the car manufacturer's recommendation is to purchase different springs rather than to rely on rubber inserts intended to provide reinforcement. Some mechanics claim that the attachment of rubber supports on coil springs introduce stress points which can hasten a fracture.

You should also look in the vehicle owner's manual because these sometimes include sections on towing. A few

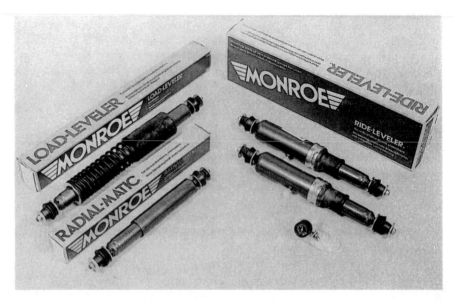

Monroe 'Load Levellers' incorporate a variable rate coil spring which increases its resistance progressively; 'Ride Levellers' involve an inflation principle.

(courtesy of Monroe)

manufacturers e.g. Vauxhall, are becoming particularly aware of the increase in trailer and caravan ownership and the need to give advice and offer accessories. To this end, Vauxhall has produced Towing Guidebooks.

Among the different ways of overcoming tail-end sag, one popular answer is to add subsidiary springs. For instance one manufacturer produces auxiliary coil springs which are mounted ***inside*** the standard coils. There are also products where additional springs are mounted round the body of shock absorbers. The Monroe 'Load Leveller', for example, incorporates a variable rate coil spring which progressively increases its resistance as the load increases. This replacement unit provides the dual function of shock absorption and springing.

Alternatively the Monroe Ride Leveller is a shock absorber unit which incorporates an inflation facility to increase ground clearance. The units can thus be adjusted to suit solo driving or

towing. A pressure gauge indicates the level selected and the units are joined by plastic tubing to an inflation point. This is positioned so that a standard air line or foot pump can be connected to provide inflation. A de-luxe version of this Ride Leveller system includes a compact on-board 12v compressor with a dashboard control switch.

Strengthening devices include products to suit coil, torsion bar and leaf spring suspension systems. However, the suspension on a towcar is rather more involved than the other topics discussed in this chapter; a product which works well when towing might be less appropriate to leave in place when driving solo. For this reason, it is worth seeking advice from a main dealer.

Chapter 4

CARAVAN CHASSIS AND RUNNING GEAR

Chassis developments
Eagerness to reduce the weight of caravans has led to various developments including the advent of the lightweight chassis. The need to minimise weight is driven by the fact that car manufacturers are producing lighter vehicles, which in turn is one of many measures for improving fuel efficiency.

Using the latest computer aided design systems, caravan chassis manufacturers are able to create maximum structural integrity using the minimum amount of material. The sophistication in design is also backed by improved methods of construction. For instance, fold backs on the edges of major sections forming the structure contribute significantly to their strength.

This diagram of a typical Al-Ko chassis shows how the main chassis members are mounted in direct alignment between the coupling head and the outermost ends of the axle.
(courtesy Al-Ko Kober)

The most beneficial location of each component is also recognised in the design. On present day lightweight chassis, it will be noticed that the main longitudinal members achieve continuous alignment between the tow ball on the car and the outermost ends of the caravan axle.

At first sight, today's lightweight chassis look very similar. However, this is deceptive and each model has its own unique purpose-built chassis. The designers take into account features like furniture layout, weight distribution and specific dimensions. The position of the axle is another consideration. For instance if a caravan manufacturer is designing a model with an 'end kitchen', the calculated axle position will ensure a normal noseweight is achieved.

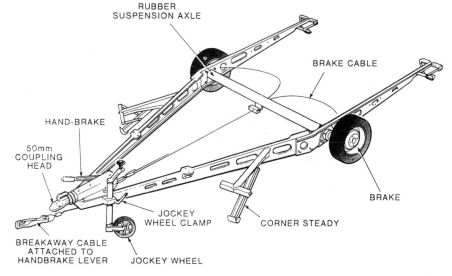

RUBBER SUSPENSION AXLE

BRAKE CABLE

HAND-BRAKE

50mm COUPLING HEAD

JOCKEY WHEEL CLAMP

BRAKE

CORNER STEADY

BREAKAWAY CABLE ATTACHED TO HANDBRAKE LEVER

JOCKEY WHEEL

With the floor panel inverted, the construction of this new caravan begins when the main chassis members are bolted into place; wiring and other services are added next.

Changes in chassis design have also led to changes in caravan assembly. Some years ago the caravan builder would start with a welded chassis and running gear, then adding wooden joists and a plywood floor. Today, however, most manufacturers start with the floor section which comprises a bonded sandwich of plywood and a block foam insulant. This is inverted, whereupon chassis members and the axle are then assembled and bolted to the floor; throughout the assembly no welding is involved.

The use of bolt-together sections makes it easy for these components to be transported in Euro pallets to the caravan factory. Although a few manufacturers e.g. ABI have favoured a one-piece chassis, this is less common. But in either case, the strength of a modern caravan is dependent on the integration of both the chassis structure **and** the sandwich floor itself.

In the 1960s and 1970s, caravan manufacturers ordered chassis from specialists such as

Ambergate, Bird & Billington (B & B) and Peak. However, CI Caravans in Newmarket made their own chassis, albeit with running gear supplied by B & B, Harrison or Peak. All chassis during this period were robust, comparatively heavy and usually painted. Many caravans are still being used today with this type of structure forming their foundation; the accompanying

Before the arrival of lightweight chassis in the 1980s, caravans were built on heavier structures which used coil spring suspension; the B & B type shown here was especially popular.

(courtesy Al-Ko Kober)

illustration of a B & B chassis shows a typical example.

The changeover occurred in the early part of the 1980s when Al-Ko, a German Company, took over B & B. Even though CI continued to manufacture its own chassis for the remaining part of the decade, most caravan manufacturers soon changed to the lighter structures. This was also accompanied by a radical change in suspension systems described in the *Axles and suspension* Section.

Changes in caravan chassis also coincided with equally major changes in the construction of caravan bodies. Indeed it was the development of the bonded floor which helped to hasten chassis evolution. The bonded sandwich system is dealt with in Chapter 5 and even if today's caravans still look similar externally to models made in the sixties and seventies, their structures are different.

The significant saving in weight of a modern chassis and bonded sandwich floor is beyond argument. Moreover, the chassis members manufactured by Al-Ko have always been galvanised which eliminates the maintenance associated with painted chassis. However, there are some

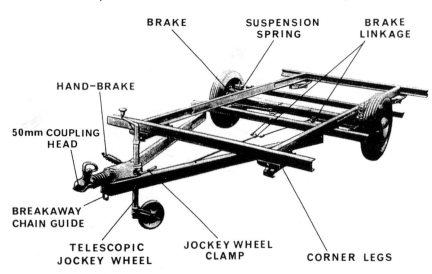

BRAKE   SUSPENSION SPRING   BRAKE LINKAGE
HAND-BRAKE
50mm COUPLING HEAD
BREAKAWAY CHAIN GUIDE
TELESCOPIC JOCKEY WHEEL   JOCKEY WHEEL CLAMP   CORNER LEGS

disadvantages. For example, computer aided design eliminates unnecessary bulk but this means that any lightweight chassis manufactured in the 1980s can only be drilled in exceptional circumstances and in particular positions. This has repercussions if an accessory like a stabiliser support bracket needs to be fitted. Strict procedures must be observed and these were discussed in Chapter 3.

But now the requirements are even more stringent. No drilling of any kind is permitted on a 1990s Al-Ko Kober chassis and disregarding this instruction will invalidate the chassis warranty. Meanwhile in Holland and Germany, drilling a chassis is deemed illegal unless the altered design is submitted for special Type Approval.

Notwithstanding these general changes, a few caravan manufacturers adopt different practices. For instance some of the caravans from Lunar, Swift and Cotswold (which is now part of Swift) are built on an aluminium structure. Lunar caravans are built on a TW chassis made in Lostock Hall, Preston; a number of Cotswold and Swift models are built on a Syspal chassis manufactured in Broseley, Shropshire. As a general rule, these aluminium chassis are assembled using Al-Ko Kober running gear.

CI caravans made in the 1970s and 1980s were built on the manufacturer's own welded steel chassis. The strategy was reviewed in 1990 and several of CI's 1991 models were built on a German lightweight chassis with undergear supplied by Knott (UK) Ltd.

In view of the diversity of chassis types, this chapter cannot cover the entire subject

The order of assembly in which construction starts by building a rolling chassis was still adopted by CI Caravans in 1990.

in depth. Owners of caravans built post 1982 will find further information in the Al-Ko Kober *Service and Maintenance Instruction Spare Part List* from which several diagrams and captions are reproduced here with the manufacturer's permission. Caravan handbooks are another source of data for older models. Where these have been mislaid, Owners' Associations can often provide information.

Chassis maintenance

A modern galvanised chassis is almost maintenance free. However, when it's new, the galvanised members sometimes suffer from a surface discolouration referred to as 'white rust'. In reality, this is not 'rust' but something called 'wet storage stain'.

Galvanised components need time to cure completely, during which time the coating changes from a shiny finish to a duller grey. If used prematurely on a salted road during winter, a new chassis should be washed-off after use in order to prevent 'white rust' forming on the surface. In practice this doesn't cause the chassis to deteriorate, but it does give an unsightly

appearance to chassis members.

Wet storage stain may also be noticed after a caravan has been parked for a prolonged period, especially if air circulation around the chassis members has been restricted. Some caravan skirts and front 'spoilers', for example, can hinder air movements. If this occurs, you can remove unsightly deposits with a stiff nylon brush.

In time, however, the zinc coating on a new chassis reacts with the atmosphere, and changes to a dark grey. This shows that the zinc treatment has developed its full protective potential and further incidence of wet storage stain is unlikely.

The protective benefit of galvanising is notable. Indeed it should never be painted because this tends to allow moisture to become trapped between the galvanised surface and the subsequent layer of paint. In any case, neither paint nor any other form of sealer will adhere satisfactorily.

At most, the owner merely needs to brush away road dirt. If the chassis gets damaged, however, repairs should be carried out by a specialist. This

is especially true if part of a chassis gets damaged in an accident. In the case of a modern sectional chassis, the specialist is sometimes able to unbolt and replace a damaged component and check alignment. Without question, this is not do-it-yourself work.

With regard to an **aluminium** chassis, owner maintenance is more necessary, particularly if the caravan is used on salted winter roads. Whilst it doesn't rust, the surface of aluminium can become pitted and coated with oxide. Salt will aggravate this condition and its effect on aluminium can be particularly harmful. It should therefore be hosed off at the earliest opportunity.

Another problem arises when steel components are attached to an aluminium chassis. As moisture accumulates, the two metals react as a result of electrolysis and in time the chassis can get damaged. In effect a rudimentary accumulator has been created in which the dissimilar metals are acting as an anode and cathode. This can happen if the 'L' bracket for a spring leaf stabiliser is bolted direct to an aluminium chassis 'A' frame. To avoid chassis damage, large 'neoprene' spacer washers have to be fitted to prevent metal contact; both Bulldog and Scott stabilisers can be supplied with modified 'L' brackets to suit an aluminium chassis.

Owner care and maintenance is different in respect of a painted steel chassis. There are a lot still in active service though many have been neglected. A close inspection often shows rusty areas where paint has peeled away, especially on the forward faces of cross members which have received the brunt of chippings thrown up by the tow car.

Before contemplating repainting work, the caravan needs to be safely elevated. One

In order to gain access to a chassis and undergear, it is important to ensure that the caravan is elevated safely.

method is to drive it on to a scaffold plank, and progressively adding two or three more. An alternative is to use axle stands. Start by elevating one side of the caravan with a jack, making certain that the handbrake is on, corner steadies are **raised**, the wheel on the far side is firmly chocked and a steady balance is provided by the jockey wheel. A stand can then be inserted under the axle, inboard from the road

wheel. The procedure is then repeated on the other side. Once the 'van is elevated, corner steadies can then be lowered, using wood blocks where necessary.

It is important to acknowledge that corner steadies are **not** strong enough to act as jacks. If this is ignored they will get damaged, together with the floor section and other chassis members as well.

Once a caravan has been raised on a safe platform, corner steadies can be lowered using wood blocks where necessary.

A modern lightweight chassis must NOT be jacked up under the main members. Lifting points are either on the axle tube or under the heavy plates (arrowed) which locate the axle.

Another point of concern relates to lifting points. On older caravans, chassis members have sufficient rigidity to provide a number of jacking points. But this is not the case with a modern chassis. Ideally a jack should be placed under the central axle tube, but it can also be placed under the plates which connect the axle assembly to the main longitudinal members of the chassis. Anywhere else is likely to get distorted.

For work at home or for emergency roadside repairs, the Al-Ko scissor jack has been purpose made. It features a special support which matches the profile of a modern axle tube. Hydraulic bottle jacks sold in auto stores would be suitable if they included a similar support but they usually lack a lifting plate.

An even better system being fitted to some of the latest caravans is a side operating jack. Attachment holes to receive this optional unit were first punched into the side members of Al-Ko chassis for certain 1992 models.

From 1992 onwards, several caravans have been manufactured using the Al-Ko Kober side jacking system

Van Royce and Elddis were among the first caravan manufacturers to offer this as an optional feature.

To renovate an old type of chassis, jack the caravan as described and then insert axle stands and planks under the wheels. ***Never* rely on a jack alone when crawling underneath your caravan.** All surface rust must now be removed using a wire brush. A

rotary brush driven by an electric drill is better than a hand brush, **but it is essential to wear safety goggles.** Filaments of wire often become detached and fly in any direction.

There are several treatments available including products which leave a coating of phosphate as a base for subsequent applications of undercoat and cellulose topcoat. Another popular treatment is a special protective metal paint called Hammerite. Available in both smooth and 'hammered' finishes, this can be painted directly on to bare or rusty metal in one thick coating. The product dries quickly and is justifiably popular; however, Hammerite instructions must be carried out correctly.

Corner steadies
It was mentioned earlier that if corner steadies are used to elevate a caravan they will distort. This damage can also extend to other chassis members and on a modern caravan the sandwich floor can split as well.

Even when used correctly, the threads on the central spindles are prone to rusting. Not unusually, the front steadies deteriorate more quickly on

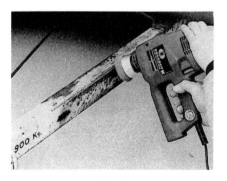

If an older chassis has started to accumulate rust and peeling paint, a rotary wire brush is useful for preparing the surfaces for refurbishment.

The mechanisms on corner steadies must be kept lightly greased; but do not over-grease the spindle because it will then hold road dirt.

account of road dirt thrown up from the towing vehicle. The mechanisms must therefore be lightly greased on a regular basis and the steadies raised and lowered as often as possible, especially during a long period of outdoor storage. Be careful not to over-grease the spindle because this will hold road chippings.

If corner steadies can be locked in the lowered position, this is a deterrent to the tow-away thief. With this in mind, Al-Ko has introduced a locking spindle kit in which the standard unit is replaced by one which incorporates an integral lock. Other devices rely on a padlock though these are usually less successful; a competent criminal can force a padlock in seconds.

Variations on standard corner steadies include hydraulically-operated units and electrically-controlled systems. Their advantages are recognised by anyone who has had to set up a caravan in the dark when it's raining. Both types consist of replacement steadies which are made for DIY installation or factory fitting.

As regards the Saltofix hydraulic system, this comprises four replacement steadies, complete with hydraulic piston, and a central pump. If required, it is also possible to purchase a hydraulically-operated jockey wheel.

The accompanying photographs show a Saltofix steady system being installed. Provided the original corner steadies can be detached easily, the conversion is straight forward. As regards the main pump and control unit, this is best situated in a locker box where it is unaffected by adverse weather. On older caravans with heavy chassis structures, the pump can also be fitted on the caravan draw bar.

By operating the pump handle, all four steadies are lowered in unison. Alternatively

i) The new corner steadies are lowered by a hydraulic piston and raised by a spring; these replace the original units.

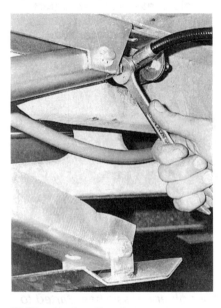

ii) The hydraulic pipes are specially made with a union which is bolted directly on to the piston assembly.

iii) All connecting pipework from the pump to the steadies is fixed securely to the underside of the floor.

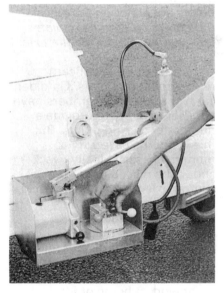

iv) The pump unit can be supplied in a metal box to fit on the draw bar. It is better, however, to install it in the front locker box.

when the pressure switch is released, heavy duty springs on each of the steadies lift them back to the stowed position. Maintaining the system involves keeping corner steady pistons lubricated to prevent rust forming on the surface. Similarly, the spring mechanisms need to be kept clean. Overall, this is a product offering particular benefits to elderly or disabled caravanners.

Another automatic system, called the Caralevel, is electrically-operated and 12v motors are attached to each corner steady. In addition, a computer monitors progress and ensures that the legs are lowered correctly and completely. The Caralevel rig shown at caravan exhibitions gives a very clear demonstration of the way that each motor is brought into a sequential operation in order to facilitate the levelling process.

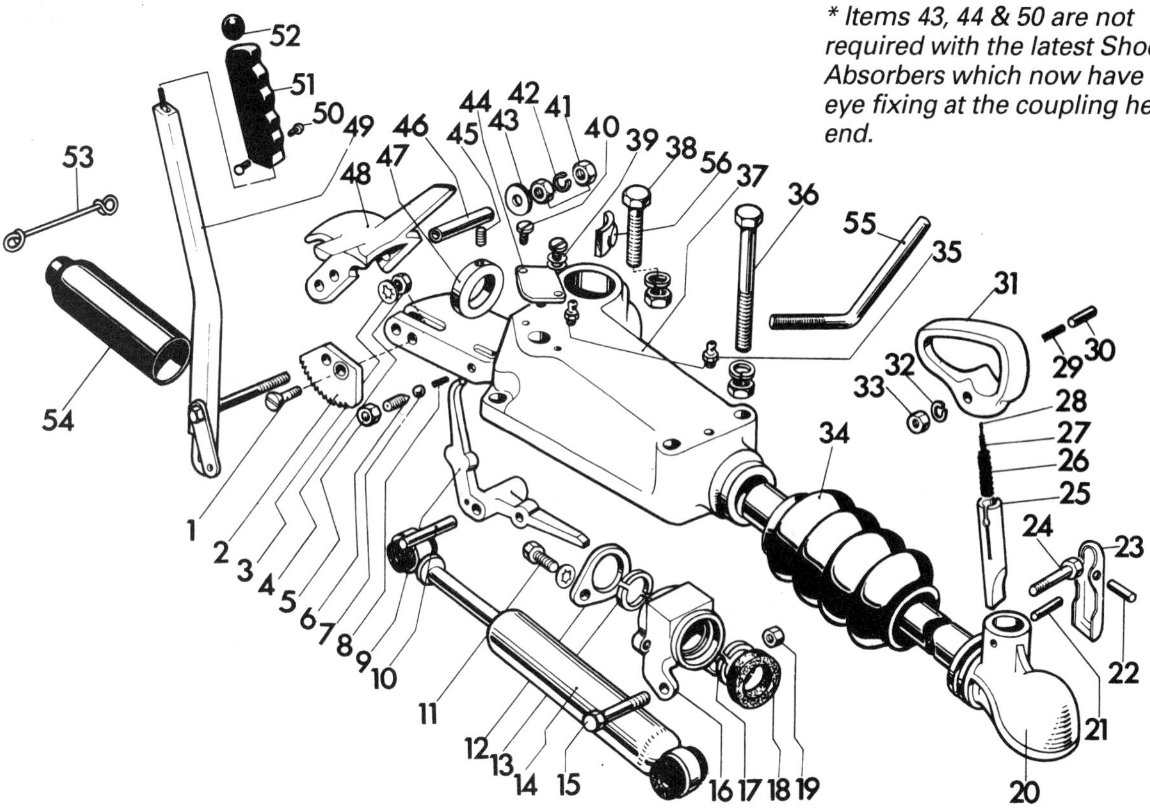

The Beta 4 hydraulic overrun coupling was used on many caravans up to 1972; it was usually matched with the 8 in mechanical brakes shown later. Spares are still listed in the Al-Ko Kober catalogue.

(courtesy Al-Ko Kober)

1 ⅜" UNFX ⅞" CSK Set Screw
2 Ratchet Plate
3 Shake-Proof Washer
4 ⅜" UNF Locknut
5 ⅜" UNF Locknut
6 Cone Point Screw
7 ¼" Diameter Ball
8 Spring for Reverse Catch
9 Reverse Lever
10 Mills Pin
11 ¼" UNF x ½" Hex S Screw
12 Retaining Washer
13 Split Ring
14 Hydraulic Damper
15 ⅜" UNF x 2¼" Hex Bolt
16 Damper Bracket
17 Split Ring
18 Rubber Washer
19 ⅜" UNF Binx Nut
20 Assembled Head and Shaft
21 Mills Pin
22 ⎰ M.S. Pin
23 ⎱ Safety Catch Assy
24 ⎰ Safety Catch Bolt M10 x 50
25 50mm Plunger
26 Outer Spring
27 Middle Spring
28 Inner Spring
29 Spring
30 Nylon Plunger
31 Release Handle

32 Single Coil Washer M.10 S.C.
33 Full Nut M.10
34 P.V.C. Boot
35 Grease Nipple
36 Fixing Bolts plus Spring Washer & Nut
37 Body Casting
38 Fixing Bolt plus Spring Washer & Nut
39 ³/₁₆" Washer (was SP 481)
40 ³/₁₆" x ⅜" Screw
41 ⅜" UNF Locknut
42 ⅜" Single Coil Washer
43 ⅜" M.S. Washer*
44 Solenoid Cover Plate*
45 ¼" UNF x ⅜" Socket Set Screw
46 M.S. Pivot Tube
47 Collar
48 Overrun Brake Lever
49 Handbrake Sub-Assembly
50 Drive-in Rivet*
51 Black Plastic Grip
52 Release Knob
53 Wire Tie
54 Dirt Shroud
55 Locking Handle (Jockey Wheel)
56 Pressure Pad (Light) Pressure Pad (Heavy)

* Items 43, 44 & 50 are not required with the latest Shock Absorbers which now have an eye fixing at the coupling head end.

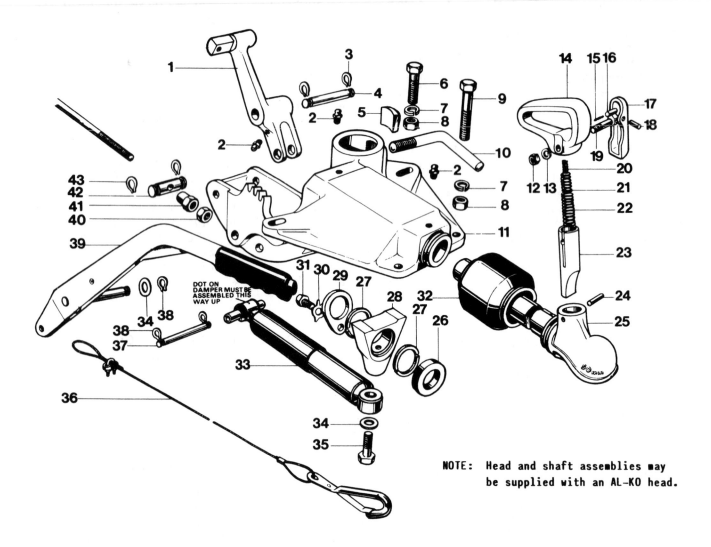

DOT ON DAMPER MUST BE ASSEMBLED THIS WAY UP

NOTE: Head and shaft assemblies may be supplied with an AL-KO head.

The Swedish Sigma Mk II was used on a large number of caravans made between 1971 and 1982. Spares are still listed in the Al-Ko Kober catalogue.
(courtesy Al-Ko Kober)

1 Overrun Lever
2 Grease Nipple
3 Iron Clip
4 Overrun Pivot Pin 12mm
5 Pressure Pad
6 Rear Bolt, Fixing M.12 x 30
7 Washer
8 Binx Nut M.12
9 Front Fixing Bolt M.12 x 120
10 Jockey Wheel Clamp Handle (Metric)

11 Body Casting
12 Full Nut M.10
13 Single Coil Washer M.10 SC
14 Handle
15 Spring
16 Plunger Nylon
17 Safety Catch Assembly
18 M.S. Pin
19 Safety Catch Bolt M.10 x 50
20 Inner Spring
21 Middle Spring
22 Outer Spring
23 Plunger 50mm
24 Mills Pin
25 50mm Head & Shaft Assembly
26 Bump Rubber
27 Split Ring

28 Damper Bracket
29 Retaining Washer
30 Tab Washer
31 Bolt M.6 x 12
32 Gaiter
33 Damper
34 Plain Washer M.13
35 Locking Bolt M.10 x 50
36 Breakaway Cable
37 Damper Rear Fixing Pin
38 Iron Clip
39 Hand Brake Sub-assembly
40 Binx Lock Nut $^5/_{16}$" UNF
41 Reach Nut $^5/_{16}$" UNF
42 Brake Rod Swivel Pin
43 Iron Clip

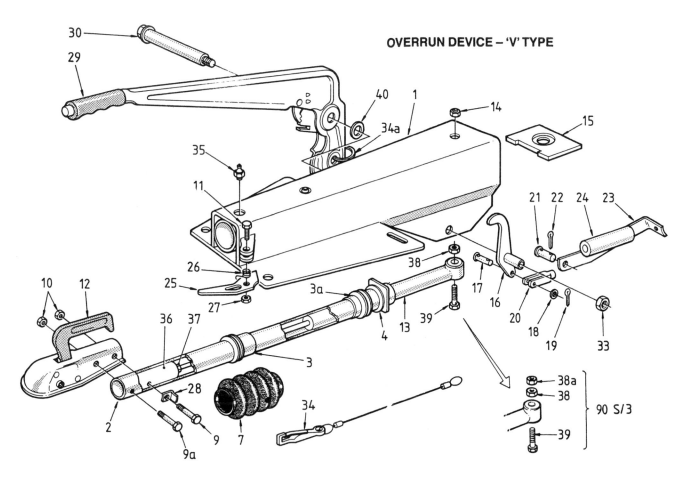

OVERRUN DEVICE – 'V' TYPE

When asbestos was banned in braking systems in 1989, a large proportion of light caravans were subsequently built with the Al-Ko 90S/3 ('V' type) coupling, matched with a 1637 braking system.

(courtesy Al-Ko Kober)

Part Description
1 Hitch body
2 Draw shaft
3 Bearing bush
3a Bearing bush } sets only
4 Damping rubber
7 Gaiter
9 Hexagon bolt
9a Hexagon bolt
10 Hexagon nut
11 Hexagon bolt
12 Coupling head
13* Shock absorber
14 Hexagon nut
15 Plate
16 Overrun level
17 Bolt
18 Washer

19 Split pin
20 Yoke end
21 Bolt
22 Split pin
23 Tension Bar
24 Spring cylinder
25 Reverse Lock
26 Torsion spring
27 Hexagon nut
28 Bracket
29 Hand brake lever
30 Pivot pin
33 Hexagon nut
34 Break away cable
34a Burst Ring
35 Grease nipple
36* Connecting bolt
37* Hexagon nut
38 Hexagon nut
38a Hexagon nut
39 Hexagon bolt
40 Washer

* Items 13, 36 & 37 are not required with the latest Shock Absorbers which now have an eye fixing at the coupling head end.

Overrun assemblies
Like caravan chassis, overrun components have also changed in the last decade. When products like the Peak and the B & B chassis were in production, coupling heads, for example, were made from a heavy casting. Nowadays, however, the majority are made from pressed steel.

All caravans are manufactured with a special overrun braking mechanism, which in turn affects the design and fixing of the coupling head. Changes have occurred, however, since the arrival of automatic reversing brakes.

In addition to technical improvements, legislation has also brought about changes in design. For instance in EEC countries, caravans manufactured from October 1982 onwards are not permitted to have braked couplings which incorporate spring mechanisms.

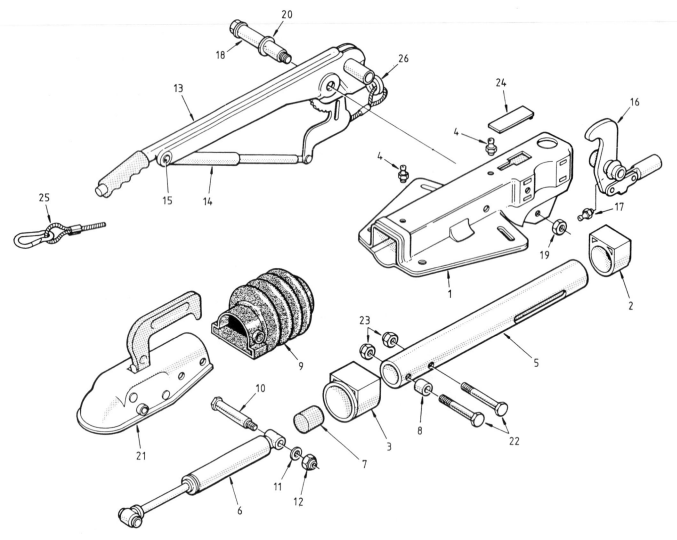

Many larger caravans built from 1989 onwards have been equipped with the 161S Al-Ko overrun system, matched with a 2051 non-asbestos braking unit.
(courtesy Al-Ko Kober)

1 Body Assembly
2 Rear Bush
3 Front Bush
4 Grease Nipple AM8xl
5 Drawshaft Tube
Drawshaft Assembly
6 Damper
7 Buffer
8 Spacing Bush
9 Gaiter
10 Damper Fixing Bolt
11 Washer Ø 13
12 Locknut M12
Handbrake Assembly
13 Handbrake Lever
14 Gas Strut

15 Fixing bolt
16 Overrun Lever Assy.
17 Grease Nipple AM6
Lever & Pivot Assy.
18 Pivot Pin
19 Lock Nut M12
20 Washer Ø 17
21 Coupling Head
Coupling Head Assy.
22 Hex. Bolt M12 x 75
23 Lock Nut NM 12
24 Cover Plate
25 Breakaway Cable
26 Burst Ring

The ruling now requires that couplings should incorporate a hydraulic damper instead. Further information on the braking principles are given in the *Braking systems* Section.

As a general rule, a caravan overrun assembly is designed so that the coupling head can be operated with one hand. On the earlier cast versions, it was necessary to press a small lever situated on one side of the coupling head so that the handle portion could be lifted vertically, thereby releasing the mechanism from the tow ball. More modern pressed steel versions operate slightly differently. There are several types in use, but these generally feature a small trigger release under the handle which has to be depressed. Older models have a small button on the side of the coupling handle. Either way, lifting the handle upwards and forwards effects disconnection.

Most pressed steel coupling heads can be fitted with an anti-thief device which prevents the locking cam inside the enclosure from being moved. Security is achieved by locating a small brass insert into a purpose-made aperture. An example of the type used for caravans made in the mid 1980s is shown in the accompanying photograph.

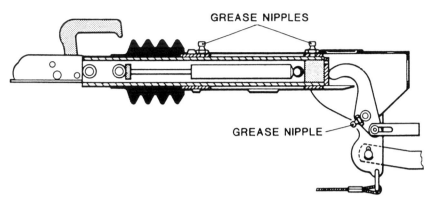

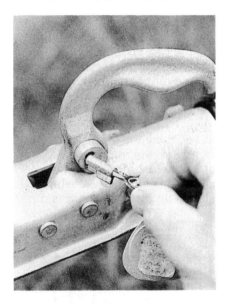

Some pressed steel coupling heads can be fitted with an anti-theft device which prevents the locking cam inside the enclosure from being moved.

Other types of anti-theft device which completely cover the coupling head are also available. Two examples which are especially robust are the Bulldog Hitchlock and the 'Keep it'; these come in various versions to suit different makes of coupling.

In addition to keeping all the moving parts on an overrun assembly lubricated, it is sensible to cover the entire assembly with a waterproof plastic sack or purpose-made cover whenever the 'van is laid up for a long period. This is especially appropriate during the winter months. However, you should endeavour to attach the cover in such a way that air can circulate around the unit. When storing the 'van, you must

It is important to keep an overrun system lubricated and nipples are provided so that the shaft bearing can be greased.

also ensure that the brake is left in the **off** position, using wheel chocks if parked on a slope.

Another point to note is that coupling heads must **not** be drilled in any way. Earlier stabilisers like the Mongoose which relied on a drilled coupling head are no longer available on account of this problem. Lastly the caravan owner should note that when lifting a 'van upwards by the handle, it is important to ensure that the lever is depressed **prior** to commencing the lift.

Axles and suspension

Since the early days of caravanning, several types of suspension system have been used. The idea of using leaf springs has been tried, but the system has not been used for many years. Torsion bar suspension has similarly had a short life, even though it has been successfully used on small vehicles like the Renault 5.

Coil springs with telescopic dampers have had a longer period of popularity and were common on famous chassis like the B & B 'Independent' units. Many are still in use and there is little to go wrong. On the other hand, the hydraulic dampers need checking for leaks and should be replaced if there is evidence of fluid loss. Service

and maintenance instructions for B & B suspension systems, B & B chassis and Sigma back-up braking systems are currently available on request from Al-Ko Kober Ltd. But the products are sufficiently old for this information to be discontinued at some time in the future.

Nowadays the suspension system employs lengths of rubber rather than leaf springs, coil springs or torsion bars. The principle involves rubber which is forced into a state of compression. If you look closely at an Al-Ko axle, you will notice that in cross section it is a hexagonal shape. The accompanying diagram shows that within the six sided tubular axle are three lengths of compressible rubber which are seated within an inner tube with tri-lobal flutings.

Extensive testing has verified the effectiveness of a rubber compression system and since it is self-damping, shock absorbers are not normally needed. Only with a heavy caravan, a Continental model, or one with a Delta axle are you likely to find additional hydraulic dampers. When the caravan is laden and on the road, the Al-Ko Kober suspension is designed so that the trailing arm will settle at 5 degrees below the horizontal position.

With regard to the complete extent of permissible movement, an Al-Ko axle moves through an arc of 45 degrees. This ranges from 25 degrees

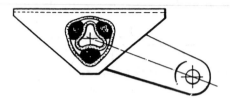

**REBOUND OR
FREE POSITION**

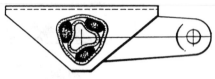

**NORMAL LADEN
POSITION**

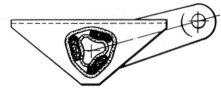

MAXIMUM BUMP

The Al-Ko rubber-in-compression system is maintenance free and its damping characteristics eliminate the need for shock absorbers. The diagrams show the deformation of the rubber in different ride positions.
(courtesy Al-Ko Kober)

below the horizontal when the caravan is jacked up, to a position of 20 degrees above horizontal at the maximum bump angle. Obviously a severe overloading could increase the permitted turning range of the suspension arm and the rubber elements would probably be damaged in consequence. It is most important, therefore, to pay particular regard to the load margin given with the manufacturer's specification data or shown on the axle plate. To exceed the limit is dangerous and in Germany the offence will result in a severe 'on the spot fine'. This amounted to 300DM (£190.00) in 1990.

When looking at the modern hexagonal axle, it is also important to recognise that its sturdy tube structure contributes strength to the chassis as well. But there are also variations in its basic design. For example, Al-Ko has introduced the 'Delta Axle' into the United Kingdom. The axle with its prominent arrow-head shape has been used for some time on the

The Delta Compound Axle has been introduced into Britain by Al-Ko Kober; its design achieves a notably high degree of stability.

Continent and is now being fitted to some British caravans e.g. the ABI Award range. Research has shown that the Delta-shaped axle achieves a higher degree of stability compared with the standard design. This improvement is particularly evident when a car and caravan are negotiating a sharp bend. In this situation, the caravan wheel on the outside of the corner increases its toe-in and negative camber angle, thereby producing an improved alignment between the vehicle and the trailer.

Without doubt, the technology in axle design has advanced significantly in recent years. So, too, has the suspension system and it is difficult to anticipate what might replace the present compressed rubber principle. Its operation is long lasting, efficient and trouble free; moreover, there is nothing needed in respect of routine maintenance.

Notwithstanding these

remarks, the owner can extend the life of a suspension system by taking certain precautions whenever the caravan is being unused for a long period. Recognising that rubber will always return to its original shape once the load has been removed, the manufacturer strongly recommends that a caravan is lifted on to axle stands so that its weight is no

Whereas supporting a stored caravan on PGR Winterwheels will take the load off the tyres, it will not relieve pressure on the rubber suspension.

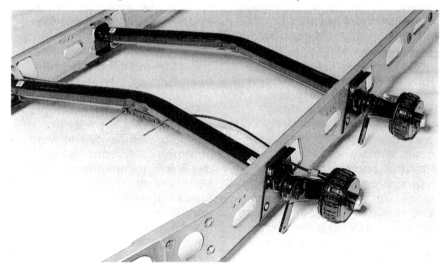

longer borne by the wheels. You are advised to carry this out whenever the caravan is left over the winter. Some caravanners pursue a similar strategy to extend the life of the tyres by fitting products such as 'Winter Wheels'. However, whereas these special brackets support the 'van in place of its wheels, they do not take the load from the suspension system. This can only be done using axle stands.

Braking systems
Unlike the axle and suspension systems described in the previous section, brakes **do** need regular maintenance. Similarly the brake shoes may need replacement from time to time, and this is a job which the competent do-it-yourselfer could tackle at home.

Virtually all caravans employ a drum brake system. Other brakes have been tried, however, and the German chassis makers, Peitz, introduced a disc brake in the 1980s. Cotswold was the first British caravan manufacturer to fit these units and the 1986 Celeste could be ordered with Peitz disc brakes fitted as an optional extra. However, caravan disc brakes are substantially more expensive than the drum alternative and they have not been fitted to many models.

Efforts have also been made to introduce an independent brake on caravans which is switch-operated by the driver. Such a device would be invaluable if brakes failed on the towcar. In recognition of the potential danger of brake failure, an emergency system was introduced in the 1980s called the Elken brake actuator. It worked on a vacuum principle, using a connecting tube fitted to the induction manifold on the towcar. The concept was clever, but few owners fitted the unit.

For most caravanners, the only way to apply its brakes is via the automatic overrun system. Since this takes a significant load which would otherwise be borne by the towcar, it is most important that all parts of the overrun mechanism are maintained regularly.

The overrun braking principle is an important contributor to safety. For instance when towing a caravan downhill, there is a tendency for it to push against the rear of the car. It is the overrun system which applies the caravan brakes and reduces the 'shove in the tail'.

To achieve this operation, the caravan coupling head is mounted on a shaft which moves like a piston within the forward part of the overrun device. When the caravan starts to catch up the car, the shaft is depressed. It subsequently makes contact with the overrun lever which in turn connects up with the brakes. In consequence the caravan brakes are applied whenever the shaft is depressed, which happens when you drive down a hill.

Unfortunately, however, the shaft also becomes depressed when a caravan is reversed. An over-ride facility is therefore needed and a disabling system was introduced on old style chassis like the B & B in the 1960s and early 1970s. Many caravans still have this arrangement, but it isn't very convenient because someone has to get out to operate the disabling lever so that the brakes don't come into operation when the 'van is backed. At least the device releases itself automatically as soon as the vehicle starts to pull forwards again.

To simplify procedures, a few caravanners purchased an electrically operated device for engaging the reversing catch. This employed a solenoid and had to be fitted into a purpose-made recess in the overrun device or in the coupling body (Beta type IV). Control was carried out from the driver's seat throughout the manoeuvring operation and the system was much liked. However, these solenoid switching systems are no longer available.

The 'breakthrough', however, came in the early 1970s when auto-reverse brakes were invented; not surprisingly these are now fitted to all modern caravans built to British Standards. The operation of an auto-reverse brake is no different from a conventional caravan brake. When descending a hill and applying your foot brake, the caravan will tend to overrun the car, thus depressing the shaft behind the coupling head. This in turn operates the caravan brakes via a rod and/or a Bowden cable system. However, the piston will be similarly depressed whenever the outfit is being reversed and for a brief moment, the brake shoe will bear against the drum. But as soon as the reverse rotation of the wheel is detected, the trailing shoe will then react by withdrawing automatically from the bearing surface.

In AP Lockheed brakes, the key to the operating mechanism is the fact that the trailing shoe is fitted within a supporting carrier as shown in the accompanying illustrations. These drawings show the A.P. Lockheed caravan reversing brake and are reproduced with the manufacturer's permission. When the brake operates normally, it is the carrier which is pressed outwards by the expander assembly; the carrier encloses the brake shoe which is then forced against the drum.

When the caravan is reversed, the same action occurs, at least to begin with. But as soon as the trailing brake shoe makes contact with the drum – now turning in the opposite direction

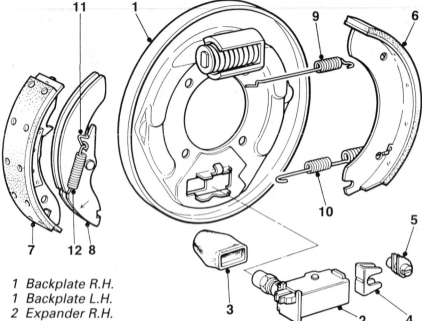

1 Backplate R.H.
1 Backplate L.H.
2 Expander R.H.
3 Rubber boot
2 Expander L.H.
3 Rubber boot
3 Rubber boot (2 off)
4 Mask
5 Micram
6 Leading shoe (2)
7 Trailing shoe (2)
8 Trailing shoe carrier
9 Pull-off spring (Black)
   Single coil R.H.
9 Pull-off spring (Red)
   Single coil L.H.
10 Pull-off spring double coil R.H.
10 Pull-off spring double coil L.H.
11 Carrier link (2)
12 Carrier spring (4)

A key component in the AP Lockheed reversing brake is the 'carrier' i.e. the component in which the trailing brake shoe is housed; when reversing, the shoe moves within the carrier and pulls away from the drum.
          (courtesy of AP Lockheed)

– it is pushed backwards. On account of the angled shape of the carrier, the brake shoe which it cradles then withdraws from the bearing surface of the drum. Nevertheless, as soon as the caravan is then pulled forwards again, a spring pulls the shoe back to its original position in the carrier so that normal action can be resumed.

The Al-Ko Kober auto reverse brake – fitted to around three-quarters of home market caravans – is completely different in operation. The key component which causes the brake shoe to withdraw from the drum when the wheels rotate backwards is pointed out in the accompanying photograph.

This is a spring loaded lever (Component 16 in the following diagram) which normally pushes the brake shoe against the drum. However, when reversing, the brake shoe starts to displace in the **opposite** direction as soon as it bears against the drum, thereby causing the spring loaded lever to pivot. It is this rotation in the lever, which causes the shoe to fall inwards, to lose contact with the drum, and to allow the backing manoeuvre to continue.

When the caravanner drives forward again, a spring (Component 21 in the following diagram) reinstates the lever into its normal operating position. A fuller description of the components in a typical Al-Ko Kober brake is given in the next section.

This 8 in brake unit was usually matched with the B&B MkIV overrun mechanism fitted to many pre-1973 caravans.

i) With the wheel removed, followed by the grease cap, the cotter pin must be withdrawn from the castellated nut on the stub axle.

ii) Once the castellated nut is undone, the outer bearing is easily withdrawn from its seating within the brake drum.

iii) The drum can now be removed, taking great care not to inhale any dust; this may contain asbestos.

Of the remaining caravans, some are fitted with Knott brakes which are again slightly different, although the broad principle of operation is much the same.

Routine servicing and brake shoe replacement is something which a competent owner might tackle. Procedures are often outlined in caravan handbooks and the accompanying sequence of photographs shows the shoes being replaced on a 1970s caravan built on a B & B chassis.

This is the spring-loaded lever which allows the brake shoe to withdraw from the drum in the Al-Ko Kober system.

The components of the Al-Ko Kober automatic reversing brake.

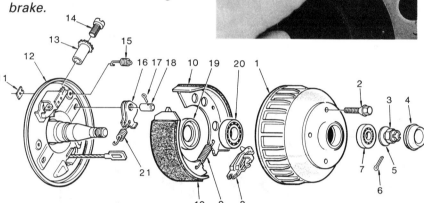

Description of Al-Ko system

Some brake units are fitted cable over and some cable under to cater for differing positions of the expanding clutch.

The wheel hub brake unit comprises, a wheel hub backplate (12), handed left or right, assembled to a central axle stub shaft. The plate is drilled to accept various items of the brake unit.

A handed transmission lever (16) is attached to the adjuster box by a floating pivot pin (18) secured by a split pin (17). The fulcrum of the transmission lever (pivot pin) is set to work against a tensioned spring (21) attached to the backplate.

An adjusting nut (13), commonly called the starwheel, slots into the other end of the adjuster box and is held in place by an adjusting screw (14).

This sub-assembly forms the spring-loaded auto-reverse mechanism. Its various functions are entirely dependent upon the position of the fulcrum in relation to the expanding clutch and brake shoes.

The brake shoes (10), joined together by a tensioned spring (9), are secured to the backplate using pressure springs (15) held in place by cover plates (11). The expanding clutch (8) is inserted between the trailing

edges of the shoes and is floating. The eye on the end of the Bowden cable attaches to a hook fitted as part of the clutch.

An oil seal (19) and bearing (20) are fitted to the brake drum hub before the brake drum (1) is fitted over the shoes and secured to the backplate.

Finally, a taper roller bearing (7) is fitted to the stub shaft and held in place by a lock washer (5) and castellated nut (3) secured by a split pin (6). This subassembly is covered by a grease cap (4). Axial play of the wheel hub bearing can be removed by adjustment of this castellated nut.

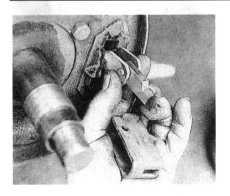

iv) Once the shoes have been removed, the housing for the expanding mechanism is slid away to reveal the actuating lever.

v) A small application of light oil to the inner section of the lever assembly was needed at this point.

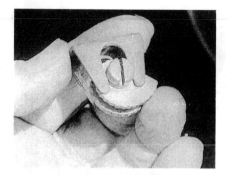

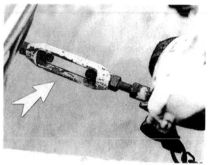

requires less maintenance, but it is prudent to keep it checked regularly and to lightly grease all moving parts. If the cable itself needs replacing, this is not difficult. The drawings opposite show how to replace the type of Bowden cable fitted to asbestos-free brake units.

vi) The micram brake adjustment cam had seized up and had to be removed for loosening off and cleaning.

ix) Only when the brakes have been adjusted at the drum should attention turn to the bottle screw on the operating rod.

If a Bowden cable needs replacing, these step-by-step instructions explain the procedures.
(courtesy Al-Ko Kober)

Fitting a Bowden Cable
The Bowden cable for the new asbestos free wheel brakes can be inserted externally.

Only an original AL-KO Bowden cable should be used for this task. These are embossed with the legend, AL-KO.

vii) Prior to reassembly, the micram brake adjuster (arrowed) is placed into the slotted end of a new shoe. The shoes were the type fitted to Morris 1000 cars.

x) On this project, the adjustment had to create a clearance of 30 mm (1¼ in) between the over-run piston and the actuating lever.

(a) *Remove the steel sleeve from the support collar and detach the upper part of the Bowden cable support.*
(b) *Insert the press-in nipple of an AL-KO Bowden cable into the insertion eye. Pull back the outer sheath of the cable so that the nipple engages correctly with the eye.*
(c) *Insert the upper part of the Bowden cable support into the opening of the brake plate. Ensure that it is fitted flush with the welded, lower portion of the cable support.*
(d) *Push the Bowden cable end bush over the complete support throat of the collar until it can go no further.*
(e) *Visually confirm that the nipple is inserted correctly, then tighten the wire of the Bowden cable.*

viii) The new shoes, held together by both springs, are re-located over the backing plate one side at a time.

A further useful source of information is the AP Lockheed Service Manual (M13/1, 1990, *Reversing Brake for Caravans & Trailers*). Pocket versions of this Lockheed Manual have been distributed as free inserts within some of the national caravan journals.

As regards the connection between the drawbar shaft and the brake units, this may be via rod and/or Bowden cable. Rod systems were popular on B & B chassis and all linkages need to be lightly greased periodically. More up-to-date caravans usually have a rod and Bowden cable system instead. This

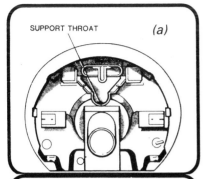

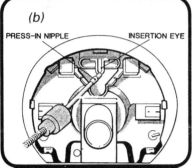

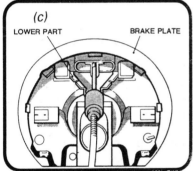

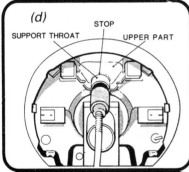

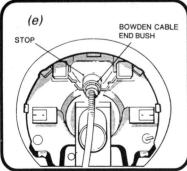

Brake Linkage Adjustment

Apply the handbrake two or three times to ensure that the brake shoes are centralised on the drum. Recheck shoe clearance at the wheel brake.

Centre brake rod – check that there is full thread engagement in the fork end of the overrunning device. Secure the locking nut.

At the axle, ensure that the compensator plate is parallel to the axle by adjusting the nuts on the bowden cables. Lock the nuts.

Adjust the centre brake rod at the rear nut so that there is no clearance between the overrun lever and the drawshaft and plate. Secure the locknuts.

Correct adjustment of the linkage is checked by operating the handbrake lever so that it engages the second tooth of the ratchet and confirming that a slight braking force is felt at the wheels.

On completion, tighten the self locking nut to give 1mm clearance between the nut and the spring cylinder. (Ignore this instuction if a gas strut type handbrake lever is fitted).

Reversing will be difficult if either the wheel brake or the brake linkage is over-adjusted.

Procedures for making a brake linkage adjustment.
(courtesy Al-Ko Kober)

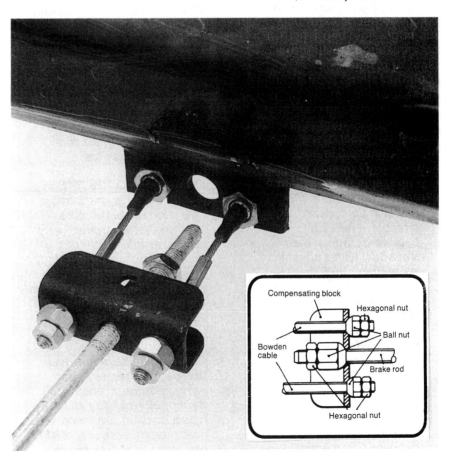

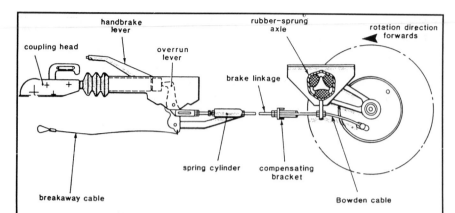

Procedures for adjusting the Al-Ko Kober Automatic Reversing brake.

(courtesy Al-Ko Kober)

1 *Ensure the towing shaft of the overrun is pulled fully out.*
2 *Ensure the handbrake is in the fully off position. If the handbrake will not go down the whole way because of obstruction from the fairing, then the fairing must be cut away to give this desired position. You will never set up a braking system properly where the handbrake is not in this fully off position.*
3 *Jack up one side of the caravan, placing the jack under the axle, also placing an axle stand under for safety.*
4 *Remove the plastic bung from the backplate to expose the 'starwheel' adjuster.*
5 ***ALWAYS*** *rotating the road wheel in the forward direction –* ***NEVER*** *backwards, adjust the starwheel with a suitable screwdriver until there is resistance in the wheel movement.*
6 *Slacken until the road wheel turns freely in the* ***FORWARD*** *direction.*
7 *Check the adjustment at the end of the Bowden cable where it is secured to the plate on the centre of the axle. When the inner cable is pulled out it should extend between 5 and 8 mm.*

8 *Repeat for the other wheel or wheels.*
9 *Ensure that the compensator is pulled evenly – apply and release the handbrake three or four times to centralise the brake shoes.*
10 *Check that the brake rod support bar (fixed to the caravan floor)* ***IS*** *supporting the brake rod evenly and not just at one end.*
11 *Adjust the brake rod so the overrun lever butts up against the end of the towing shaft, leaving no clearance. Secure all brake rod locking nuts.*
12 *Adjust the locking nuts to give 1 mm* ***ONLY*** *clearance on the spring cylinder. (if the overrun is fitted with a gas strut handbrake there is no spring cylinder fitted and therefore ignore this paragraph.)*
13 ***CORRECT ADJUSTMENT*** *of the linkage is checked by operating the handbrake lever so that when the second or third tooth of the rachet is engaged a slight braking force is felt on the wheels.*
14 ***OVER ADJUSTMENT*** *of either the wheel brakes or linkages will make reversing difficult or impossible.*
15 *Finally if you have removed the road wheels, retighten using a torque wrench to 65 lbs ft or 90 Nm – (on all M12 wheel bolts) in sequence, ie, north, south, east, west* ***NOT*** *clockwise or anti-clockwise.*

Over a period of time, a brake cable will stretch and the brake shoes will start to wear. Adjustments will therefore be necessary. The initial tightening adjustments should always begin at the brake drum assembly before turning attention to the linkage. On the older B & B 'mechanical' system with a rod operating principle, some caravanners do nothing more than to adjust the bottle screw which is just behind the handbrake lever. This is wrong; only final adjustments are made here after you've tightened the brakes at the drum.

Whilst the method of making adjustments at the brake drum may vary, many brakes incorporate an access point on the backing plate (e.g. Al-Ko) or on the brake drum (e.g. Lockheed or Girling). The opening is just large enough for a screwdriver to be inserted so that a tightening wheel or notched cam can be turned.

In addition to brake operation via movement of the coupling head and shaft, the mechanism can also be operated by the handbrake on the draw bar. If the brakes are correctly adjusted, the movement of the handbrake should not be excessive. For example, if you have Al-Ko undergear fitted on your caravan or trailer, it is recommended that when the caravan is parked on level ground, your brakes should start to engage on the second click of the hand lever.

On a reverse incline, however, it is most important to pull the brake lever ***much*** further. This is because the auto-reverse system may disengage the brakes if there is any slight backward movement when the shoe contacts the drum. To ensure this does not happen, the handbrake must be pulled backwards until it is vertical. This demands a sustained pull, in which the initial effort is needed to compress a coil

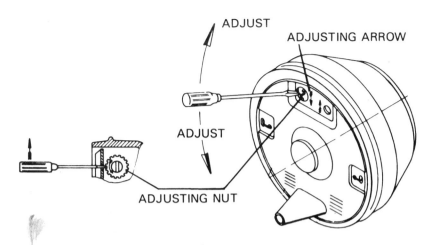

ADJUST

ADJUSTING ARROW

ADJUST

ADJUSTING NUT

Adjustments to the shoes on an Al-Ko Kober drum brake are carried out via an access port in the backing plate.

spring in the brake rod assembly. But once you have done this, if the caravan starts to roll backwards slightly and the auto-reverse brakes begin to disengage, the spring in the brake rod which you compressed will then react, imposing further force to re-establish braking.

In spite of this operating principle, it is still wise to carry wheel chocks; in fact in Germany, they are a legal requirement. Purpose-made chocks can be purchased from caravan accessory shops and Al-Ko units are supplied with a stowage rack which you screw underneath the floor of the 'van.

It is sensible to carry wheel chocks with a caravan or trailer; in fact this is a legal requirement in Germany.

Acknowledging that a handbrake demands a reasonable amount of strength to engage fully, Al-Ko Kober has developed a gas spring version which can be fitted as a replacement for the original overrun assembly. It is possible for a competent do-it-yourselfer to carry this out, although most owners would prefer to have the new mechanism fitted at an Al-Ko Service Centre. The great benefit of this handbrake is the fact that a gas piston forces it firmly into a fully engaged position as soon as the brake button is operated. It takes a certain amount of pressure to return the lever to its normal unbraked position later, but the technique of doing this is mastered after a little practice. Overall the gas spring handbrake is a great help for anyone uncertain about their ability to secure a caravan parked on sloping ground.

Wheels
A surprising variety of wheel types is fitted to caravans. This need not concern the owner too much, except when it comes to purchasing a spare wheel or having replacement tyres fitted. A more important matter is to inspect the wheel rims periodically to see that they are not badly damaged or distorted; when towing for the first time, it is not unusual to strike a kerb by accident. Also important is the

need to check that the wheel nuts (or bolts) are completely tight. Letters to caravan magazines often report frightening experiences where a wheel has become detached.

The reason for loosening wheels is unclear; there is even a belief that nearside wheels are more likely to come undone. But none of the research carried out has revealed irregularities. Moreover, the Caravan Club has conducted enquiries and collated data from members who have experienced this hazard but no conclusive evidence has been forthcoming. The matter has also been referred to Government and relevant technical organisations.

One related subject which has been addressed is the fact that the corner steady brace supplied with a pre-1988 caravan is usually inadequate for tightening the wheel fixings properly. With this in mind, changes have occurred within the National Caravan Council Certification scheme; this recognises British Standard 4626 and the August 1987 amendment regarding running gear. As a result, all 1988 and later models have been supplied with a suitable wheelbrace as part of the criteria for gaining NCC approval.

In addition, user's handbooks are also required to contain details about the correct torque for tightening wheel fixings. To assist even further, Al-Ko has introduced a purpose designed torque wrench for caravanners. Not only is it a risk to undertighten wheel fixings; they can be *overtightened* as well.

At one time, caravan wheels were secured by nuts on a threaded stud; nowadays wheel bolts are used instead. This is not necessarily considered to be a safer arrangement but a bolt securing system is claimed to be easier to manufacture accurately. Moreover, it has implications for tightening. If your caravan wheels are held in place with nuts, Al-Ko recommends that on their own products they are tightened to a torque setting of 8.0 kg/m (60 lb/ft). Meanwhile, if bolts are used, these must be slightly tighter and Al-Ko recommends 9.0 kg/m (65 lb/ft). If you own a caravan built on either an Ambergate or a CI chassis, the recommended settings are 9.0 kg/m (65 lb/ft). But irrespective of which setting is needed to suit your 'van, the appropriate tightness may not be easily achievable using the corner steady brace.

It is also necessary to recognise that there is a correct sequence to be followed when tightening wheel nuts. If your caravan wheels have a four stud fixing, the tightening sequence related to the figures on a clock face are 12, 6, 3 and 9. On a five stud wheel, you should tighten each opposite nut in succession.

As a further warning, alloy wheels can become detached more easily than pressed steel rims. Therefore owners must be even more vigilant in checking the tightness of the fixings. In practice, alloy wheels are unusual on caravans although they were fitted to the 1982 Bessacarr Melton.

Making a regular check of wheel nut tightness is discouraged by the current fashion of covering the entire wheel with a decorative wheel trim. Moreover, some trim covers have a poor method of attachment and disappear unknowingly when a caravan is towed along bumpy roads. A few manufacturers overcome this by securing the cover using brackets which couple up with the wheel bolts themselves. However, there should **never** be any other object or material between the nut (or wheel bolt) and the wheel rim.

When comparing wheels, three technical terms are used for diameter measurements. The 'nominal diameter' of the wheel is the diameter measured from one side of the rim to the other. The 'bore' diameter describes the size of the central hole. Finally a most important measurement is the 'pitch circle diameter' (PCD). If a circle is drawn through the centre of each fixing hole, the PCD measurement is the diameter of this circle. On a four stud fixing, this is the same as the measurement from the centre of one stud hole to the centre of the opposite one (but NOT the adjacent one). In the case of a 5 stud wheel, the procedure for working out the PCD is to measure the distance between the centre of **adjacent** stud holes and then to divide this by 0.557755.

Caravan wheels have sometimes been found to be faulty and examples from one batch of French made Delachaux products **must** be replaced. At worst, these wheels are believed to disintegrate. Some may still be in use because the product was fitted by several British manufacturers. The suspect batch made by Delachaux SA are four studded and have a PCD of 100 mm. They are stamped H4 27 and date stamped 01-84 and 06-86.

Having a spare wheel is essential, although many manufacturers supply this only as an optional extra. Some caravanners scour car breakers' yards looking for a compatible car wheel. But it is rare to find a suitable wheel from a car. Neither the 'nominal diameter' nor 'pitch circle diameter' are likely to match and it is much wiser purchasing the correct spare from a caravan dealer. In cases of obsolete models, the addresses of three specialists who may be able to help are given in the Appendix.

When changing a caravan wheel, there is a strict procedure. You also need a suitable jack as discussed in the

Chassis maintenance section.

Wheel changing procedure:

1. Apply the caravan handbrake firmly and chock the wheel on the opposite side.
2. Lower the jockey wheel, but keep the corner steadies **raised**.
3. Slightly loosen the wheel fixings.
4. Locate the jack under the axle and elevate the 'van.
5. Fix an axle stand in place to replace the jack; never use bricks.
6. Lower the corner steadies.
7. Undo the wheel fixings completely and remove the wheel.

Notes:
Jacking points: On older, heavy chassis (e.g. B & B) the robust side members are usually strong enough to act as alternative lifting points. However, the side members on a modern lightweight chassis are **not** strong enough. The only lifting points on a modern chassis (e.g. Al-Ko) are;

i) directly underneath the sturdy plates which enclose the axle and which are bolted to the side members just behind the wheels.
ii) underneath the axle tube.

After replacing a wheel, the fixings must be tightened up to the correct torque and in the order previously described. Regarding wheel loss, mentioned earlier, it is believed that some problems occurred because the final tighten up, when the caravan was lowered back to the ground, was overlooked.

Tyres
Recognising that the safety of road users can be in jeopardy when a vehicle has substandard tyres, the legal requirements are strict. Tread depth requirements apply to caravan tyres just as they do to car tyres and in 1991

the law required a depth of 1.6 mm across the central three quarters of the breadth of the tread. This is likely to become more stringent in future and caravan owners must keep abreast of changes in legal requirements.

In practice, however, few owners use their caravan enough to create significant tyre wear. Of course there may be damage caused by kerb collision or road debris. But as a general rule, the *age* of a caravan tyre is the element which leads to replacement rather than tread deterioration. It is recommended that tyres should be replaced after 5 years; if this is ignored, under no circumstances should the tyres be used for longer than seven years.

If you find that a caravan tyre is wearing unevenly, this can be caused by several factors. Wear on the *inside* is usually the result of persistent overloading which causes the tyre to assume an incorrect camber. If there is wear on the *outside* of a tyre, this is usually an indication that the caravan is running out of track and in consequence the tyres are 'scrubbing'. This is often caused by an impact accident such as hitting a kerb. The cure is to have the axle removed and re-aligned by the manufacturer. It is not a job for the 'do-it-yourself' repairer.

On a caravan, tyres are subjected to different conditions from the tyres on a car. For example the weight per tyre on a single axle caravan is almost twice that of the loading per tyre on the average saloon car. Tyres are also subjected to irregular use, and if a caravan is left stationary for long periods, tyres can get damaged.

During a winter lay-up period, supporting a caravan on axle stands is recommended. If this advice is not followed, the 'van should periodically be moved a short distance in one direction and then the other. This ensures that different parts of the tyre wall are distended by the weight of the caravan.

Damage during a lay-up period can also occur if the tyres are exposed to the sun. Covering them will help, though it is better to remove them for storage away from bright light.

Today's caravans are almost all supplied with radial tyres. However, in the 1960s and early 1970s, cross ply tyres were fitted. Caravans are also subject to the same legal requirements as cars, in so far as a radial tyre must *not* be mixed with a cross ply tyre. Bearing in mind that cross ply tyres are virtually unobtainable in many countries abroad, British caravanners have always been strongly advised to fit radial tyres before travelling in Europe.

In making the switch, changes to the tyre pressures are needed, too. For instance a cross ply tyre marked as 155 SR 13 should be inflated to 33 pounds per square inch (psi) whereas its radial tyre equivalent should be increased to 35 psi.

It should also be noted that when radial tyres are fitted in place of original cross ply tyres, the caravan will assume a lower ride height. Radial tyres have a lower profile and in some cases the ride height may be reduced by as much as 50 mm (2 in).

As regards pressures, the recommendations are usually quoted for speeds which do not exceed 62 mph, which is fine in Britain where the maximum speed on motorways and dual carriageways is 60 mph.

However, caravanners touring abroad may be in a country where higher speeds are permissible. In this case, modifications to pressures may be needed; different tyres may also be desirable to withstand sustained fast driving.

Some owners adopt the strategy of fitting a *larger* tyre in order to permit a greater loading capacity. But this is ill advised and in some instances it could prove dangerous. One problem, for example, concerns the clearance between the extremity of the tyre and the wheel boxes on the caravan. British Standards require that there must be at least 30 mm ($1^3/_{16}$ in) of free space at all extremes of wheel movement. Obviously when larger tyres are fitted, this dimension could be reduced unacceptably.

Information on tyre pressures is normally given in caravan handbooks. It is also available from any reputable tyre supplier. To give an example of information provided by a manufacturer, the accompanying table is reproduced with the permission of Compass Caravans Ltd. It relates to a selection of models in the 1990 Omega Range, whose exterior lengths vary from 4.213 m (13 ft 10 in) to 5.685 m (18 ft 8 in).

Wheel rim sizes for all models in this particular range are $4^1/_2$J x 13; wheel type is Dunlop LP 1317, pitch centre diameter 100 mm, 4 wheel bolts.

Omega Range

Model	360/2	400/2	430/4CT	510/5
Exterior body length	4.213 m 13 ft 10 in	4.619 m 15 ft 2 in	4.898 m 16 ft 1 in	5.686 m 18 ft 8 in
Tyre size	165 SR 13	175 SR 13	175 SR 13	175 SR 13 C6 PLY
Tyre pressure	36 psi	36 psi	36 psi	54 psi

Part of the Compass Caravan Handbook, 1990, reproduced with the permission of Mr. R. Cook, Managing Director, Compass Caravans Ltd

A cut-away illustration of the wheel fitted to 1990 Elddis caravans shows how a Tyron safety band is located in the well portion of the rim.

Accessories

There are a number of accessories related to caravan chassis and running gear. For instance some caravanners fit Tyron Safety Bands to the wheel rims and the accompanying photograph shows how this steel band is positioned in the well portion of the rim.

With a Tyron band permanently fitted, the beads of a punctured tyre are prevented from falling into the rim well which means that the tyre is more likely to remain in its normal position. The metal rim of the wheel is thereby prevented from making direct contact with the road surface. A large proportion of the tyre tread will remain in contact with the road surface, too, thus allowing the caravan, to have considerably greater stability.

The Tyron safety band is a useful asset, but it doesn't eliminate the importance of carrying a spare wheel.

However, stowing a spare wheel can be a problem.

On the older type of chassis, its design leaves little under-floor space where a spare could be stowed and no wheel carriers are available. However, a space is available alongside the gas cylinder compartment if you fit a SuperLocker discussed in Chapter 5, but this is likely to cause excessive noseweight. An inconvenient answer is to carry the wheel inside, on the floor of the caravan, or in the car boot. It

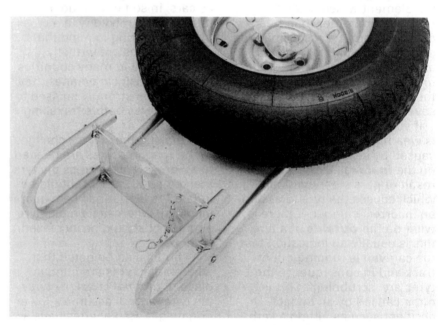

An Al-Ko Kober spare wheel carrier can be purchased as a kit to fit all types of Al-Ko caravan chassis.

is **not** safe to build a rack on the rear of the 'van because this would seriously upset stability on the road.

There is no problem on modern chassis like the Al-Ko units and a purpose designed spare wheel carrier is available as an accessory. This can easily be fitted by the DIY owner and an Al-Ko chassis has pre-punched mounting holes in the main members. These are intentionally positioned so that the wheel will be mounted as

Holes are punched in the main chassis members at the time of manufacture so that a carrier assembly can be fitted.

The Al-Ko Kober spare wheel carrier comprises a wheel platform and a pair of telescopic tubes.

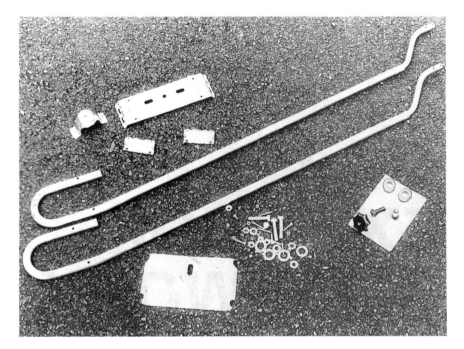

near to the axle as possible.

The design employs telescopic tubing so that when access to the spare wheel is needed, a security bolt is released and the support section can then be withdrawn sideways. The carrier can be fitted to offer access on either the nearside or the offside, depending on whether the caravan is used mainly at home or on the Continent.

Another useful underfloor item is a fold-away step but this should not be attached to the chassis. Fitting a step is usually straightforward and in Chapter 14, illustrations show a Morco 'Slide-away' caravan step being installed on a 1985 caravan.

Lastly, a jockey wheel often gets damaged but replacements are stock items at accessory shops. If a caravan has been neglected, it may also be necessary to fit the complete assembly and these are equally available.

To avoid damage when towing, many owners of modern caravans remove the jockey wheel assembly whenever they

take to the road. This merely involves undoing a securing clamp. On some models, however, the design of the drawbar fairing makes detachment less easy; certain models of Bailey caravan, for example, are harder to deal with.

The simplicity of a clamp release system also makes it easy to fit a different type of jockey wheel assembly. There are models with a pneumatic tyre for improved manoeuvrability. You may also

find a model once manufactured by Al-Ko which incorporates a spring balance on the column for checking noseweight.

Lastly there are electrically powered jockey wheels and others which have a lever operated drive arrangement. Both are useful for disabled or elderly caravanners.

In summary, many important changes have occurred beneath the floor of caravans. The next chapter shows that changes have also been occurring ***above*** floor level as well.

When the carrier is assembled, the position of the cross member on which the wheel is mounted (arrowed) can be adjusted as required.

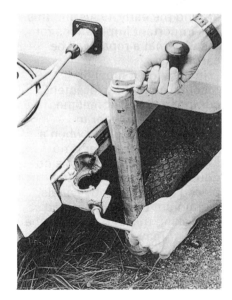

On many modern caravans, the jockey wheel can be unclamped and removed completely; many caravanners prefer to stow the wheel away when towing.

Chapter 5

EXTERIOR BODYWORK

Owner repairs and maintenance

Most caravans sustain body damage at some point in their working life. On occasions the damage is sufficiently serious to require expert help. However, other repairs can often be tackled by a competent owner.

Before tackling body repairs on a caravan, you need to have a clear understanding about the way it is built. Major changes in caravan construction occurred around the early 1980s and this has important implications for the way that a repair will be carried out.

In addition it must be recognised that replacement components are sometimes difficult for an owner to purchase, particularly when a caravan manufacturer is no longer in business. There's no doubt that a dealer is better placed to source body panels, aluminium trim sections and so on. Taking this into account, the amateur may decide not to attempt a home repair; but having the knowledge of what is involved means that an owner

can check if a professional repair has been carried out correctly.

Changes in caravan construction

With the lack of registration documents, it is difficult to assess the age of a caravan. However, a number of clues betray its approximate year of manufacture and a guide in the Appendix traces changes that have occurred since the 1960s.

It is also important to note that there are still many caravans being used which were manufactured in the early 1970s. Caravan sales were remarkable, partly because touring 'vans were not subject to 'purchase tax' at this time. A peak was reached in 1972 when production for the home market was around 67,000 tourers, an output not exceeded since then. In fact the annual production figures from **any** year in the 1980s failed to attain 50% of the 1972 peak figure.

Recognising that the method of building a caravan changed radically around 1980, it is important to be able to ascertain

a caravan's age. When viewed from the side, pre-1980 caravans are usually symmetrically shaped. In addition, their chassis is a substantial structure made from sturdy steel sections which are welded together. The sections are usually painted.

Caravans from this period were single glazed with window frames made of aluminium. This changed when it became illegal to fit non-safety glass in 1978 and clear acrylic materials proved the ideal alternative. This material could be moulded to include a lip which meant that there was no need for an aluminium frame. In addition, the acrylic could be used to form sealed double-glazed units. This represented a significant step forward in reducing the problem of condensation. In consequence, virtually all models launched at the turn of the decade were equipped with acrylic double glazed units.

As regards body construction, the floors of a 1970s caravan were built of treated plywood which was usually around $1/2$ in (13 mm) thick. The ply sheets

Acrylic double glazed windows have been fitted since 1978 when legislation banned the use of non-safety glass.

were mounted on longitudinal timber joists which in turn were located on the main chassis members. Structurally the floors were sound even if they were fairly heavy by today's standards. They also lacked any form of insulation which meant that the winter caravanner would frequently have the discomfort of cold feet.

To solve this problem, several owners have fitted slabs of polystyrene under the floor ply, positioning them between the joists. Materials used in the building industry for cavity wall insulation may improve the level of thermal insulation quite considerably. Products like Jablite polystyrene slabs are an example.

Looking at the walls, caravans built in the 1970s usually had a skeleton framework of softwood. On the inside, this would be clad with decorative wallboard and faced hardboard was popular. The exterior was covered with a smooth skin of aluminium sheet. The void between these inner and outer skins was packed with glass fibre wool. In practice this gives only a limited degree of thermal insulation and in time it slumps in the cavity, leaving cold spots. Roofs were built in the same way, with both flat and pitched profiles. Lantern roofs with small side windows were becoming less fashionable on all but the very expensive models.

It was partly the quest for a higher standard of insulation which led to the changes which followed. At the close of the 1970s, Fleetwood was one of the pioneering manufacturers who started to experiment with a different type of floor construction. Chassis were also being reviewed and computer aided design was showing that

considerably lighter structures could be constructed.

Starting firstly with the floor, the new structures consist of a composite slab made up of a sandwich of a solid foam, bonded on both faces with thin plywood. A typical composition is made up of 23 mm ($^{15}/_{16}$ in) foam and 5 mm ($^{3}/_{16}$ in) plywood. When the components have been coated with special adhesives, the structure is placed in a press and subjected

Bonded sandwich construction used for modern caravan floors features a foam insulant bonded between layers of plywood.

to compression forces of some magnitude. The result is a rigid laminated panel.

Sometimes lengths of timber are bonded between the ply sheets to provide sound fixing points for furniture units and there is also a timber surround to provide an anchorage for wall panel fixings.

Faults sometimes occurred when this change was introduced. It was not unusual, for example, for parts of the ply sandwich to lose its bonding and become detached from the foam. Methods of reinstating delaminated panels of ply are dealt with later in this chapter.

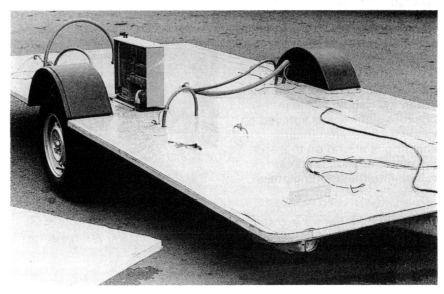

Nevertheless the merits of the sandwich system were clear and this construction system was subsequently employed for caravan walls.

When manufacturing a composite wall panel, the interior layer is usually made with 3 mm (¹/₈ in) decorative plywood. Faced hardboard lost favour with manufacturers on account of its extra weight, instability and higher level of flexibility. As regards the outer material of the sandwich, sheet aluminium is used. This, too, is bonded to the foam with special adhesive.

A bonded sandwich panel offers a high level of thermal insulation, but its strength needs careful consideration by the designer. Unlike a composite bonded floor, caravan walls have many openings. The door in particular represents a weak spot and reference is made later to problems occurring in caravans built with an 'end kitchen'.

Window apertures are a similar area of weakness and strengthening is needed. Hence these are usually lined with a wooden surround cut to the requisite pattern.

Prior to entering the press, wall panels are usually assembled on a large jig so that strengthening timber can be located accurately within the sandwich. Wooden battens in key positions are important because they provide the anchorage for furniture which needs to be fastened to the wall. When everything is laid in position, adhesive is sprayed on to the surface, aluminium sheeting is placed on top, and the whole section is sent on rollers into the bonding press.

Strengthening timber and slabs of foam are assembled on a jig before this wall section is coated with adhesive and fed into the press.

One problem with this process is the fact that the foam core compresses more than internal timbers. If you look closely at the external aluminium surface on a sandwich wall, you can sometimes see where the main structural timbers are located. This may look unattractive and it is one reason why many manufacturers use aluminium sheeting with either a stucco effect or a reeded moulding on the surface.

It is also claimed that aluminium with a surface pattern is stronger than plain aluminium sheeting. This means that a thinner skin of aluminium can be used without reducing the strength of a composite sandwich panel. The strategy also has cost implications as well. Nevertheless, as techniques improve some manufacturers (e.g. Avondale and Compass) are reverting to plain aluminium once again.

In spite of the benefits of bonded construction, a few 1990s caravans e.g. the Cotswold Celeste, are constructed in the more

When completed, bonded sandwich wall panels are stored in readiness for delivery to the production line.

traditional manner using a wooden framework. Once the timber skeleton is complete, this is skinned with aluminium sheet and interior decorative plywood. The sheet is pre-stretched before being offered up which helps to reduce the tendency for aluminium to billow out in hot weather. Although prefabricated bonded panels facilitate mass production, caravans like the Cotswold are built individually, appealing to customers who are willing to pay the price for traditional craftsmanship.

As regards caravan roofs, their contoured shape makes the integration of bonded sandwich panels quite difficult. A few manufacturers manage to do this e.g. Bailey, but loose-laid glass fibre wool is more commonly used as an insulant. The wool compresses easily, providing space for the wires serving ceiling mounted lamps.

Most roofs comprise a timber framework lined on the inside with decorative plywood, skinned on the outside with aluminium panels and filled with glass fibre wool in the void.

Caravan roofs are usually made with a timber structure which is skinned on top with aluminium; glass fibre wool insulant is used in the void.

However, some manufacturers (e.g. Avondale and Castleton) use a glass fibre moulded roof. A single section of glass reinforced plastic is inclined to be heavier than aluminium but its lack of joints produces a notably leakproof arrangement. On the other hand, seamless single sheet aluminium has recently been used by CI on some of the 1991 models. A few other manufacturers had used this technique in the 1980s as well.

Whereas the lantern style of caravan roof has almost disappeared, both flat and pitched constructions are

equally popular. The pitched form is more expensive to produce but sheds rainwater more efficiently. It also creates greater headroom inside, which is beneficial for the taller owner.

Like variations in roof construction, the fronts of caravans vary, too. Less expensive models employ a slab front composed of bonded sandwich material whereas more expensive caravans are

Rather than using a pre-bonded flat panel, the fronts of many caravans are made from moulded material such as GRP or ABS plastic.

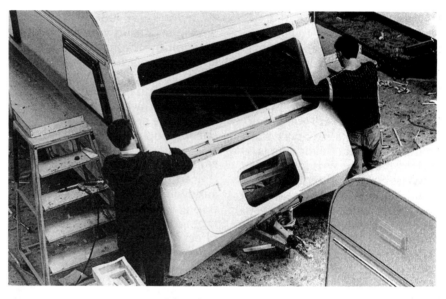

built with a contoured front. This is formed with a plywood and softwood framework and many fronts are then covered with a glass reinforced plastic (GRP) skin. Others use a form of plastic called ABS (which is easier to say than acrylonitrile-butadiene-styrene). However, in the closing years of the 80s, acrylic moulded panels were introduced as a third alternative. This is both lighter and cheaper, but a damaged panel has to be completely replaced whereas GRP can be repaired as described in the *Repair work* Section.

Other distinguishing changes

Individually laminated glass fibre fronts are more costly than acrylic moulded panels, but the advantage of GRP is the fact that it is repairable.

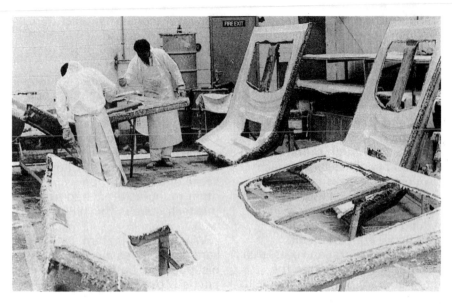

of recent caravans include the wedge shaped profile to improve petrol consumption, albeit to the dismay of the awning manufacturer. Integral external lockers appeared in the mid 1980s to replace the gas bottle box on the caravan drawbar. In the 1990s, separate lockers with external access were introduced so that a battery could be stored separately from gas cylinders. Fairings on the drawbar were also a feature of British caravans and these are often made in GRP i.e. 'fibre glass'.

In the future, it is likely that more manufacturers will provide a gas locker on a side wall so that the weight of cylinders is nearer the axle. This idea has already been tried by a few manufacturers and it is consistent with recommendations for loading a caravan.

A final clue to the age of a caravan is its type of rooflights. In order to achieve good thermal insulation, most of the current units feature a double layer of plastic material. In contrast, caravans made in the 1970s had rooflights made from a single layer of plastic. The condensation which forms on the underside, particularly in cold weather, is extremely inconvenient.

Caravans constructed in the early 1990s provide external compartments for batteries and electrical items which are separate from the gas locker box.

Having surveyed developments in material technology, methods of construction are also useful to understand. If models were once built individually, many modern factories now have a production line where pre-fabrication has speeded up output significantly.

Method of assembly
Since the introduction of bonded sandwich panels for caravan floors, caravan construction methods changed. This took effect in the early 1980s and coincided with the advent of the lightweight, computer designed caravan chassis. The assembly

of a rolling chassis, floor section and running gear is described in Chapter Four.

By commencing assembly with the floor panel inverted, underfloor cables, gas pipe and water service pipes can be fitted without any access problems. Once the chassis is rolling, it is inverted and taken to the assembly line.

Major appliances are one of the first things to be installed on the assembly line; so, too, are cabinet units and furniture which has been pre-fabricated in separate workshops. In many modern factories, these items are craned from above and fitted

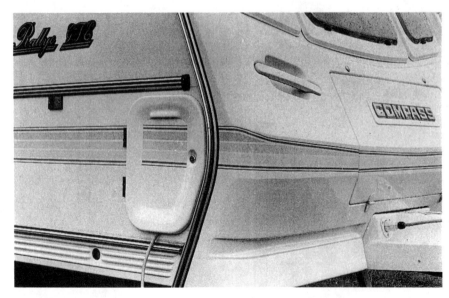

Many interior items of furniture are fixed to the floor panel, before the exterior walls are added.

At the corners of a caravan, the aluminium skin is dressed around the joins between side and end sections and stapled in place.

before the walls of the caravan are added. Like the furniture, wall sections will have been prefabricated prior to reaching the assembly line.

Side walls are easily fitted to the floor section, but the front wall together with its integral locker box involves much more attention. To begin with, the timber framework needed to support a single piece of GRP or acrylic panelling has to be strong. It is much the same for the roof structure which is usually constructed at the same time.

As a general rule, a number of key items are 'bought-in' by caravan manufacturers. For instance, double glazed acrylic windows are often imported from Holland. Most manufacturers 'buy-in' the external door – and the cabinet fronts for furniture as well. There have been exceptions, of course, and CI manufactured external doors throughout the 1980s.

Upholstery is much the same and most caravan manufacturers have cushions and curtains made by a soft

furnishings specialist. The trend has implications when buying replacement spares and sometimes you can purchase items e.g. a replacement double gazed window, directly from a

In many modern factories, caravans are assembled on a construction line using items like furniture which have been prefabricated in a separate workshop.

specialist manufacturer or importer. This can be most helpful if a caravan manufacturer has gone out of business.

Overall, production line assembly techniques are a feature of the industry. But there are still a few manufacturers whose products are custom built. Caravans like the 'Buzzard', for example, are bespoke models which are all individually made to customer specification.

Internal bodywork faults
In spite of sophistication in the manufacturing process, a caravan is not necessarily immune from bodywork faults. For example, rot in caravan walls is surprisingly common. At first it may pass unnoticed, but if repairwork is delayed, the cost of major work sometimes exceeds the value of the caravan.

The ingress of rainwater is not necessarily eliminated if you own a modern caravan built with sandwich construction walls. Indeed the problem can sometimes be worse when water gets trapped in a bonded panel.

Without doubt, prevention is better than cure and it is essential to prevent rainwater from entering the structure.

Keeping out the rain

To meet British Standards, the external construction of a caravan should adequately resist the penetration of rain, damp, and insects. This relates to a caravan at the time it leaves the factory and the British Standard gives no indication how long it should fulfil this expectation.

As a general rule, roofs are not prone to problems – except at the perimeter join with the walls. On the other hand, the front panel is much more vulnerable. For instance if you watch the flow of rainwater when your caravan is parked, a considerable amount discharges from the roof and runs down the front. This is particularly evident now that more and more caravans are built with a wedge shaped forward end. In addition, when you are towing in wet weather, it is again the front of the 'van which meets the onslaught of rain and spray from the towcar.

The rear panel is the second most likely source of leaks whereas the side walls are less vulnerable. However, any wall is susceptible to leaks where there are fittings and trim strips screwed into place. Sealants and mastics on which these are bedded don't last for ever and if you have doubts about the integrity of a particular external fitting, look at it closely.

In the caravan industry, there are principally three types of mastic in common use. Oil based products are used a great deal and have a life expectancy around six years. Mastics based on an acrylic formulation are likely to last at least twice as long, whereas silicone based mastics have a normal life expectancy of twenty years. This presumes that a liberal application was used at the time of manufacture and that the sealant hasn't been dislodged in the course of normal use.

Close inspection frequently shows that rain running down the face of a panel disappears behind a trim piece or fitting. Typically it tracks along the rear of the trim, draining into the body panel via the holes made by screws which keep the strip in place. A preliminary cure is to apply a bead of silicone sealant along all the edges of the fitting. An external grade sealant is needed and it is advisable to purchase a gun dispenser and

Leaks can often be tracked down to trim strips on the front or rear of a caravan. Failed bedding sealant means that rainwater creeps behind the trim, entering the body via the fixing screws.

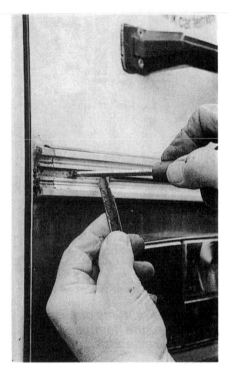

To release trim strips in readiness for rebedding them on new sealant, plastic insert strips have to be removed to reveal the fixing screws.

cartridge rather than a small tube. If the application of sealant looks untidy, a rag dipped in methylated spirits will smooth over any larger blobs. Do this quickly before the sealant starts to set, and try to create a neat chamfer. Inevitably some sealant will be wasted in the process, but skill with a cartridge dispenser improves with practice.

If this fails to effect a cure, it is necessary to remove the trim piece or component completely and to re-bed it. For instance if a refrigerator grill loses its original snug fit, unscrew it and remove it. Take care to prise it away gently because plastic fittings often become brittle with age and can crack if flexed too much. Once removed, a plastic ventilator should then be re-bedded on a sealant like W4 flexible tape. This is a paper backed ribbon which should be placed around the aperture

before you return the fitting to its original position. When the item is screwed down again, trim away any surplus sealant that exudes from around the sides with a sharp cutting knife. This usually cures the problem, but for even more certainty, you can follow this up by applying silicone sealant around the perimeter as well.

The same approach should be followed if new items like awning eye plates or a TV aerial are fitted to the body. In the long term, keep a check on the route taken by rain or dew as it discharges from the roof. Tell tale marks will be helpful; in each case, look at trim pieces which are met by the discharging water, no matter how modest the flow. These are the vulnerable areas.

Moving inside, showers are the next area of weakness. Shower trays often flex and breaks can develop in a cover strip of sealant. The same problem occurs in a bathroom at home and in both cases the cure is the same. Joins should always be checked, damaged sealant removed and a new application of silicone sealant dispensed. Look carefully as well at the join in the wall panels which form the cubicle; movements during towing often break the continuity of the sealant.

When more serious problems develop, structural repairs will fall outside the scope of the inexperienced owner. On the other hand, several keen woodworkers achieve pleasing results and even the removal of a complete fibre glass front panel is daunting in prospect, but not particularly difficult in practice.

Faults in bonded sandwich floors and walls
As regards the old type of floor described previously, there is little to go wrong with this system during a caravan's normal life expectancy. But bonded sandwich floors are less trouble-free.

Though it offers good thermal insulation, a bonded floor can occasionally suffer from delamination problems. For instance, areas subjected to heavy use, e.g. around the door, are especially vulnerable.

Similarly, the interior ply of a wall panel has also been known to delaminate. In practice, most problems occur with caravans built in the early 1980s when sandwich construction was in its infancy. Nowadays, the method of manufacturing bonded floor or wall sections is greatly improved.

In the past, the cure for a delaminated area was one of three strategies; inject more foam, add a new plywood overlay near the damaged area, or in the case of floors, add strengthening timber underneath to reduce flexion. Whilst these approaches achieve a reasonable measure of success, an even better technique is now employed using chemical injection.

Curing delamination in wall or floor panels
To cure delamination, a series of small holes are drilled in the interior panel around the faulty area. These need to match the size of the nozzle on a special injection syringe and would not normally exceed 4 mm ($^5/_{32}$ in). An epoxy resin two part adhesive is then used such as Apollo Chemicals AX8136 Part A and B. The compound is injected into the panel so that it percolates around the interior. On a wall it would disperse downwards. Any surplus accidentally settling on the surface must be removed immediately because it becomes rock hard when it sets. For the same reason it is recommended to plug the injection holes temporarily using woodscrews as soon as the syringe is withdrawn.

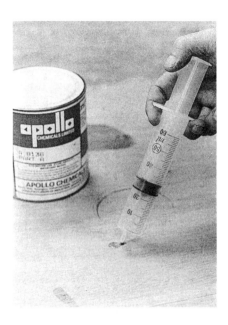

Once mixed, a compound from Apollo Chemicals is injected into a small hole drilled in the ply of a sandwich floor in order to re-fix an area troubled by delamination.

Any surplus chemical left on the surface of a delaminated panel must be removed at once; it will become rock hard if allowed to set.

When a repaired area has been treated, you should try to cramp or compress the panels together. This may mean adopting some makeshift

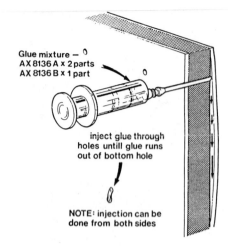

Glue mixture — ○
AX 8136 A x 2 parts
AX 8136 B x 1 part

inject glue through
holes untill glue runs
out of bottom hole

NOTE: injection can be
done from both sides

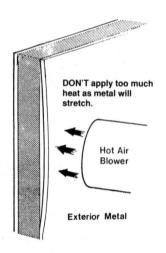

DON'T apply too much
heat as metal will
stretch.

Hot Air
Blower

Exterior Metal

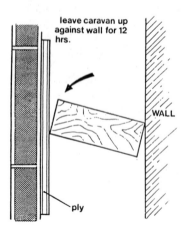

leave caravan up
against wall for 12
hrs.

WALL

ply

To reattach delaminated aluminium on a wall, a similar injection process is involved using epoxy resin two part adhesives.

arrangements such as wedging a prop against a wall, or the ceiling, so that it applies pressure to a piece of scrap plywood positioned over the repair. This pressure must be maintained until the chemical has set.

The Apollo product is an important repair substance because it doesn't attack the foam core and its ability to re-bond delaminated sections is quite extraordinary. Further details about the product are contained in a technical data sheet obtainable direct from Apollo Chemicals Ltd. (See Appendix address list.)

Dealing with dents

Even the most careful owner is going to have a dent in their 'van at one time or another. Whether a caravan is built from a sandwich or aluminium cladding system, panel beating is out of the question. To begin with, aluminium stretches and cannot be tapped back into shape like steel. In a severe accident, sections of wall may need replacing, and this is a structural task which many owners would prefer to entrust to a specialist in body repairs.

However, a surface dent or hole in the outer aluminium skin is easier to deal with. In a traditionally constructed caravan with hollow walls, it usually means replacing the distorted panel with a new section of aluminium.

In a sandwich wall, the first task is to fill the depressed area. Traditional resin based fillers used in the automotive trade can be tried, but these sometimes react with the foam insulant causing its cells to disintegrate. When this happens, the area of foam coming into contact with the resin filler looks as if it is dissolving. In consequence, many caravan repairers will use Apollo A5045 two part adhesive instead. This can act as a filler, and should be applied with a scraper; it is also a bonding agent. For instance if a new section of aluminium is pressed or clamped against a damaged area which has been filled and coated in A5045, adhesion will be satisfactory after two hours. However, the section should be left for the full cure time of 24 hours.

As regards the procedure for *covering* damaged external wall surfaces, the first job is to

Apollo A5045 two part filler has excellent bonding property and does not react unfavourably with the foam insulant in walls or floors.

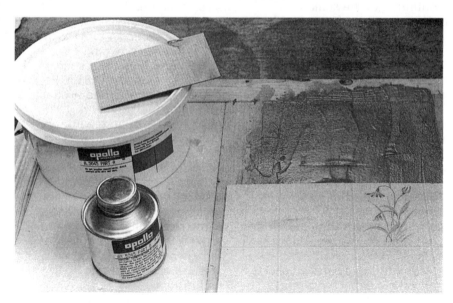

remove any surface irregularity. Having done this, most repairers usually bond a new secondary skin on top of the original surface. There is no point in trying to remove the old skin first because this merely pulls away parts of the foam filling.

In this approach, it is most fortunate that caravan walls are usually divided up into distinct zones, bounded by trim strips. This means that smaller sections can be fixed rather than having to use huge aluminium panels to cover the entire side. By butting up the new skin against a length of trim, or by covering its edge completely with re-fastened aluminium trim, the fact that there's a double skin is unlikely to be discernible.

Notwithstanding the visual success of the system, the repairer is still faced with a problem of colour matching, especially if the original panel of aluminium was finished with decorative coach stripes that had been pre-painted. Fortunately, however, most leading manufacturers keep stocks of exterior pre-painted panels for their different models and these can be specially ordered. For example the accompanying photograph taken at CI Caravans shows an extensive collection of

Many caravan manufacturers can supply matching, prepainted aluminium to suit models made in the last 5 to 10 years. This is the stock at CI caravans.

aluminium cladding material in the after sales department to suit models going back a number of years.

Regrettably this doesn't help the owner of a caravan whose manufacturer has long ceased trading. In this case, an unpainted replacement panel will have to be fitted and then sprayed. But all is not lost because several automotive paint specialists listed in the

Yellow Pages operate a mixing service for colour matching. Small quantities of cellulose paint can be prepared and a personalised colour can even be supplied in an aerosol spray can. If specialists offering this service are hard to find locally, a similar service is now available from Holts; information is included in the Appendix address list.

In order to obtain a spray can of touch-up paint with an exact colour match, specialists like Holts can specially mix up a product to suit any caravan.

In order to attach a second skin, a special contact adhesive is required. For a small area, a piece of aluminium could be bonded using impact adhesive, e.g. Evo-Stik. However, the professional uses a sprayable product like Apollo A11. The adhesive is built up with several skim layers from a spray gun rather than being applied in a single thick coating.

Prior to adding a new skin over an area previously damaged, a coating of Apollo A11 adhesive is sprayed over the receiving surface.

The instant touch of a new panel of aluminium previously coated with Apollo A11 impact adhesive makes it essential to have the help of an assistant.

Like all contact adhesives, Apollo A11 produces instant touch bonding. So the repairer needs an assistant to help with a large section so that it can be accurately positioned before the wall and panel are mated. Once in place the sheet is then pressed hard against the entire receiving surface with a rubber roller.

Fractured wall panels

Once the principle of 'over-cladding' is understood, another serious fault can be dealt with. This is the problem of wall fracture.

In sandwich constructions, an insufficient distribution of internal timber reinforcement can lead to structural inadequacy. At worst, this can result in a wall section fracturing at a stress point. An example of this sometimes occurs in caravans which have an end kitchen, and a side door situated to the rear of the axle. Bearing in mind that kitchen appliances e.g. fridges, ovens etc. are the heaviest fixtures in a caravan, a design in which they are built at the back is less sound from a structural viewpoint than locating them centrally over the axle.

It stands to reason that a trailer caravan pitching fore and aft on a bumpy road surface, will receive significantly greater stresses where there are heavy appliances rising and falling at the rearmost extremity. In addition, if there is a doorway in the rear part of the 'van, this opening represents a zone of considerable weakness whenever there's a pitching action on the road.

In this design arrangement, the small section of bodywork directly above the doorway is

put under enormous tension. When the caravan is being towed on an uneven road, this part of the body is subjected to a considerable pulling effect every time the rear kitchen drops sharply. Not surprisingly, a number of owners have found that two large fracture cracks appear in the walls directly above the top corners of the doorway. Internal damage to the foam core may not be visible, but splits in the exterior aluminium skin are clearly evident.

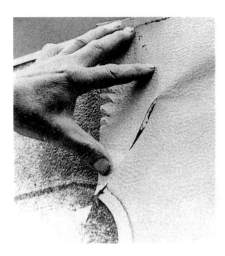

The weight imposed by an 'end kitchen' can sometimes lead to a structural split in the aluminium skin over the top of a caravan door.

This weak spot is now recognised, and many manufacturers building caravans with a rear kitchen and rear entrance include a section of timber in the sandwich core over the door instead of using normal foam. Fortunately, an earlier caravan which lacked this provision can have a strengthening portion added if splits have occurred.

The strengthening procedure shown in the accompanying illustrations involves the installation of a plywood infill block directly over the doorway. Its thickness should match the dimension of the original foam (i.e. approx. 22 mm) and it should be cut to the shape shown in the diagrams. In other words it should not only bridge the section ***above*** the opening but should also extend a small amount on either side of the doorway as well.

Before making this modification, the caravan door must be removed. Then it is necessary to detach the door frame, awning rail and the longitudinal trim strip which runs over the top of the side windows. When the infill block has been cut to shape, it should then be offered up to the caravan to act like a template. This enables the repairer to

The dimensions of a typical
timber insert needed to
strengthen an area of weakness
over a caravan door.
(courtesy Compass Caravans)

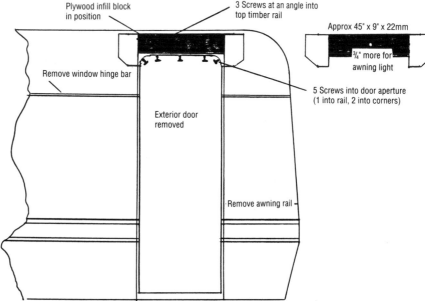

Plywood infill block
in position

3 Screws at an angle into
top timber rail

Approx 45" x 9" x 22mm

¾" more for
awning light

Remove window hinge bar

Exterior door
removed

5 Screws into door aperture
(1 into rail, 2 into corners)

Remove awning rail

*Once the torn aluminium skin
and foam of a damaged portion
has been removed from over a
door, strengthening repair work
involves inserting blocks of
timber (arrowed) and Apollo
adhesives.*

pencil around the block so that
its future position is precisely
marked. Then the existing
aluminium skin and foam is cut
with a sharp Stanley knife and
removed. However, special care
should be taken not to cut
through the decorative plywood
forming the inside walls; this
should be left intact because it
provides a base on which the
block will be mounted and
bonded.

The infill block can now be
fixed permanently using an
impact adhesive. However, one
of the best products for this job
is Plusbond 140 from Chamtek
Adhesives on account of its
notable bonding properties.

If the infill block introduces
any discrepancy in the level of
the wall surface, you are advised
to use a filler, skimming over the
area with a plastic applicator. An
ideal product for the filling and
smoothing operation is Apollo
A5045, which was mentioned
previously in the *Dealing with*

dents section. Where a caravan
is equipped with an awning light
above the doorway, the infill
block must also be drilled and a
feed wire buried in place.

Additional fixing can also be
achieved if screws are angled up
through the top of the infill block
and driven into the top timber
rail which runs along the
intersection of the wall and roof
panels. Further screws can be
driven upwards through the
aluminium surround of the
doorway and into the block.

When the integrity of the new
section has been re-established,
the entire upper section of the
wall has to be re-skinned with
new aluminium sheeting. This
will be carried out using the
procedures described in the
previous section. Its upper
edge will be hidden when the
awning rail is replaced at the
top; its lower edge will also be
covered by the longitudinal trim
strip which runs along the top of
the windows. When carried out
correctly, the finished repair
should be imperceptible.

Moulded plastic panels
Dealing with damaged fibre
glass involves completely
different procedures compared
with aluminium repairwork.

Mouldings made of glass
reinforced plastic (i.e. GRP or
'fibre glass') can be damaged
either by deep surface
scratching or by more severe
structural damage like cracks
and splits. However, these can
be repaired fairly easily.
Regrettably, this is not the case
with other plastics and some
manufacturers are now using
acrylic plastic for front panels
rather than GRP; this is not
normally repairable. Neither is
ABS plastic which is often used
for air dams, wheel arch covers
or side skirts; these have to be
replaced completely.

To establish if a damaged
plastic section is GRP and
repairable, look at the reverse
side. Evidence of a rough
surface suggests that GRP has
been used and what you can see
on the back is the chopped
strand matting which gives
strength to the resin.

Working with GRP is
something within the scope of
the amateur and this is very
thoroughly covered in Chapter 7
of *The Car Bodywork Repair
Manual* by Lindsay Porter,
Haynes Publishing Group.

Chemicals used in GRP repairs
can be damaging to human
tissue; moreover, they must be

stored appropriately since some polyester products are a fire hazard. Information on safety and the use of polyester resins is contained in a series of free leaflets available from Trylon of Wollaston, Northamptonshire. These are well worth obtaining and you should read them most carefully; Trylon is one of the best known suppliers of polyester materials, tools and associated products to amateur repairers and hobbyists. Polyester chemicals, catalysts and cleaning fluids are sold in small quantities for repairing cars, building canoes, lining fish ponds and so on.

GRP lamination explained
Caravan body panels made from glass reinforced plastic (GRP) are produced in a mould. The mould itself is usually made from GRP as well, and is a replica in reverse. Its inside surface has to be meticulously polished so that the product made within it can be released easily when the chemicals have set. The shiny surface will also be evident on the final body panel.

When manufacturing a product in GRP, three main constituents are involved. These consist of the first chemical applied to the mould called 'Gel Coat'. When this is dry – but tacky to the touch – polyester laminating resin is added next. So, too, are layers of glass fibre matting which absorb the resin and give it strength.

There are many variations on this theme according to whether you require rigidity, flexibility, waterproof qualities and so on. But in all cases there will be a shiny face on the finished panel, together with a rough surface on the reverse showing the glass fibre mat.

In the caravan industry, GRP panels are usually pre-coloured during manufacture. This is achieved by adding a colourising pigment paste to both the gel coat layer and the supplementary layers of laminating resin. The advantage of colourising at the mixing stage means that the panel doesn't have to be painted later.

In terms of their constituents, gel and laminating resin are very similar. The way they are prepared for use is much the same, too. However, gel coat has a thicker consistency whereas laminating resin is more liquefied and can be poured from its container.

Both products usually contain an 'accelerating' chemical which means that their shelf life is unlikely to exceed nine or ten months. Quite often, polyester resin is designated as pre-accelerated (PA) resin which means that the manufacturer has already added accelerator. In spite of this addition, you also have to mix in a further chemical known as catalyst as soon as you want to use the resin or gel coat. In the automotive trade, 'catalyst' is always referred to as 'hardener' and is usually supplied as a paste. But in most plastics workshops the catalyst is a liquid which has to be measured out carefully using a graduated cylinder.

Catalyst is especially hazardous; under no circumstances should it be splashed into the eyes by accident. Accordingly, **safety goggles are an essential part of the GRP laminator's personal equipment**. In the event of an eye accident, water must be poured liberally into the eyes and the patient taken to a hospital casualty department at once.

Polyester resins are not pleasant either, and when buying materials from a supplier like Trylon, it is important to order some 'barrier cream' for wiping on the hands ***before*** starting work; in addition you should also purchase a special hand cleaner which is used afterwards. Even though barrier cream and cleaner affords a measure of protection, plastic gloves are also recommended, particularly when you cut glass fibre matting to its required size.

In caravan repair work, it is normal to use a 'chopped strand' glass mat and this can be particularly irritating. 'Fibre-glass itch' is most uncomfortable and may take a day or two before it clears up. This may also be accompanied by a skin rash.

Brushes and laminating tools (e.g. rollers) also have to be cleaned and acetone is sold for this purpose. The kind used in GRP workshops is an industrial version of nail varnish remover; but it is infinitely cheaper. If you run out of acetone, an expensive laminating brush can be saved from irreparable damage by cleaning it in nail varnish remover. However, this is a costly emergency and 'borrowing' someone's remover may not be regarded too favourably.

When a GRP panel is produced, its thickness will be determined by the number of layers of glass mat used in the lamination. If flexibility is required, glass fibre cloth or man-made woven fabrics like 'Kevlar' and 'Diolen' are used. But in caravan manufacture, panels need rigidity rather than pliability. Instead of using a cloth material in the lamination process, a chopped strand mat is chosen instead. This is often listed as 'CSM' in catalogues.

For laminating work, polyester resin is a liquefied chemical. However, when a polyester paste is needed for dealing with dents, this can be made by mixing filler compounds into the laminating resin. An example of a filler which does not react with polyester resin is powdered aluminium; another compound is chalk. Since talcum powder is a form of chalk, you can mix this into polyester resin as a makeshift arrangement to produce filler. But a surprising amount will be needed and taking someone else's talcum powder is likely to provoke as much anger as taking nail varnish remover. Purchasing these items from a supplier like Trylon is much to be preferred.

Repair work

Repairs to damaged glass fibre panels fall into two categories. Firstly there are repairs to a badly scratched gel coat surface; these are dealt with from the shiny 'face side' of the panel. Secondly there are more serious cracks or splits in the material; these are repaired from the reverse face i.e. the rougher side.

In automotive repairs, a dent is often repaired using a polyester filler paste. The filler is mixed with catalyst paste (i.e. 'hardener') and then applied to the damaged area with a decorators' knife. When dry, it is then rubbed down with a succession of progressively lighter grades of abrasive paper until a smooth surface is produced. The area then needs finishing off with several coats of matching paint and reference has already been made to Holts special paint mixing service in the _Dealing with dents_ section.

Although this is a satisfactory way to effect a repair on a caravan, a more certain method of producing an 'invisible repair' is to purchase some colourised gel coat. For example, colour matched gel coat is available from Compass Caravans Ltd for all their models and this is a most useful 'back-up' service. The first step, therefore, is to enquire if the manufacturer of your caravan operates a similar supply service.

To fill a deep scratch, you need to take a small quantity of gel coat, put on some goggles for eye protection, add a few drips of catalyst, and stir thoroughly. The prepared gel

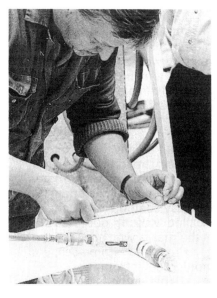

Once catalysed gel coat has been applied to a damaged area, a strip of sellotape must be placed over the repair to retain the chemical and to keep it airtight.

coat is then applied to the scratched area with a small stick, or a brush. A strip of sellotape is then applied to the repaired area so that the gel doesn't drain from the crack; it also prevents air from reaching the gelcoat. If you leave gelcoat exposed, it doesn't dry properly and remains tacky.

On a vertical surface the sellotape needs to be ready for a hasty application before the gel drains out of the depression. Repair work is much easier to carry out on a horizontal surface and if a damaged panel can be removed and transferred to a work bench, so much the better.

Depending on the ambient temperature and the amount of catalyst used, the gel should be dry in an hour. In hot weather it may dry in a quarter of the time. You are not advised to undertake GRP repairs in temperatures less than 12 deg C (around 55 deg F), although if you direct a hot air gun around a repaired surface to give very gentle warming, this achieves results in cold temperatures.

An old pair of kitchen scales with graduations in grams enables the mix of laminating resin and catalyst to be calculated exactly.

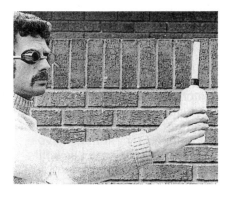

Even when a special dispenser is used, it is essential to have full eye protection whenever measuring out catalyst for the gel coat or laminating resin.

To be strictly accurate, a quantity of gel coat would normally need a 2% addition of catalyst on a weight-for-weight basis. Since 1 cc of catalyst weighs 1 gram, the usual procedure is to weigh the gel in grams and then to measure out the catalyst in a graduated cylinder marked in ccs. There are special catalyst bottles – as shown in the accompanying photograph – which include a measuring cylinder as an integral part of the screw cap. You can also purchase inexpensive plastic syringes which have graduated markings on the side.

To give an example of a mix, 100 grams of gel needs 2 cc of catalyst. This 2% mix is adhered to strictly when a GRP panel is manufactured, but in repair work where the tiniest amount of gel is needed to fill a crack, a drip or two of catalyst acts as a rough and ready measure. Moreover, on hot days, the quantity of catalyst should be reduced, especially if the sun is shining on the panel requiring repair.

In contrast, a split or a crack needs attention from the back. If the damaged panel can be removed, so much the better. However, access from behind isn't too difficult if you are repairing a front body skirt or a wheel arch cover.

As a preliminary, you should align the cracked pieces and then hold them in place using sellotape. Whereas PVC tape is strong, it usually deforms and stretches when it reacts with polyester resin. The rear of the damaged area must be roughened up next to achieve a good 'key'. If the area has splits, there are likely to be 'keying-in' areas already. Otherwise you can rough-up the surface using the sharp corner of an old wood chisel. A wood rasp is even better.

The chopped strand mat must now be cut to size with some old scissors and mat designated as 100 gram, (or 1 oz mat) is thick enough. Alernatively 150 gram (1½oz) mat is fine as long as it is impregnated thoroughly with resin. You should now cut two or three pieces of matting to cover the area of damage.

Normally there's no need to colourise resin used for repairs. You will need a glass jar which should be weighed empty. Then a small amount of laminating resin is poured into the jar and it

is weighed again. An old pair of kitchen scales with graduations in grams is ideal. A manageable quantity would be 100 grams of resin, to which must be added 1 cc (1%) of catalyst. Note that this is less than the 2% quantity used for gel coat.

Using a paint brush, the damaged area is then coated with resin. In addition, the first layer of chopped strand mat is laid on some old newspaper and similarly coated with resin. This is called 'wetting-out'. As soon as the mat is wet, and **before** it starts to shred into pieces, you should peel it from the newspaper and position it on the back of the damaged area. This is where you will need plastic or rubber gloves, or a liberal coating of barrier cream on your fingers.

Once a damaged area has been coated with laminating resin, the repair mat should then be 'wetted out'.

Once in place, the mat should be stippled thoroughly with the brush. This helps to draw the resin through all the glass fibres; if you see any white strands, you have failed to impregnate the glass mat sufficiently. Another test of good lamination work is to see if the fibres in the mat have started to curl. If they retain their original straightness, continue stippling the surface

When laid in position on the back of a damaged panel, 'wetted out' chopped strand mat must be thoroughly stippled with a brush or treated with a laminating roller.

until curling takes place.

One layer of glass mat is unlikely to provide much strength to the cracked area and a second layer is usually needed as well. As a general rule, two layers of 150 gram (1½oz) mat are sufficient, or three layers of 100 gram (1 oz) mat. Depending on the temperature, the repair is likely to be dry in half an hour or so. When the panel is firm again, you will have repaired the damage from a structural point of view. But the cracks will look chipped and ragged on the all-important face side. So your attention will now turn to the shiny side and you will hack away stray fibres. You should also start to create grooves using a sharp instrument in readiness for the application of some colourised gel coat. The finishing work will then involve the procedures already described in the earlier part of this section.

Obtaining a shine on the dried gel coat is finally achieved by smoothing off the surface using 'wet and dry' abrasive paper. This process is repeated using a succession of finer papers; you can then use car chrome cleaner. An even milder abrasive can also be used such as toothpaste. By this time a shine will be appearing on the new gelcoat. Finally use polishes, starting with something mildly abrasive like 'T' Cut and then progressing to a conventional car polish. If you follow this progression, it will be possible to recreate a 'like-new' shiny surface.

Although this repair method is strongly recommended when a panel is cracked, split or shattered, you can also produce a quick strength repair using David's U-POL 'B'. This GRP repair material was formerly manufactured under the name of P40 and consists of polyester resin and a mulch of glass fibres. The strands of glass fibre not only provide the strength; they also help to bond the resin into a convenient workable paste. All you need in addition is a wallpaper knife, some acetone cleaner and a scrap of plywood to act as a mixing board.

On account of its consistency, the material is scooped out of its tin with the knife. A typical workable quantity to transfer to the mixing board would be about the volume of a golf ball. The catalyst, which is provided in paste form, is supplied in a tube. As regards mixing proportions, the descriptive instructions recommend that three blobs of catalyst about the size of garden peas are needed where a quantity of paste about the size of a golf ball is being used. The two components should be mixed together thoroughly using the knife, and the pink colour of the catalyst helps to show when this has been achieved.

Although it will vary according to temperature, working time is usually brief. Therefore the material should be applied to the damaged area quite briskly. The decorators' knife is an ideal tool for transferring the material to the reverse side of the panel, spreading it and then smoothing it over; but don't forget to clean

it with acetone, together with the mixing board, as soon as you've placed the material.

On account of its paste-like consistency, U-POL 'B' doesn't run down a vertical panel like a normal polyester resin; this is a distinct advantage. However, whilst this material is a suitable alternative for dealing with small splits, larger areas are better repaired with resin and chopped strand mat as described previously.

Cutting and shaping glass fibre panels

On occasions it may be necessary to cut away small sections of glass fibre. This occurs, for example, if you want to fix a blade type of stabiliser which includes a bracket that has to be fixed to the drawbar. Many caravans have a glass fibre fairing on this forward part of the chassis, and it is likely to need trimming in order to make space for the additional bracket.

Similar trimming work has to be carried out if you want to fit a new locker box on the draw bar, an improvement project which concludes this chapter. Trimming GRP is easy to carry out, though it must not be forgotten that glass fibre dust can act as an unpleasant irritant.

A hacksaw is the usual tool for cutting a panel; on a really thin section it is sometimes possible to make rough cuts with a pair of tin snips. The edges thus produced now need cleaning up and a Surform or wood rasp are both useful. Thereafter, you should use coarse glasspaper, followed by finer abrasive papers to create a tidy finish. This is shown in a practical way in the photographs which accompany the next improvement project.

Fitting a new drawbar locker box

A good improvement project when refurbishing an older caravan is to replace the gas

locker box. This is dealt with here since it involves many of the techniques discussed in the previous sections. Provided you purchase a good quality replacement locker box, installation can be quite straightforward.

A full range of suitable locker boxes is manufactured by Lamplas of Co. Durham. This is a plastics specialist whose glass fibre panels are used by several leading caravan manufacturers. For example, many GRP front walls are made under contract at the Lamplas works for caravan manufacturers who prefer to 'buy-in' plastic panels rather than undertaking lamination work themselves. The company's association with the industry is one reason why the locker boxes are popular in the after-sales market. The products are smart, robust and sensibly designed.

The accompanying photographs show a model known as the 'Super Locker' being fitted to a 1972 Lynton Caravan. This is a large capacity locker offering storage for two gas bottles, a spare wheel and sundry other items. It incorporates two 'parking points' for 12N and 12S plugs and two catches which can be locked by padlock. The only word of caution is to urge anyone fitting a Super Locker to keep a vigilant eye on its implications for caravan noseweight. It is an excellent space carrier for loading up large, but light, items like a plastic bucket, beachballs or a spare washing-up bowl. But you mustn't use the space for jamming heavy items into every available corner.

The old box which it replaced was removed first. The old self-tapping screws holding the original locker in place were so rusty they had to be cut with a builders' club hammer and bolster. Having exposed the drawbar, the steel sections of the old B & B type chassis had to be wire brushed, and treated with rust inhibiting paint and a new topcoat.

When fitting one of these lockers, the unit has to be offered up against the front wall, recognising that it is going to need trimming to suit the caravan's profile. A cutting line has to be pencilled on the glass fibre surface of the Super Locker and excess material can then be trimmed away. Trimming can be done with a hacksaw although an electric jigsaw fitted with a blade for cutting plastic is quicker to use.

Trimming accurately may involve several checks and cutting adjustments in order to copy the line of the caravan front exactly. When doing this, it is important to leave a gap of about 19 mm (^{3}/$_4$ in) between the locker and the caravan body itself. When towing, there is considerable flexion on a drawbar, and a closer fit could result in the locker chafing against the caravan wall.

The accompanying photograph shows the tidying processes which follow the saw cutting. The rounding-off work has already been described. The Super Locker is supplied with plastic trim for covering the glass fibre edges, and this is anchored by metal barb clips fitted around the perimeters.

The locker shown here was attached to the drawbar using sturdy self-tapping screws.

A jigsaw set at a slow speed and fitted with a blade to cut GRP was used to trim the Super Locker to match the caravan profile.

A wood rasp was used to trim rough sections left by the jigsaw, prior to smoothing down the cut edge with abrasive paper.

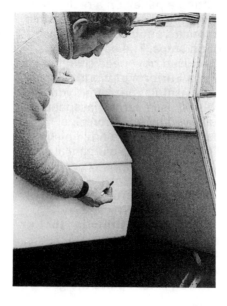

Sequence of 4 photographs showing a GRP 'Super Locker' being fitted to an older caravan.

When the old locker had been removed, the Super Locker was offered up and marked so that it could be trimmed to fit.

Once fitted, the Super Locker offers considerably more space, although it is important to check that noseweights are kept within acceptable limits.

However, a stronger fixing is a self-tapping bolt which has a hexagonal head. These are often used in the automotive trade for attaching the front wings on many modern cars; a trip to a breaker's yard is recommended. But there is one note of caution. Whereas older types of heavy steel chassis can be drilled to accept a locker box, this strategy should **not** be adopted on a modern lightweight chassis. In consequence, Lamplas can supply special clasp bolts instead. These are standard fixings used in the roofing industry for attaching profiled roof panels to a steel framework. The hook section grasps the fold-back on the chassis member whilst the opposite end features a threaded portion with a large washer and nut. The hook bolt is tightened from inside the base of the locker box.

Overall, this is a straightforward improvement project and several sizes of locker to suit different caravans are available from Lamplas direct or can be ordered from a dealer. The address is given in the Appendix.

Relacing a double-glazed window

Repairing windows in older caravans can present difficulties

and this is not a job which many owners would want to tackle. Modern double-glazed windows are different. If a window is damaged, a replacement can either be purchased direct from the caravan manufacturer or through a dealer. In addition, there are specialist suppliers such as D. J. Russell (Sales) and the Exhaust Ejector Co whose addresses appear in the Appendix.

The hinge of window units is usually held in a groove of the aluminium trim piece which runs along the head of the opening. To carry out the replacement, you first remove the plastic insert from the trim strip to expose its attachment screws. The screws are removed so that the trim section can be lifted away from the body. The damaged unit is then slid out of its retaining groove; the replacement is returned in the same manner.

The trim piece should be rebedded on sealant and it's advisable to inject sealant into the holes used by its attachment screws. All the catches are then transferred to the new window.

Conclusion
This chapter has described how to repair aluminium and GRP bodywork. As suggested at the

beginning, many repairs are best left to experienced service engineers. Other tasks, however, can be tackled by competent owners. Either way, it is helpful to have **some** knowledge of repair techniques so that you can confirm if work is being carried out in accordance with good practice.

(iii) The trim strip has to be carefully prised away from its mastic bedding, so that it stands proud of the window recess.

(i) The plastic insert has to be removed from the aluminium tim strip mounted above the window.

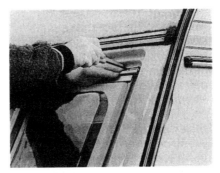

(ii) Screws that are revealed below the plastic insert have to loosened.

(iv) Once its plastic end stop is unscrewed, the window unit can be slid out of its groove in the trim strip.

Chapter 6

INTERIOR MAINTENANCE AND IMPROVEMENTS

Interior matters

Many people choose a new caravan on account of its layout, furnishings and fixtures. Without question a caravan interior is very important, but after several seasons it will start to show the inevitable signs of wear.

This is especially evident when purchasing a second-hand model; whilst the general structure may be sound, interiors often look disappointingly shabby. Fortunately, however, it isn't difficult to refurbish an interior and many owners achieve pleasing results. With this in mind, the intention here is to consider both furniture and fabrics and to look at repair work, maintenance tasks and improvement projects.

Furniture construction

With regard to furniture, a caravan manufacturer is concerned with three key issues, strength, weight and appearance. There are other matters, of course, like cost and speed of assembly. However, the construction of caravan furniture is different from domestic furniture and this has implications for repair work.

In some instances, the quest to save weight leads to a compromise in strength. It isn't unusual, for example, to find that a bed support collapses and an urgent repair has to be carried out. Examples of a poor original design are not unusual and owners with woodworking skills are often able to make improvements.

The point to emphasise, however, is the fact that a well-meaning repairer should never resort to using heavy timber or boards when carrying out repairs. Weight watching is always important.

Timber and adhesives

Light structures are achieved in several ways; for example fitted furniture usually comprises a skeleton framework which is clad in decorative 3 mm plywood. Frameworks are made from light softwood like obeche, and there will be a notable absence of hardwoods like mahogany or teak which are unacceptably heavy.

Interior surfaces of walls, doors and furniture are usually built from very thin plywood which is covered with a decorative finish. In earlier caravans, hardboard was used, but this is no longer favoured because of its additional weight, tendency to expand and billow, and its excessive flexibility.

As regards decorative surfaces, some early 1970s caravans e.g. Lynton models were finished in a real wood veneer; this can be revitalised easily with a light grade of glass paper. Nowadays surfaces have a mock grain effect in which a printed paper has been applied to bare plywood. Rub this in error using glass paper and you'll have a nasty shock as the ply suddenly loses its fraudulent facade.

Plywood is strong and light. Veneered chipboard, however, is unacceptably heavy and whereas it it used for domestic furniture, it should never be used in a caravan.

Overall, the caravan cabinet maker employs great guile in

disguising his product. Cupboard fronts and locker doors often have a fine look of robust solidity. Their shaped lippings aroung the perimeter and mouldings on the panel face bestow a look of heavy quality. But there's a surprise in store for anyone who undoes the hinges and removes a cuboard door from its location. Appearances bely the true structure and doors which look convincingly solid are usually hollow.

The accompanying photograph shows a typical cabinet door with its interior exposed; the void between the front and rear ply faces is immediately evident. If you plan to refurbish a caravan, it is most important that you follow this building strategy. A hollow door can be easily formed using a softwood frame which is sandwiched between two pieces of 3 mm plywood. An interior grade PVA woodworking adhesive like EvoStik Resin W is ideal for the job, though you will need several G-cramps to hold the sandwich assembly in position. When making doors up in this way, you must also make sure that they are situated in a level position when cramped-up. A twist created at this stage is virtually impossible to rectify later.

Hollow cupboard doors are easy to construct by cramping 3 mm ply to a frame of softwood.

prepared on a precision saw bench. A well equipped woodworker might also use a router or a spindle moulder, to create a decorative moulding on the lipping. Since the trim is unlikely to be thicker than 6 mm ($^1/_4$ in), you can use hardwood without adding too much weight to the end-product. This is one instance where caravan manufacturers allow final appearances to take priority over weight constraint.

An alternative is to use a veneer to cover the exposed edges of doors and cupboard fronts. This can be purchased in narrow rolls with a pre-coated

If a door or cupboard front is cut open, it will almost certainly have a hollow interior to save weight.

Purpose-made lippings to cover the edges of hollow doors can be cut to size using a circular saw table.

When a door is released from its cramps, the edges will need trimming. A circular saw table is ideal for removing the main surplus, though a handsaw will also do the job, albeit more slowly. Lastly a smoothing plane is needed to square everything up completely. The exposed edges now need covering, and DIY Superstores usually carry an array of edge mouldings in different profiles. Alternatively, purpose-made lippings can be

glue blacking. When a strip is cut to length, it is applied with a hot iron but unfortunately the results are not always a long term success. It is often better to coat them with an impact adhesive like EvoStik. This approach is also recommended if you purchase sheet veneer and cut it to size with a woodworking knife

When making up your own doors, it is important to ensure that within the core, the softwood perimeter frame is wide enough to provide a fixing for the screws which hold the hinges. In the case of catches, you may also find it necessary to

A timber insert can be glued into a hollow door which has been reduced in size; this also ensures the edge is substantial enough to accept screws holding the hinges.

insert a block in an otherwise hollow door to provide a good fixing for a handle or lock assembly. Similar measures are needed if it is intended to fit a weight bearing item like a mirror or a coat hook.

Inevitably it takes longer to build a hollow door than to fit a pre-made wardrobe door from a DIY Superstore. But the experienced caravan cabinet maker is aware of the subtle accumulative effect of mounting weight. If you don't have time to make your own hollow doors, consider the following approach.

Most caravan manufacturers 'buy-in' their interior cabinet and locker doors from abroad. Similarly they keep stock of hollow units used for earlier models. Some manufacturers e.g. Compass Caravans distribute extremely comprehensive spare parts catalogues to their dealerships. In the case of CI caravans, the spare parts listings are held by their dealers on microfiche. By placing an order, a complete door replacement can be undertaken. If there are problems matching size, purchase larger units specifying doors which don't have face mouldings. These can cut down as required, inserting and glueing new core timber where necessary. Any exposed edges

are finally trimmed with veneer or lipping.

Catches, hinges and handles

Door fittings in caravans are not always robust; handles, locks and catches often need replacement. Hinges are suspect, too. For example, the 'piano hinge' used for items like a hinged work top or a tilting wash basin often rust badly. This is because some manufacturers fit cheaper 'brassed' hinges; these are not solid brass but coated steel. A brassed hinge soon develops surface rust in the damp atmosphere of a caravan; plastic

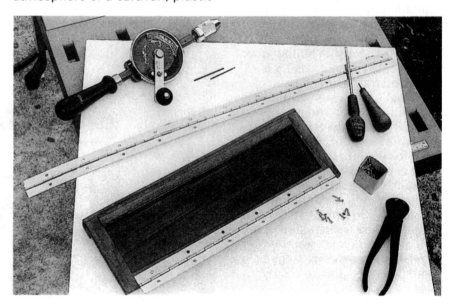

If continuous 'piano hinge' starts to rust, it is worth replacing with a solid brass replacement. In a caravan, 'brassed' steel soon deteriorates.

piano hinge is better, but many manufacturers attach this with steel screws which go rusty.

Rusting hinges often occur on bed box locker lids as well. This subsequently discolours the lining material on the underside of seat cushions and the problem is aggravated if they become damp. This happens when a cushion is used as a bed mattress because condensation forms on the underside at night.

A lightweight drop flap stay is a typical item which should be available from any well-stocked caravan dealers – or even a DIY Superstore.

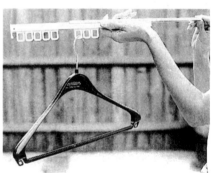

Many unusual fittings are shown in the catalogue from Woodfit of Chorley. Extending rails for wardrobes, for example, are not easy to obtain from other sources.

When replacing catches and hinges, it is worth noting that DIY superstores are starting to stock lightweight fittings which are suitable for use in caravans. There are also specialist suppliers like Woodfit of Chorley. The Woodfit catalogue is a worthy starting point for anyone engaged in caravan renovation. It includes items like wire cage storage shelves, self-assembly drawers, all sorts of hinges and a prodigious array of knobs and catches.

Shelves

There are several ways to build a shelf which is both strong and light. Caravan manufacturers often create a hollow shelf in the same way that a door is constructed. Two pieces of 3 mm ply are held apart with a softwood insert at either side with a void in the middle.

Another method is to use a single length of ply which is reinforced along its forward edge using a grooved batten. The purpose of the groove is to house the plywood tightly and this can be formed using a circular saw or a grooving plane.

This technique not only provides a useful leading edge to prevent items slipping from the shelf; thin plywood which would otherwise be unacceptably flexible assumes notable rigidity when glued into the slot. Quite often it is useful to fit a similar grooved batten at the rear so that the shelf can be screwed to the wall of the caravan and supported at the back as well.

Wood stains and colourisers

Even if reinforcements to shelves are made in white softwood, these can be given the appearance of hardwood with a wood dye. Manufacturers like Colron produce a large range of colours and these stains are simply applied with a rag.

In addition to the darker stains, you can also purchase pastel tints in the Dulux Woodtones collection. Moreover, Ronseal 'Woodstyle' range includes subtle shades like applewood, barleywood and peachwood. These can bestow a light and delicate appearance to any interior finish.

Rebuilding

When embarking on a radical rebuild, it will often be noticed that much of the original furniture was held together with staples. In the hands of a professional, staple guns speed up assembly. The DIY builder, however, is probably able to achieve better workmanship using more traditional fixings.

When considering which screws to use, modern twin-threaded 'Supascrews' are more rust resistant than conventional steel screws. You are also advised to use brass screws in locations where there is likely to be moisture. They are recommended, for example, if you are replacing a piano hinge on a drop flap in the kitchen.

If you intend to use panel pins, the type with a sherardised coating are suitably rust resistant. Brass panel pins used by boatbuilders are equally successful but are normally only available from a marine specialist. Lastly, a few extra long veneer pins are useful for fine work. It takes a little skill to avoid bending a veneer pin when driving it home with a hammer. On the other hand, by nipping of its head it can be used as a 'throw-away' drill bit in a hand drill. This is a good way to form tiny pilot holes in timber, especially in moulding strips made from a whitewood like Ramin which splits easily. Once pre-drilled, a moulding strip is easy to fix into position using glue and veneer pins.

Lastly, reference has been made to decorative 3 mm plywood. This is not usually stocked in DIY stores and it has to be ordered through a caravan dealer. There are two types. Firstly there are wood veneer patterns which are normally used for caravan furniture. Secondly there are plywoods with white surfaces for ceilings

Having strengthened a thin ply shelf with a sturdy softwood batten across the front, this is being prepared for fixing into the sides of a cabinet.

Ordinary deal used to reinforce the front of a shelf can be finished quickly and effectively using one of Colron's wood dyes.

or walls. Both are ideal for their purpose and are better than hardboard with a glazed white surface.

When cutting 3 mm plywood to size, a saw is inclined to leave a ragged edge. It is better to place the panel on an old piece of board and to use a sharp woodworking knife and a long steel rule. An even better cutting guide is a Rabone Chesterman Measuring and Cutting Scale. This is stocked in many DIY Stores and comprises a straight edge a metre in length and a central handle. It is safer than a normal rule because the cutting knife is less likely to jump the

Decorative 3 mm plywood used by caravan manufacturers is sufficiently thin to be cut accurately using a woodworking knife and a steel rule.

edge. This is equally true if you use it to cut some carpet or plastic vinyl. Several passes across the surface with the knife produces a clean edge.

Caravan upholstery – foam fillings

Although spring interior mattresses were announced as an optional extra for several 1993 caravans, most cushions are made with synthetic foam.

Some foams, however, have been known to be hazardous in fires, and toxic fumes are particularly dangerous. As a result of 1988 Safety Regulations, filling materials and coverings in newer caravans have to meet special requirements regarding resistance to cigarette and match ignition. Earlier caravans are unlikely to have fire resistant foams, and it is strongly recommended to upgrade the filling at the earliest opportunity. In the literature available from specialist caravan and boat upholsterers, it is important to select a 'Combustion Modified'

foam which meets current fire regulations.

Fire resistance is important; so too, is comfort. Many caravans are fitted with an inexpensive foam which is comfortable at the time of purchase. But it doesn't last. A mattress filled with this type of foam tends to lift at either end if someone sits in the middle. Moreover, after several seasons it loses its resilience and starts to 'bottom'; there can be quite a jolt when sitting down and making contact with the solid base beneath the mattress.

When foam has degenerated, there are several measures which

can be taken. If the budget is limited, one strategy is to give it a boost by adding a 'topping', a job best entrusted to a professional caravan upholsterer. It involves unstitching the cover material, removing the foam and then bonding a thin layer on the top with a special adhesive. This adds to the overall depth, of course, but since the original foam will have compressed over the years, this can generally be accommodated in the original covers. Where upholstery buttons are fitted, this soft layer allows them to bed down neatly. Some specialist caravan upholsterers like Caralux of Alfreton can make up any multi-layered cushion to order, and if required, a bottom layer can be added, too.

The addition of topping is a good revitalising strategy but a better long-term answer is to replace the original product with a 'High Resilient' (HR) foam. This retains its shape and body much longer and contains fire retardants described earlier. Specialists like Caralux supply the product with a five year guarantee.

For even greater comfort, HR foam can be topped with a thin layer of polyester Dacron. This is sometimes used as the padding in quilted anoraks and it doesn't add a great amount to the price.

Some caravan cushions are a simple symmetrical slab, whereas in more expensive models, the forward edge has a raised portion. Upholsterers refer to this as a 'knee roll' and it is an easy addition for the expert to provide. It involves bonding a pre-shaped length of foam on to the forward edge of the mattress.

Replacing the foam in cushions is a sensible idea if you want to renovate a second hand caravan to a high standard. It may be quite a costly element in a refurbishment scheme but sleeping in comfort is important

The forward edge of a caravan cushion can be increased in depth by bonding on additional strips. This produces what upholsterers call a 'knee roll'.

A specialist such as Caralux Upholsterers can bond together foam to create any shape, width or length required by a customer.

on any holiday. Owners who can use a needle and thread with skilled patience might tackle the job themselves. To help the do-it-yourselfer, some upholsterers e.g. Caralux are willing to supply filling materials; 'Foam for Comfort' of Cookridge, Leeds is another specialist which cuts foam to order.

Caravan upholstery – stretch covers

On a second hand caravan, the cushion covers are often worn or discoloured. The cheapest way to deal with this is to have some stretch covers made to measure. This may not produce

the smartest answer, but it costs far less than having new tweed or velour covers made to suit the cushions. Stretch covers are also easily removable for cleaning – an important consideration if young children use the caravan.

Stretch cover specialists usually supply enquirers with samples, some of which may be reversible fabrics. The covers can also be supplied with either tie tapes or zips according to preference. Advertisements for stretch covers appear regularly in caravan magazines and it is worth 'phoning for a catalogue.

A disadvantage with these products is that with use, they often tend to slip around seat cushions. This can be overcome if the manufacturer is asked to make-up some matching upholstery buttons with elasticated tags. After taping the tag to a skewer, this can be pushed completely through the foam, leaving the button on the face and with the tag appearing on the underside. This helps to prevent the material from sliding about although it adds more work when the cover has to be removed for washing.

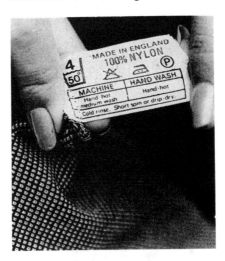

Caravan stretch covers are usually machine washable which can be useful if an accident occurs; 100% nylon fabrics are quite common.

Stretch covers can be held in place with tie tapes; however, covers with zips are more convenient.

To prevent a cover from slipping around the foam core, a specialist can make up matching upholstery buttons which the owners can fit themselves.

Caravan upholstery – replacement covers

Whereas stretch covers are competitively priced, the best results are achieved if a caravan's cushions are re-covered by a specialist. After sending for samples, fabrics may be recognised as the ones being used in the latest models. Several upholsterers e.g. Beauvale, who supply the caravan manufacturers, recognise this is a seasonal industry and deal with the public individually during slacker periods.

An advantage of going to a specialist is that they are able to

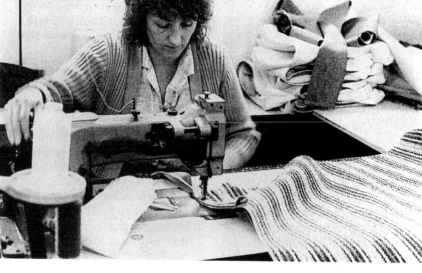

Provided the owner is working with a generous budget, best results are achieved by getting a specialist to make a completely new set of permanent covers.

With the help of an industrial quality sewing machine, a skilled operator can manufacture a new cushion cover at remarkable speed

A good caravan upholsterer has no difficulty covering unusual cushions – like split folders – and can often supply curtain material to complement the other fabrics

deal with unusual cushion covers like 'split folders'. These units open rather like a book, for example a split folding seat back is often converted into one of the base mattresses of a bunk bed. Needless to say, the do-it-yourself upholsterer would find these cushions hard to tackle.

Caravanners wanting to have this work done can either send the cushions to the factory by carrier, or book an appointment to call themselves. Several companies have carparks where you can stop overnight in your caravan and many customers combine a factory visit with a short holiday in the area. The fact that several specialists are based in Pennine woollen areas means there's attractive scenery nearby. Alternatively the cushions can be taken in a large car, though it may not leave space for passengers.

In all cases, it is essential to book a visit in advance because most of the specialists have busy periods when factory staff are making a bulk order for a caravan manufacturer. However, visiting in person means you can discuss matters like backing fabrics and ruche.

'Ruche' is the name for the decorative beading material around the edges of seat cushions and seat backs. Upholstery tape is a cheaper alternative. For caravans with an ornate decor style, 'cut ruche', which has a frill effect, is usually affixed around the top seams. 'Flat ruche' is often put around the bottom corners and is a popular match with velour materials. Both types come in a variety of colours.

With regard to backing fabrics,

A special machine is used to re-stitch a replacement backing fabric to the main part of the cushion cover, although ruche is usually added as well.

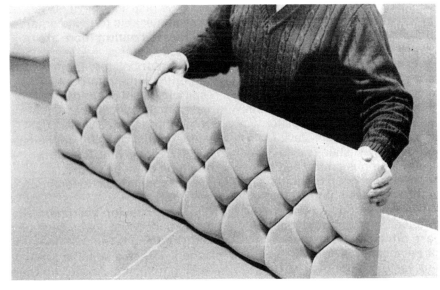

dark materials are less prone to showing stain marks left from under-mattress condensation. And cotton is better than synthetic materials which are inclined to 'fluff-up' against the lids of bed boxes.

On some caravans, upholstered seat backs are screwed to the walls, particularly on an end wall near the dining

A purpose-made machine stitches ruche around the perimeter of a caravan cushion in a matter of seconds.

Padded seat backs in caravans can easily be made to suit customer requirements by a caravan upholstery specialist.

area. These can be re-covered by a specialist but the panel has to be detached. It is usually fixed with screws and since the head gets lost amongst the pattern, a little detective work is needed.

Additional soft furnishings
Since the furnishings are

conspicuous in a caravan, re-upholstery gives a startling face-lift. Specialist companies can also make matching scatter cushions to enhance the interior even further.

Curtains and padded pelmets are another element which might be considered. Many upholstery specialists hold stocks of curtain fabrics whose patterns can be matched against the cushions. By arranging to visit the factory, complementary colour schemes can be chosen. Moreover, working direct is usually less expensive than making a purchase through a caravan dealer. A closer communication also ensures there are no misunderstandings over preferred fabrics and finishes.

Routine maintenance
Curtains are the easiest item to keep clean. Cotton prints can be washed by hand but should be treated with care; moreover, modern detergents should be avoided because they may affect the fabric's fire retardancy qualities as well as the colour. Traditional soap flake treatments are recommended.

Velvet curtains normally need dry cleaning. If washed in water, there's a tendency for the velvet to shrink at a different rate from the lining material.

As regards upholstery, stains can often be removed with a proprietary cleaner. Stain Devils, for example, are available from most chemists and the range includes treatments to deal with marks such as biro ink, tea stain, red wine, grass stain, lipstick and so on. The Stain Devil for removing rust stain is also useful if hinges on the bed box have left marks on the underside of the mattress lining fabric.

There are many other general cleaners, working on a foam base principle. Sometimes a carpet cleaner is equally successful on upholstery, but

check the instructions. It is always advisable to test a small area first to confirm there are no adverse reactions.

Modern upholstery fabrics are inherently flame retardant as a result of special chemical treatment. Products like Scotchguard from 3M are often used, and these can be applied in an older caravan. The work should be done outdoors, observing all instructions about user-safety.

If a large cushion becomes heavily soiled, the cover must be unstitched and taken to a dry cleaners; it is **not** suitable for a washing machine. According to

Scotchguard specialists, cushion covers can be dry cleaned up to three times before this fire retardant treatment is affected.

Obviously, prevention is better than cure; if there are young children likely to leave marks, a few inexpensive stretch covers may be worth purchasing.

Interior blinds and fly screens

As a final improvement project, combined window blinds and fly screens may be worth fitting. These are standard fittings in de-luxe caravans, but are not difficult to install. This presumes there is enough space around the windows to house the roller assemblies at the top and bottom and for the guide channels on either side.

A good example is the Remis roller blind system available through most caravan accessory suppliers. The product incorporates a blind for complete privacy which is mounted on a roller above the window. The fly screen is a separate fabric which is mounted on a roller at the bottom. However, the attraction of the system is the fact that rails at the extremity of the two fabrics can be clipped together and scrolled. Once linked, it is possible to scroll the material to cover the window with part blind and part mosquito gauze.

These units are particularly popular with caravanners who visit hot places. For example it is possible to sleep with a window wide open, with the mesh playing its part in keeping out insects and the normal curtains preserving one's privacy.

The Remis system is available with over a dozen different sized units and it there are no obstructions around the window, they are easy to fit. Sometimes the curtain trackway may need repositioning and it may be necessary to fit ply packing pieces to ensure the units stand proud of the interior

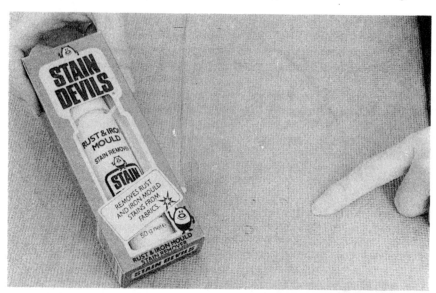

The rust and iron remover made by 'Stain Devils' is ideal for dealing with marks left by hinges on the underside of cushions.

Foam based carpet cleaners like this 'Stain Devils' product are equally suitable for dealing with marks on caravan cushions.

Combined window blinds and fly screens are often fitted to deluxe caravans; but many owners would find Remis blinds easy to fit themselves.

The lower section of a Remis blind – which contains the roll of decorative mesh fabric – is clipped into the side channelling.

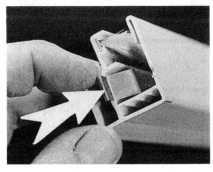

Spring clips hold the sides and tops in register. When screwing the four sections around a window, checks must be made to see that the framework is square.

wall to clear the window catches and locks.

The sections can be attached to the ply inner skin of a wall using self-tapping screws. However, it is important to make sure that the framework is mounted squarely and this must be monitored when the four sections are being assembled.

Conclusion

The interiors of old caravans frequently look shabby whereas new models look sumptuous. However, with time, effort and some funds set aside for improvements, you can easily transform the interior of a caravan quite impressively. The only cautionary note is to point out that some tasks like re-upholstery are usually the preserve of the professional.

When an installation is complete, Remis blinds and flyscreens are particularly useful in holiday venues where mosquitoes and midges become a nuisance.

Chapter 7

LOW VOLTAGE SUPPLY SYSTEM

Introduction to electrical provision

Modern caravans have two completely separate electrical systems. One circuit serves 12v DC appliances, whereas the other provides power for 240v AC equipment. Some caravanners find this confusing, particularly the fact that there is a degree of inter-relationship.

Even though the circuitry is totally separate, a mains supply is often used to charge a 12v battery or it can be fed through suitable safety devices into a transformer/rectifier to be converted into a 12v DC supply. Nevertheless, the two supply systems are wholly independent of each other and it would be exceedingly dangerous if this were misunderstood. With this in mind, the present chapter is concerned solely with low voltage 12v DC provision. The subject of 240v AC mains current is dealt with separately in Chapter 8.

The developing sophistication of caravan electrics has occurred over a number of years and by looking at the original electrical

items fitted in a caravan you have a clue to its age. However, it isn't difficult for owners of older caravans to update this electrical provision and several suggestions are given later in this chapter.

When carrying out work on

An inexpensive 12v circuit tester costing a little over £1.00 from many Auto DIY stores is a most useful asset.

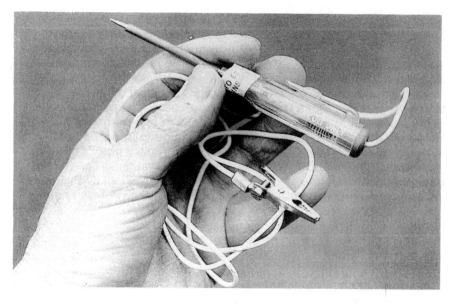

the low voltage system, a 12v circuit tester is almost indispensible. Arguably a multimeter is better, but a much cheaper tester available from car DIY shops can be used instead. A wire stripper is needed too, particularly the type with an adjustment for dealing with insulations of different thickness.

When you have to join lengths of wire, you will need a crimping

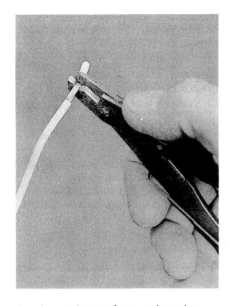

A wire stripper for cutting the insulation from wire cleanly and quickly is another invaluable tool.

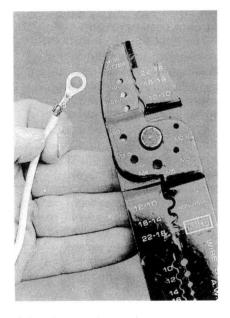

Crimping tools can be purchased from Auto DIY stores together with a selection of terminals.

tool together with a selection of crimp terminals. Starter kits are usually available from auto specialists such as Halfords.

The development of low voltage supplies in caravans
When LabCraft, an electronics specialist, introduced fluorescent lights for caravans, their benefits were instantly acknowledged. Nearly all caravans manufactured in the early 1970s had at least one fluorescent light as standard provision, though some models retained a gas lamp as a stand-by. Gas lighting, however, soon disappeared.

At first, the 12v supply for fluorescent lights was provided by the towcar battery. The connection used Pin 2 of the 12N socket as described in Chapter 3, and some owners with older caravans continue to use this arrangement. If used judiciously, a single tubed fluorescent light seldom causes a serious drain on a 12v battery. Moreover, its light output is better than a tungsten bulb of the same wattage.

Once the full potential of a low voltage supply was recognised, manufacturers subsequently introduced electric water pumps, reading lamps, a TV connection point, and other electrical items. No longer could the caravanner rely on a towcar to provide the power. This reliance all-too-easily leads to a discharged battery and car starting problems; it also means that caravan occupants are left without power whenever the towcar is taken off-site. The problem was resolved when owners started to install a second battery inside the caravan, an arrangement discussed in the *Inboard Batteries* Section.

The introduction of more and more 12v appliances also led to the development of fused distribution systems. These take a 12v supply and feed it into separate routes to serve selected categories of appliances such as lights, water pump, and auxiliaries e.g. a socket for a TV, or a power source for a stereo. Separate circuits are also fitted with a fuse of an appropriate size. This orderly distribution makes it much easier if you are trying to track down a fault and nearly all caravans built since 1980 employ this system.

Some distribution units in the early 1980s featured a prodigious array of switches, digital displays and light emitting diodes. No attempt was made to hide these; on the contrary, some owners preferred elaborate facia controls. More recently, however, the trend has favoured a more discreet arrangement and a corresponding simplification of the control panel.

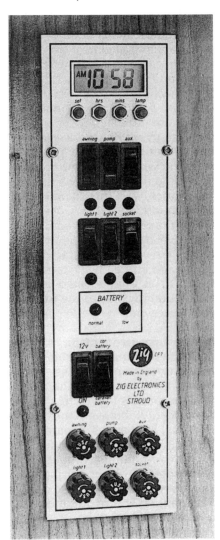

Produced in the early 1980s, the Zig CF7 was bristling with switches, fuses, light emitting diodes – and also a digital clock.

Today's low voltage provision is properly planned, carefully protected, and eminently useful. However, an owner of an older caravan could plan a supply system and fit new appliances without too much difficulty.

Power from a towcar

Provided that the only electrical item fitted in a caravan is a fluorescent light, it is acceptable to draw power from a towcar battery using the 1.0 mm square, 8.75 amp blue wire which forms part of the 12N multicore cable. This was discussed in Chapter 3. However, caravans fitted with a wide range of electrical appliances need a 12S system as well, and the way in which this is connected has been discussed in *Fitting a 12S socket* Chapter 3.

The aim here is to focus on the system within the caravan itself. After the 12N and 12S coupling with the car, the supply is fed into the caravan via the appropriate 12N (black) or 12S (grey) multicore cable. Once inside the fabric of the 'van, the wires which make up the two cables are usually separated and connected into a plastic terminal strip. This is often located in a bedbox quite close to the front of the caravan.

In-line fuse protection

After the terminal strip, the wiring arrangement varies according to the age of the 'van. In older models in which fluorescent lights were the only electrical appliances, separate feed wires would often be fed direct to lamp units without any fuse protection. Recognising that 12v current *can* cause a fire if something shorts out, this is potentially dangerous.

It is true that if a permanent live feed has come via the car's fuse box, this offers a measure of protection in the event of a short circuit. However, modern practice commends the

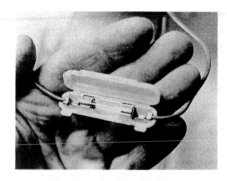

The simplest way to provide protection between a 12v appliance and a caravan circuit is to fit an in-line fuse.

inclusion of fused protection in the caravan as well. If you are modernising an old model, the simplest expedient is to fit an in-line fuse within the positive feed wire. This should be located as near to the point of entry into the caravan as possible, and a 10 amp glass tubed fuse is recommended if the supply is just for lighting. Inexpensive fuse holders are stocked at car accessory shops.

Fuse box

Whilst the installation of an in-line fuse is fine just for lighting, a purpose made fuse box is needed if there are several appliances. When introduced in 1986, the FDU12 fuse box manufactured by Metofax provided just the answer. It offered individual protection for up to nine appliances and a number of owners fitted the Metofax product when upgrading their caravans. But in spite of its merits, wall-mounted fused control panels proved more popular and the Metofax fusebox was withdrawn.

Simple fused distribution units

Basic models of fused distribution units are only a little more elaborate than a straight forward fuse box. A popular example often fitted in mid-price caravans is the Zig CP3. This model lacks the facilities

included in more elaborate distribution units, but it meets many caravanners' requirements. It is compact, simple to fit and there are horizontal and vertical versions (CP3V) available.

The Zig CP3 is designed to accept 12v power from both an inboard battery and a car battery. These separate supplies should be wired up to the unit and the selection switch then enables the user to decide which battery will provide the power. The three position switch can also isolate the circuits completely; when left in its middle position, both supplies are disconnected. Under normal circumstances your choice of power source on site would be an inboard caravan leisure battery. However, it is useful to have the chance to switch to the towcar battery briefly if the inboard battery is running low.

The Zig CP3 also informs the owner about the state of the feed batteries. A green light on its facia confirms the charge is good; the red light warns that the battery is getting low.

Whatever the battery source, the CP3 divides the supply into three separate circuits – lights, water pump and auxiliary appliances. Each has its own on/off switch on the facia panel and a fuse holder as well. This control can be useful when carrying out repair jobs. For instance you can switch off a supply to an electric pump, without needing to cut the supply to the lights.

When fitting a Zig CP3, its location must be chosen with care. To begin with, room is needed **behind** the supporting facia panel for the circuit board and cable connections. Furthermore, the rear of the unit needs ventilation and must not be obstructed. However, compared with some of the larger units which incorporate a battery charger, a CP3 takes up much less space.

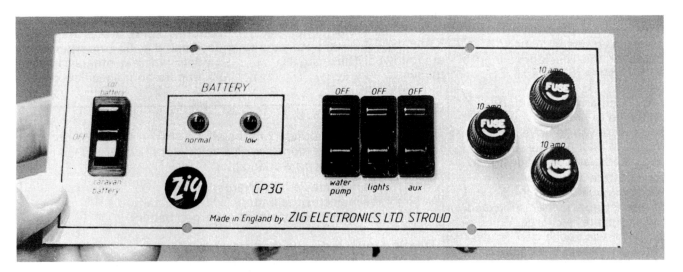

The Zig CP3 fused distribution unit was fitted into many 1980s caravans; it is compact, easy to install and perfectly adequate for most caravanners' needs.

One of the neatest ways to make a cut-out in caravan furniture for a fused distribution unit is to use a sharp woodworking knife.

Having passed a cutting knife several times across the surface of 3 mm decorative ply, it is easy to lift away the waste wood leaving clean edges around the cut-out.

Normally the metal facia is screwed into 3 mm decorative ply which is the light material used for caravan furniture. One of the best ways to cut a neat rectangular aperture in this thin material is to use a woodworking knife and a steel rule. A new blade will help and care must be taken that the knife doesn't ride up over the edge of the rule. The technique involves repeatedly passing the blade along a pencilled cutting line. Gentle pressure and five or six passes is likely to penetrate the ply. Patience is invariably safer than strong arm tactics and even if it takes a dozen strokes across the surface, the reward is a neat cut in the plywood and no need for First Aid.

Although the Zig CP3 isn't heavy, you shouldn't rely solely on four facia plate screws to provide a fixing. Support is also needed at the rear of the aperture, and this can be provided by glueing a full width batten to align with the lower part of the cutout. A length of deal with a cross section size of 25 mm x 25 mm (1 in x 1 in) is adequate for small distribution units of this kind.

Inboard batteries

Recognising that a second battery is needed to supply the

appliances in a modern caravan, many owners try to save money by using an old car battery. However, this is seldom a long term success for several reasons.

By intention, a car battery is designed to produce a sudden surge of power to drive a starter motor. In addition, the structure of its lead plates is not designed for a pattern of use where the battery is operated to the point of discharge, and then subjected to a complete re-charge. When a car battery is re-charged, some of the paste held in its plates often becomes dislodged.

To meet the needs of caravan and boat owners, battery designers have produced the 'leisure battery'. In order to cope with a life of constant discharge and recharge, its plates are constructed so that their paste is held in place much longer. Special separators help to fulfil this role and inevitably the manufacturing costs are greater.

Bearing the words 'Energy for Leisure', the batteries from Al-Ko are available in three sizes, offering different amp hour capabilities.
(courtesy Al-Ko Kober)

On the other hand, life expectancy is much improved, particularly if certain procedures are followed. These are as follows:

Condition check
A battery left for around 12 hours after a charge should be given a check across its terminals with a voltmeter to confirm it isn't reaching the end of its working life.

12.7 volts indicates a fully charged battery
12.4 volts indicates the battery is 50% discharged
12.0 volts or less indicates a discharged battery

Dealing with a discharged battery
★ A battery in a state of complete discharge must not be allowed to remain in this condition for more than 24 hours.
★ If this is permitted to happen, recharging must take place as soon as possible. If a voltmeter reading doesn't subsequently indicate 12.7 volts, permanent damage has taken place.

Procedures during a caravan lay-up period
★ When a caravan is stored or left for a long period, its battery will gradually lose its charge. The battery should therefore be checked regularly and charged periodically. A re-charge every two or three months is recommended and to carry this out, many caravanners transfer the battery into a garage or workshed.
★ Before taking out a caravan for the first time after a period in storage, a battery needs a preliminary charge. Where possible, this should be done over a period of about 15 hours, using a charger whose output is around 5 amps.
★ Trickle charging using a wind or solar powered generator may help to maintain the condition of a battery when a caravan is left unused for long periods.

When comparing leisure batteries, some makes are designated as 60 ampere-hour models, whereas others carry a 90 ampere-hour specification.

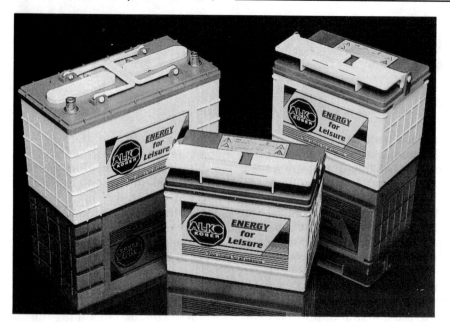

Since the latter product is both larger and heavier, most caravanners purchase a 60 ampere-hour model. However, this won't provide current for as long as the 90 ampere-hour battery and it needs to be re-charged more often.

Before buying a battery, it is sensible to establish its operating life between charges. This involves listing all the appliances and their rating in Watts. Further information about current rating is explained later in this chapter.

To give some examples, a single tube fluorescent light is typically rated at 8 watts. A spot light is likely to be 10 watts. A water pump has a much bigger rating at around 50 watts but apart from when it's used to run a shower, it is normally only used intermittently. Rather more demanding is the loading of a portable TV because this is often used for several hours at a time. A black and white TV set is typically rated at 15 watts, whereas a colour TV is likely to be rated at 100 watts.

Having noted the rating of all the appliances, you now need to work out how long they are likely to be in operation during a typical 24 hour period on site. This produces the number of **watt hours** and the calculation might read as follows:-

rated capacity of a battery deteriorates as it gets older. Other influencing factors are temperature and the speed of discharge.

Looking at temperature, the capacity of a battery is usually given for a working temperature of 25 deg C (77 deg F). However, the capacity drops by around 1% per 1 deg drop in degrees Centigrade. This means that a battery designated as a 60 Amp Hours product at 25 deg C would effectively be rated at 54 Amp Hours when working at 15 deg C (60 deg F). On a winter caravan holiday, when temperatures are much colder, its performance would be shortened even more.

In addition, the table here is

example, a battery would be able to recover completely after a 24 hour period if a charger with a 6 amp output is operated for around 6 hours (i.e. 6 amps x 6 hours = 36 amp hours). However, there are different ways to replenish a battery using both boost and trickle charge methods. These are discussed in the *Battery Boxes* section.

Most leisure batteries are maintenance-free sealed units with little risk of acid being accidentally spilt in a caravan. Some have a carrying handle which is useful when lifting a battery out of a locker box and moving it into a garage. Other batteries are referred to as 'minimal maintenance' models which means that you can check the electrolyte once a year and top up the cells if necessary. When tipped at 90 deg these are less safe than the sealed type, although they are better than expected. The 90 amp hour batteries often fall into this latter category.

Equipment	Loading in watts	Hours in use	Watt hours
Two 8 watt lights	16	5	80
Two reading lights 10 watts	20	1	20
Water pump	50	0.2	10
Colour TV	100	2.5	250
		Total watt hours	360

When the number of watt hours is divided by the volts of the battery (i.e. 12 volts), the result is the number of Ampere hours. i.e.

360 watt hours divided by 12 volts = 30.0 ampere hours

If 30 amp hours is an accurate assessment of usage during a 24 hour period, an inboard battery rated at 60 amp hours is going to provide power sufficient for 2 days before needing charging. Obviously this is only a rough guide and it is wise to expect around 10% variation. To begin with the length of wire leading to each appliance exercises a degree of influence, together with the fact that the

based on battery use being spread over a twenty four hour period. If the time over which appliances are operating is shortened, the battery will discharge even more quickly. For instance if you leave an appliance rated at 5 amps operating constantly rather than intermittently from a 60 amp hour battery in good condition, you might presume it would operate for 12 hours. In effect it operates for **less** time before the battery becomes completely discharged.

A further point to remember is that it is best to avoid working a battery until it is totally exhausted; it's better to provide **some** recharging each day. For

A leisure battery described as a 'minimal maintenance' type means that you can check the electrolyte periodically and top up the cells if necessary.

Notwithstanding its sealed design, a battery should always be operated in an upright position. Its electrolyte is dilute sulphuric acid and if this gets spilled on to clothing or skin, it should be washed off with a copious stream of water.

Like a car battery, the terminals should be coated with Vaseline or Tri-Flow grease to prevent a build-up of corrosion.

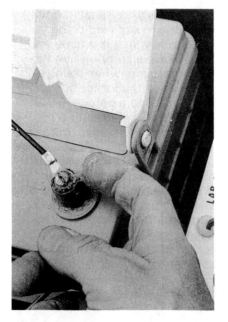

Like the terminals on a car battery, leisure battery terminals should be coated with Vaseline or Tri-Flow grease.

Similarly it is always recommended that the negative i.e. the 'earth' terminal is removed first or replaced last.

As a final precautionary measure, you should note that when a battery is being recharged, an explosive gas is given off. Ventilation is therefore essential and if the battery is being charged in a locker, a ventilator **must** be fitted so that any accumulation of gas can discharge safely to the outside of the caravan. It is also important that no metal object is likely to bridge the battery terminals by accident to cause a spark. This might cause the gas

to explode and battery specialists are well aware of this risk. It's for this reason that crocodile clips are **not** suitable for making battery connections. A more positive means of attachment is needed and special pillar clips available from caravan suppliers are recommended.

Transformer/rectifiers
An alternative method of providing power for 12v appliances is to use a transformer rectifier which is connected to a 240v mains hook-up. A model installed in some caravans as a standard fitment is the Type PA Ranger Power Pack from Breckland Trading Co. This converts 240 volts AC into 12 volts DC but for safety reasons it must be connected to a hook up using a mains socket meeting British Standard 4343. A further assurance of safety is given if a residual current device is fitted and these products are discussed in the next chapter.

The Range Power Pack, type PA8 is a transformer rectifier which converts a mains 240v AC supply to a low voltage 12v DC supply.

Breckland Trading Co also offers a **portable** version known as the DP17 Ranger Power Pack. This is supplied with a 10 or 25 metre three core mains cable and is ready to plug directly into a site supply. Since it is not a fixture, it can be transferred when a caravan is sold.

Some low voltage appliances in a caravan have to be powered by a smoothed and regulated 12v current and this requirement is met by both Ranger Power Packs. With these packs, appliances like a water pump, fluorescent lights, TV and radio can be operated. However, you should not operate a refrigerator from such a 12v supply because its level of cooling cannot be controlled in this operating mode.

Many owners feel much safer with 12 volt power in their caravan rather than mains power. Since a DP17 Power Pack is encapsulated in a weather-proof case, it can even be left **underneath** the caravan. With both a 12N and a 12S socket on opposite sides of its casing, there is plenty of versatility. But another interesting feature is the fact that the DP17 can also act as a car or caravan battery charger. Its maximum charge rate of

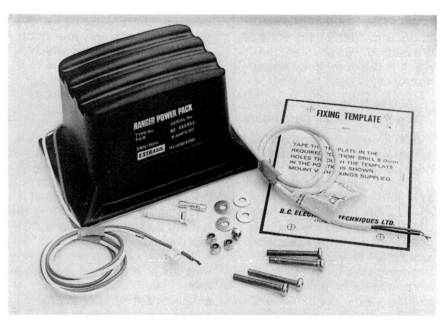

17 amp progressively reduces to 1.5 amps when the battery becomes fully charged.

The Ranger PA8 is designed to yield a continuous load of 6 to 8 amps. To put this in practical terms, typical loads for appliances are:

Fluorescent Lamp	0.7 amps
Water Pump (Intermittent)	6 amps
Black & White TV	1-2 amps
Colour TV	8 amps
Radio and Cassette player	2 amps
Battery Charging	8 down to 1 amp
Fridge on 12v operation	8 amps

Other transformer/rectifiers are available from manufacturers such as LabCraft and Powerpart. Each model differs in its design and output, so it is worth comparing products before fitting one in a caravan.

Choosing a location for an inboard battery

Many modern caravans provide a location for an inboard battery and include feed cables to connect up with the terminals. Sometimes an external locker box at the front is used but you need to check that this doesn't lead to excessive nose weight at the coupling head.

Another problem with an external locker occurs when caravanning in cold conditions. When temperatures drop below 25 deg C. (77 deg fahrenheit), the capacity of a battery diminishes significantly.

Indoor locations overcome this problem and places like the bottom of a wardrobe or a blanket box are quite popular. However, it is essential that the location is fully ventilated if charging is to take place without removing the battery. The reason for this was emphasised in the *Inboard Batteries* section and to avoid a risk of explosion there **must** be venting to the outside.

Battery boxes

To make it easier to move a battery, purpose-made carrying boxes are available. Moroever, the TP2 model made by LabCraft includes a built-in battery charger as well. Several improvements have been made to the TP2 since its introduction but in essence it includes a carrying strap, and an integral charger adjacent to the battery compartment.

When a mains supply is available, the TP2 can be directly connected using the cable provided. For example if the TP2 and battery have been carried into the house, the unit can be plugged into any 13 amp socket for recharging.

Another means of charging is via the towcar. When left in the caravan, a trickle charge can be provided while the 'van is being towed. This presumes that the 12S system has been wired-up with a controlling relay switch as described in Chapter 3. In this situation, the charge may be as little as 1 to 2 amps on account of the considerable length of wire running from the car's alternator to the caravan. In consequence you would need to tow for a long time before a flat battery becomes fully recharged.

A more effective approach is called 'boost charging' in which battery replenishment is around 6 amps. This can be achieved if the battery is transferred to the boot of the towcar and Chapter 3 gives information about the wiring arrangement. If you are using a TP2 battery box, the supply wires in the car should be fitted with a plug supplied by LabCraft for insertion into the charger socket.

When making this connection, you **must** observe the polarity of the supply wires. Polarity is marked alongside the socket on top of the TP2 charger and the plug is moulded so that it cannot be reversed by accident.

Taking advantage of the portability of a TP2 battery box

To gain the benefits of boost charging from a towcar, a caravan battery should be transferred to the boot and connected directly into the car system as discussed in Chapter Three.

and the benefits achieved by boost charging, experienced caravanners get into the habit of transferring the battery to the back of their car whenever driving around during a holiday. This keeps it in tip top condition.

As regards other features, the TP2 can be left 'plugged in' to the mains without any risk of battery damage. Built-in electronic controls prevent over charging and the 12v DC output circuits have thermal cut-out protection which comes into operation in the unlikely event of overheating. The product is also double insulated which means that the power cable which you connect up to a 13 amp household plug does not include a yellow/green earth wire.

Earlier TP2 models included a charging meter to indicate the state of the battery, although a lack of graduated markings made it difficult to take an exact reading between 10 and 12 amps. The MkV version introduced in 1986, featured five light emitting diodes along one side of the casing to indicate various conditions. These can be checked at a glance, even in a dark locker box.

The Mk V TP2 employs a light emitting diode warning system which can be especially useful when checking battery condition when it is dark.

Once the battery has been wired to the TP2 terminals via an in-line fuse, all subsequent connections are made via a LabCraft non-reversible plug which preserves polarity. One of these plugs should be attached to the main feed wires which link the battery pack with the caravan circuits; another must be fitted to the boost charge wires kept in the boot of the tow car.

When a TP2 is in the caravan but being mains charged, it is still possible to draw current for the 12v systems. However, the charging unit should not be regarded as a transformer i.e. used to provide 12 volt current **in the absence of** a battery. The battery helps to provide a stable supply and **must** be connected in the circuit.

Fused distribution units with in-built chargers

Another way to replenish a battery is to have a mains charger fixed permanently in the

caravan. Sometimes these are fitted independently; alternatively the charger is integrated within a fused distribution unit.

The fused distribution units, described in the *Simple fused distribution units* Section, dealt **exclusively** with 12v DC current. Other units, however, include a mains operated charger as well. In these versions both the control panel and the dimensions of the casing are much bigger.

Models which incorporate mains chargers display trade names such as Zig (Peter Everard Ltd), Carapart (Hawkins

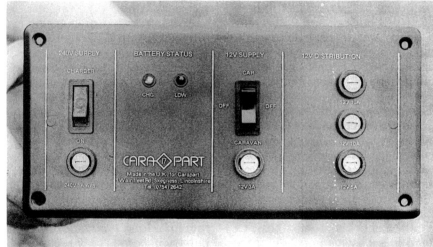

The Carapart 17 was a fused distribution unit including a battery charging facility which was fitted in many 1980s caravans – often as a DIY project.

Electrical), and Symphony (Symphony Systems Ltd). However, these units are sometimes over-printed with the name of the caravan manufacturer.

Another unit designated the Kestrel 3 (CEC Plug-in-Systems Ltd) features a Residual Current Device (RCD) as well. Since this is equally concerned with providing a fully protected mains supply, it is discussed

more fully in the following chapter.

Even though charger/distribution units are often fitted into new caravans, they can also be fitted into older models. However, the fact that there is an additional mains 240v supply for the integrated battery charger means that the caravan must have a properly installed mains supply system as detailed in the next chapter.

If the design of the system means that charging is carried out via a fused distribution unit, it would be wasteful to purchase a TP2. This would simply mean that you now have two battery

chargers in the caravan, one in a wall mounted distribution unit and another in the battery box. On the other hand, connecting up a leisure battery in a locker tends to discourage its transference into the back of the towcar for boost charging. However, there **are** carrying boxes available which are built without an integral charger; the Desmo Pacemaker is an example.

Fitting a fused distribution unit with inbuilt charger

Installing a fused distribution unit with its own built-in charger is a task which most careful do-it-yourselfers could tackle. Admittedly there are numerous wires to connect, but a methodical, careful amateur would manage without problem. In addition, most installation instructions are clearly written.

Taking the Zig C.F. 2000 model as an example, two booklets are supplied with the unit. One is concerned with 'Instructions for Fitting' whereas the other is entitled 'Instructions for Use'. Both are easy to follow.

On the rear of the casings, electrical connection strips are usually marked clearly. An example of this clarity is evident on the rear of the Carapart 17 unit which has been marketed by Hawkins Electrical Ltd. Connecting up feeds to a water pump, lights, and auxiliaries is easily undertaken.

On the rear of the casing of a Carapart 17, all connections are clearly marked.

Before starting work, however, it is important to select the best location for one of these units. For instance the control panel represents the 'tip of the iceberg' and a large part of the unit projects behind the facia controls. Ventilation is important, too, because heat from the transformer in the charger needs to be dispersed. With this in mind, your location requires free space around the

fitting and there mustn't be any risk of clothing or other possessions falling on to vents in the casing. If this happens by accident, some models include a thermal cut-out. On the Zig C.F. 2000 mentioned earlier, this re-sets itself automatically when the unit has cooled down.

To assist installers, some manufacturers offer models in both vertical and horizontal styles. This is helpful, but in either case it is best to select a location where connections at the rear of the unit can be easily coupled and no less easily checked whenever necessary.

A method of cutting an aperture to house distribution units was described in the *Simple fused distribution units* Section.

Having made the cut-out, it then needs reinforcement because distribution units with battery chargers are much heavier than the Zig CP3 mentioned earlier.

One way to do this is to prepare a piece of 6 mm ply with an identical aperture using an electric jigsaw. This can then be glued to the rear of the cut out in the caravan to strengthen the 3 mm ply which is used for most caravan furniture. The reinforcing piece can be fixed in place using an impact adhesive or a PVA woodworking adhesive like EvoStik Resin W.

Woodworking adhesive is better but takes longer to dry; you will also need a G-cramp to hold the piece of reinforcing ply in place.

It is likely that the metal casing is going to need support at the rear and this can be achieved by constructing timber supports. Alternatively you can provide support with a metal strip i.e. in the same way that a car radio has to be braced at the back.

As a general rule, you are unlikely to be able to anchor the unit finally until all wires have been fitted into the connector strip at the back of the casing. A methodical approach is needed and recommendations about the gauges of wire should be followed.

As regards the mains cable, this must be routed directly from the Residual Current Device (RCD) in the caravan, taking note of all points made in the next chapter. Fitting instructions for the distribution unit will give clear guidelines about making these connections.

Separate inbuilt battery chargers

Fused 12v distribution units with integral battery chargers were popular during the 1980s. However, caravans made in the early 1990s were often equipped with distribution units **solely** concerned with 12v control; a mains charger was then situated separately, e.g. in an external locker.

A rationalisation in layout occurred next and manufacturers like Compass purposely situated all electrical control components at the forward end of their caravans. This is both tidy as well as beneficial in keeping connecting wires as short as possible.

Earlier practice of leaving a battery space in the forward gas locker was also changed. This recognised that gas valves could leak and poor connections on battery terminals might generate a spark. For safety it is now preferred to have **separate** outside lockers, one for gas cylinders and the other for a battery and charger unit. Both have to be fitted with ventilators.

Independent mains operated chargers are manufactured by a number of specialists including Peter Everard Ltd. The Zig DCU3 is a good example. In a refurbishment project, the idea of fitting a separate charger rather than an integrated 12v distribution and charger unit has several advantages. However, it should be re-emphasised that this should only be undertaken where there's an approved mains supply system. This is described in Chapter 8.

Battery charging via wind and solar devices

Battery care is important but mains operated units are not the only devices concerned with charging. Both wind and solar power can be used to trickle charge a battery. For example, solar panels from Chronar Ltd are available in kit form for installation on a caravan roof.

The medium size solar panel from Chronar is available in kit form for installation on a caravan roof to keep its battery trickle charged.
(courtesy Chronar)

There are also solar panels manufactured by PAG Solar Technology Ltd; these are embedded in a flexible plastic and are intended for both caravan and marine markets. When mounted directly on to the deck of a boat, it is even possible to walk on a PAG panel without causing damage.

Solar units are available in several sizes, and an output is assured during ordinary daylight. Some caravanners use the benefit of a solar panel to keep a battery topped up, even when the 'van is parked and not in use.

In practical terms, a good solar panel will produce about 6 amp hours of current over a long day in good summer weather. This represents sufficient input to a discharged battery to keep two eight watt fluorescent lamps operating for over 5 hours. It is also possible for a solar panel to revive a flat 60 amp hour battery in around 10 days during a typical June or July.

Fitting solar panels involves little work. Once the panel has been secured, it is merely a matter of routing its two wires to the inboard battery. The units from both Chronar and PAG include a blocking diode which means that current can only move in one direction i.e. from the panel to the battery. The diode prevents reverse current flowing from the battery to the panel at night.

Wind generators also produce a trickle charge but are more popular with boat owners than caravanners. However, models manufactured by Marlec Engineering Ltd. (The 'Rutland' Windcharger), Wasp Instruments Ltd (The Wasp 'Genmaster') and LV Motors (The 'Aerogen' Generators) are considered suitable for keeping a caravan battery in a good state of charge as well.

When a caravan is laid up for the winter, a suitably located

At windspeeds around 19 knots, the Aero3Gen produces about 4 amps; when a caravan is stored on an exposed site, this can helpfully keep its battery trickle charged.

wind generator provides a useful trickle charge. Outputs will vary according to the model as well as the windspeed. In the case of the Aero3gen, for example, it will start to charge at wind speeds around 5 knots; at 19 knots it produces 4 amps. Where a caravan is stored at an exposed site during the winter months, this could be most useful. But whereas the idea of gaining 'something for nothing' is always attractive, their output is greatly reduced if you tuck your caravan at the side of your house.

Improvement and repair work – electrical theory

Most low voltage electrical appliances are easy to fit in a caravan and it is unlikely that the owner needs any more than a modest understanding of electrical theory.

In this section, some basic points are discussed although readers requiring further information about 12v electrics should refer to: *Automobile Electrical and Electronic Systems: Essential Theory and Practice*, by Tony Tranter, published by Haynes.

Essentially it is helpful to understand the difference between volts, amps, and watts and this is often explained with the help of a water analogy. The beginner is asked to picture a water tank in a loft which has connecting pipework feeding taps.

Amps

The amount of water which can flow out of a loft tank is greater where the outlet pipes are large. The same occurs in respect of the diameters of wires and the flow of electricity. The **amount** of electricity which flows is measured in amperes or 'amps'. This is why you need a much **thicker** wire to operate a caravan fridge which takes 8 amps as opposed to a caravan interior light which takes around 0.7 amps.

Volts

Voltage is concerned with pressure. As regards the plumbing illustration, a considerable pressure can be noted at the end of a pipe without there necessarily being a large quantity of water flowing. Moreover, in a water system, pressure will fall if the pipe routes are long and full of bends. The pipes will create a resistance to the flow of water and pressure drops accordingly. A similar problem occurs when electricity has to travel along a wire of considerable length; the volts i.e. **pressure** will be affected and there will be a voltage **drop**. This happens when an auxiliary battery fixed in a caravan is being charged by the towcar. It only receives a trickle charge of something like 1 or 2 amps. However, by moving the battery into the tow vehicle, the reduced length of

connecting wire may mean that the battery receives a charge of around 6 amps.

A loss of pressure is obviously bound up with resistance and in electrical terms, 12 volts represents a modest pressure. In consequence, you should make every effort to avoid increasing resistances when carrying out electrical improvements in caravans. Even an electrical **connection** in a wire may cause a resistance; it also occurs in 12N and 12S plugs and sockets which have dirty brass contacts. Every effort should be made to keep the contacts clean and we have already commended the use of water inhibitors such as Tri-Flow.

Watts

The unit of power is expressed in Watts. This is associated with the **rate** by which electrical energy is used and some electrical appliances are considerably more greedy than others. The energy itself represents a combination of both the **amount** of current (amps) and the **pressure** of flow (volts). Calculations use this formula:-

Watts = Volts x Amps.

Rate of consumption

The installation instructions from Electrolux specify that a fridge operating on 12v draws 8 amps of electricity; converting this to Watts establishes the rate of consumption.

The figure of 96 watts (i.e. 12 volts x 8 amps) is quite startling when compared to a typical fluorescent interior light rated at 8 watts. It explains why a fridge discharges a 12 volt battery very quickly whereas a light will operate for a long time.

It is also important to realise that a black & white TV is far less demanding on a battery than a colour set. The former may be rated around 12 to 24 watts whereas its colour

Many caravanners take portable colour TVs on holiday; but power consumption may be four times as much as a black and white model of similar size.

counterpart is often four times more demanding with a 100 watt rating.

With regard to lighting, many caravans are equipped with a mixture of fluorescent and tungsten lights. Lights which use a bulb or a festoon are examples of the latter type and have a much higher wattage than their fluorescent counterpart. This means that neither a reading lamp nor an awning lamp over the door should be used indiscriminately. This type of lighting discharges a battery far more quickly than a fluorescent lamp.

The wattage of an appliance also has implications for the size of wire needed to provide the power. If a product is connected up using wire which is unacceptably thin, there will be a high level of resistance. Returning to the plumbing analogy, this is rather like trying to draw water from a tank in the loft via a microbore pipe. However, in the electrical context, resistance in a wire also produces an increase in temperature. If several wires in a supply are taped together, the accumulative effect of a rise in temperature can sometimes lead to overheating, whereupon the insulating sheath starts to melt.

In spite of the importance of connecting up appliances with wires of the appropriate current rating, some caravan accessory shops fail to carry suitable products. Fortunately you can make the appropriate purchase by going to an auto electrician. However, in the automotive trade, wire is sometimes referred to by its cross sectional area in square millimetres. The table below clarifies the different terminologies.

As a rule, the copper filaments used for automotive wire measure 0.3 mm in cross section and this enables you to verify the current rating of a piece of wire. All you have to do is to peel back a short length of insulation and count the filaments. The accompanying table relates the number of strands to other elements.

Improvement and repair work – typical projects

Provided the structure of an old caravan is sound, there is no reason why it shouldn't be brought up to date in respect of a 12v system. Improvements should begin by installing an inboard leisure battery and its supply should then be taken to a fused distribution system. In addition, provision to re-charge the battery should be made. Thereafter it is a matter of personal choice what appliances are installed.

One task worth considering is to fit new fluorescent light fittings. In fact the alternative of trying to repair old units is *not* recommended because high voltages are involved. When a fluorescent lamp is connected to a 12 volt Direct Current (DC), a small transistorised inverter in the casing converts the input to Alternating Current (AC) and boosts it to around 125 volts. However, when the lamp is first switched on, an even higher voltage is needed to activate the gas in the tubing. So whereas it is easy to fit a complete new assembly, don't attempt to repair an old fitting.

Other additions might include extractor units in a toilet compartment; cooling fans in the kitchen are also useful in the heat of the summer. The former is one of the projects described in Chapter 14.

Another worthwhile project is to improve the provision of low voltage power sockets. These accessories are distributed by WFour Leisure Products and both flush and surface mounting two-pin sockets are available. Recognising that some portable TV sets are supplied with leads terminated with large crocodile clips, replacing these with purpose made 12v plugs is much safer.

Further improvements might include the installation of an electric pump and this is a further task which the handyperson could consider.

Wiring diagrams

If you intend to improve the facilities in a recent model, it is helpful to see a wiring diagram. Regrettably some owner's handbooks don't include any information about circuits whereas others fail to give details such as the gauge of wires supplying appliances.

But the situation is improving and the accompanying illustrations show a wiring diagram taken from a recent owner's handbook published by Compass Caravans. These are clear, easy to follow and better than the diagrams in several other handbooks. In general, there's still room for improvement in the information given to owners, especially when 12v circuits get more elaborate. It is certainly much easier trying to track down a fault when you've got a circuit diagram to follow.

No. of strands @ 0.30mm	Nominal cross sectional area in mm square	Approximate Continuous Current Rating in Amps	Typical application in caravanning
9	0.65	5.75	Feed to clock
14	1.00	8.75	Interior lights; Coloured wire in 12N multicore cable
21	1.50	13.00	Coloured wire in 12S multicore cable
28	2.00	17.50	Feed to Electrolux fridge; white earth wire in 12N multicore cable
36	2.50	21.50	Feed from relays in towcar; white earth wire in 12S multicore cable; feed to Whale Evenflow diaphragm pump

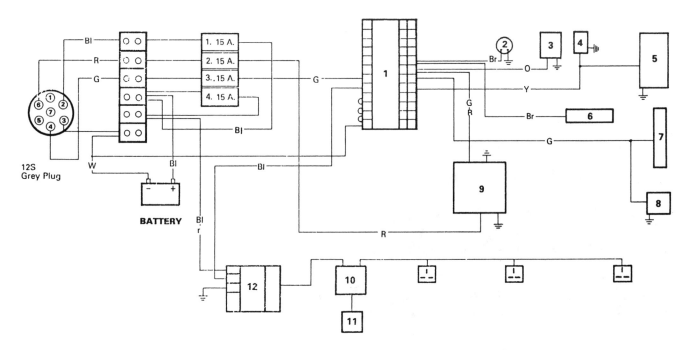

This helpful wiring diagram is taken from the owner's handbook accompanying Compass Rallye models. Regrettably some caravans are not supported with wiring information.
(courtesy of Compass Caravans)

Fuses

1	Split Charge	3	Car Battery
2	Fridge	4	Van Battery

B	Black
Bl	Blue
Br	Brown
G	Green
Gr	Grey
O	Orange
R	Red
W	White
Y	Yellow

1	ZIG CP 2000
2	T.V. Socket
3	Water Heater
4	Water Pump
5	Cassette Toilet
6	Space Heater
7	Lights
8	Berth Lights
9	Refrigerator
10	Earth Leakage Circuit Breaker
11	Mains Inlet Socket
12	DCU3 Charger

Chapter 8

MAINS VOLTAGE PROVISION

Today, more and more caravanners want to use mains operated appliances in their tourers. In response to this, almost all recent models are professionally wired at the time of manufacture.

On caravan sites, pitches offering mains electricity are popularly requested. Many sites are thus equipped and in a 1990 UK Site Guide published by *Caravan Magazine* (Link House Publishers), over 1,600 caravan sites were listed with mains hook-ups. Since that date, the figure has grown even more.

In addition to the introduction of site hook-ups, lightweight portable generators can also be purchased. Some models are notably quiet and their use can pass unnoticed. Others are unacceptably intrusive, particularly late at night on a tightly packed family site. However, when used thoughtfully, generators can be useful appliances and further information is given in the *Portable generators* Section.

The amount of electricity available

The current which can be drawn from a site hook-up is strictly limited and regulated. It also varies and you must enquire about the supply limit when booking a pitch. The site warden will express this in amps and many sites at home and abroad provide a 10 amp supply; a few, however, only provide 5 amps. If the system is overloaded, an automatic cut-out terminates the supply and the site warden will have to re-set the 'trip switch' on the feed to your pitch.

To avoid this you must establish what the supply in amps means in respect of the appliances which will be used. As a rule, the consumption of domestic appliances is expressed in Watts and in the previous chapter, it was stated that Watts = Volts x Amps. In Britain, where the electricity supply is rated at 240v, a site supply of 5 amps means that you can operate appliances up to a total of 1200 watts (Watts = 240 x 5). If you are caravanning abroad where the mains voltage is either 220 or 230 volts, the resulting calculation produces a lower figure.

The total units of power (Watts) needed by most electrical appliances is given in their instruction booklet. Sometimes it is marked on the appliance. For instance, the markings on a light bulb show whether it is rated at 40, 60 or 100 watts.

With 1200 watts available, there is no problem operating lights. On the other hand a domestic electric kettle, usually rated at 2 kw (2 kilowatts, i.e. 2000 watts) will definitely exceed the 1200 watts available. This is why caravan accessory shops sell low wattage electric kettles. They boil water much more slowly, but can be used on most caravan sites.

When calculating the consumption, you must add up the wattage of *all* the appliances being used at a particular time. This includes a refrigerator switched over to mains operation; for example, a typical fridge such as the Electrolux RM2200, has an input rating of 95 watts. When the calculation is made, it is obvious why many standard domestic appliances such as a pop-up toaster or a deep fat frier need to be left at home.

The hook-up point

Legislation plays an important part in ensuring that the supply of caravan site electricity is safe and in Britain the installation requirements are clearly prescribed. As a result, you will notice that connection points are conspicuous, housed on strongly constructed supply pillars, and suitably constructed to resist the weather.

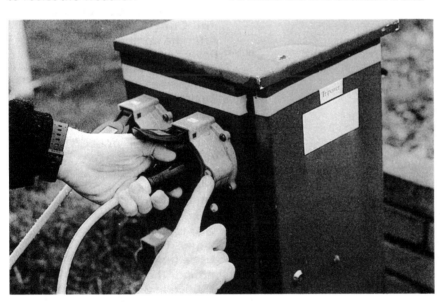

Mains connection points are housed in weather-resistant pillars; the type shown here includes a red release button to hold the plug securely.

You will also notice that the socket itself is different from a 13 amp domestic socket. It follows a 16 amp industrial specification and is the type used on building sites. The supply to each caravan pitch is protected by a miniature circuit breaker which reacts and arrests the supply when there's an overload.

Mains components in touring caravans

The mains system installed in a touring caravan must comply with the IEE Regulations. (Regulations for Electrical Installations 15th Edition: 1981) Recognising that a faulty system could lead to a fatality, caravan wiring should be checked periodically by an NICEIC qualified electrician.

In broad terms, there are four key items which ensure that a caravan linked to a hook-up supply is safe and these elements are discussed in the following sections.

The hook up cable

To make the link between a site source and a caravan, you need specially-made flexible heavy duty cable. Other kinds of wire or flex must **not** be used. The orange sheathed hook up lead comprises flexible three core cable (live, neutral and earth) where the size (expressed by cross sectional area) of each wire is 2.5 mm square to give a 16 amp (max) rating. Hook up leads are available from caravan dealers and have the appropriate plug and socket already fitted. If you buy an installation kit, the hook-up cable is often included in the package.

Hook-up cables are sold in several standard lengths up to a maximum of 25 metres (82 ft). You mustn't exceed this length, nor should you join a number of hook up leads to extend the link. It is also strongly recommended to purchase cables which are already made-up with the appropriate connectors on each end; a sleeved collar on the plug and socket grips the cable tightly giving good weather-resistance.

Two types of adaptors are sold at caravan accessory shops. For example, if the hook-up cable is fitted with British industrial connectors, a conversion lead wired with a Continental plug is needed if hook-ups abroad are going to be used. In the same way, a conversion lead is needed if you want to draw power from a British 13 amp domestic socket. Caravanners often want to connect up to a domestic socket so that a fridge can be operated on mains electricity for several hours before leaving home for a holiday.

A Continental plug is needed to couple up with the supply points on many European caravan sites.

Conversion leads are available; the upper one is needed to plug a caravan system into a 13 amp socket at home whereas the lower one is needed for hook-up points on the Continent.

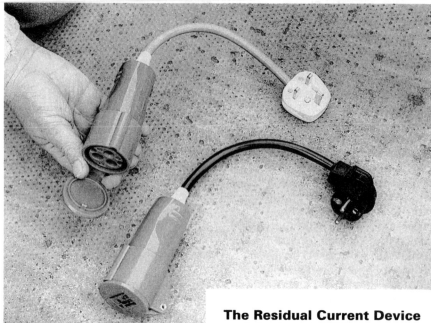

When connecting a hook up lead, you should plug into the site supply **last of all**. Make sure that the lead is sensibly routed and that excess cable is unwound **loosely** and stowed under the caravan. Never leave spare cable tightly wound on a drum; coiled mains wire can become hot when carrying a current.

Most caravanners in this country follow these procedures strictly. However, it is worrying that in some sites abroad, caravanners sometimes use ordinary twin flex and couplings made with twisted wire and tape. This is extremely dangerous yet the practices often go unheeded.

The input connection

At the caravan end of a hook up cable, the blue plug is designed with deeply recessed tubes to eliminate any chance of making accidental contact with the live connectors. On the caravan itself, the connector has pins housed within a plastic casing.

There are two main types of connector unit fitted to caravans. One version consists of a box, complete with a hinged lid, which is recessed into the wall of the caravan. The receiving socket fixed inside is thus protected from road dirt or driving rain.

The other type of input socket is supplied without an enclosure and is designed for surface fixing. In the past, these units have often been fitted underneath the floor; this is no longer approved because the socket is too exposed when towing in rain. A better arrangement is to install the component inside a weather-protected external locker box, a

A surface fixing input socket is no longer considered suitable for location under a caravan floor on account of its exposure to road debris. It may be used, however, in an external locker.

procedure being followed by several manufacturers.

The hook-up socket on a caravan is permanently connected to a residual current device and consumer unit via three core cable of 2.5 mm square cross sectional area. If accidentally severed, this length of cable offers the caravanner **no** safety against electric shock – unless the site supply has its own protection. For this reason, the run of cable has to be as short as possible, attached securely, and routed where accidental damage is unlikely.

The Residual Current Device and Consumer Unit

After the point of entry, current flows to a vital safety component in the system. This is known as a Residual Current Device or 'RCD'. Unfortunately, the RCD has previously been referred to as an 'Earth Leakage Circuit Breaker' or ELCB. This was then changed to a 'Residual Current Circuit Breaker' or RCCB. And whereas its name is finally settled as an RCD, you will invariably meet suppliers who refer to it by one of its earlier names.

The function of an RCD is to monitor the balance between a positive and negative supply. Normally the balance is perfect because the number of electrons flowing along the Live wire equals the number flowing along the Neutral wire. However, if anyone accidentally touches a live cable, the current passes via their body to earth causing a severe shock. Where the RCD has been fitted, the resulting imbalance in positive and negative feeds is detected at once. Instantaneously a trip switch is triggered, and the supply is checked. The response, measured in milliseconds, is sufficient to save life.

The danger of electrocution is

especially acute in a caravan because it comprises a body clad in aluminium, mounted on a steel chassis, and featuring four corner steadies which would provide a speedy route to earth. However, in a caravan wired to IEE standard with an RCD in the supply, the user is nearly always protected in the event of a fault. Only the hook up lead and the short length of input cable taking the feed into the RCD remain unprotected.

Recognising that an RCD **must** function correctly, the units are usually manufactured with a test button. You should check this periodically; the moment it's pressed, the trip switch should flick into the **off** position.

As a general rule, an RCD forms part of a Consumer Unit which distributes the supply into two or more separate circuits. The modern practice is to protect these circuits using small switches called miniature circuit breakers (MCBs). These are modern versions of the old re-wirable fuse.

The fact that the Consumer Unit has several similar switches might confuse caravanners who are unfamiliar with electrical equipment. But if their appearance is similar, their functions are different; the RCD protects the user against a 240v shock, whereas the function of the MCBs is to react to a short circuit in a faulty appliance which might otherwise cause a fire.

The Consumer Unit may also feature a red indicator light to warn the user that the polarity of the supply system is incorrect. Reverse polarity doesn't affect the operation of most electrical appliances, but it means that a switch on the appliance itself will only interrupt the negative return, thereby leaving it with a permanent live contact. On a light fitting, this is potentionally dangerous, especially when a bulb is being changed.

On British sites, reverse polarity is most unusual. But on Continental sites where a two pin adaptor is generally used, this can sometimes be inserted either way round. Obviously if reverse polarity is shown by the warning lamp, it is then a simple matter to reverse the plug to restore correct polarity in the caravan.

Internal wiring
In most caravans, there are two separate outputs from the Consumer unit, both of which have protection from a miniature circuit breaker (MCB). Under present regulations, 2.5 mm square 3-core flexible cable is used to connect up the 13 amp sockets. Other items such as the mains lights and a battery charger should be connected up with 1.5 mm square 3-core flexible cable.

With regard to the domestic three-pin plug fitted to appliances, you must remember to check that this is fitted with a 3 amp fuse. Quite often these are sold with a 13 amp fuse as standard but fitting a lower rated fuse is needed for the low wattage appliances that are used in caravans.

Quite often, no provision is made in a caravan for mains lighting. Just as the Building Regulations disallow an exposed

light fitting in a bathroom at home, the principle is the same in a caravan. A sink or washbasin is always near at hand and this could constitute a danger. Nevertheless, in caravans introduced for the 1991 season, several models included wall mounted lights for the first time. Without doubt, this provision is considerably safer than movable bedside lamps with a trailing lead.

If you have a mains facility, together with a charger for a 12v battery, you can use **low voltage** facilities without exercising the usual care needed to preserve battery condition. These can be used at the same time as the battery is being charged although the more appliances in use, the lower the rate of charge.

Installing a mains system – methods of approach
Installing a 240v system in an older caravan is a popular improvement project. A number of DIY kits are available, most of which have clear instructions.

However, the subject of DIY

Electrical kits from Powerpart include a Consumer Unit with RCD and MCB protection; this is already connected up inside and is supplied with trailing wires for easy DIY installation.

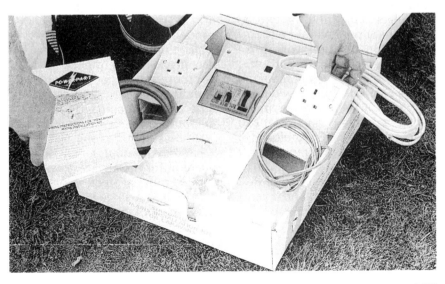

A DIY installation must be checked by a qualified NICEIC member before being connected to the mains. Thereafter, a small tester is worth purchasing to confirm the supply is sound.

electrics is one which leads to strong argument. On one hand there is the view that anything involving mains electricity should remain strictly in the hands of a qualified electrician. On the other, there's the view that since most people are called at some time or other to fit a 13 amp plug to a household appliance, if this is done competently, they should have no more difficulty wiring up a 13 amp socket.

In further support of the second view, Geoffrey Burdett wrote in a manual entitled *Home Electrics*, 'It may surprise readers of little or no experience with electrical wiring that more than ninety per cent of home electrical installation work is in fact *non*-electrical' (G. Burdett, *The David & Charles Manual of Home Electrics*, Pub. David & Charles, 1981, Page 7) It is much the same in the caravan context.

However, there is good sense in purchasing a caravan wiring kit, particularly one where the Consumer Unit and integral RCD is already pre-wired. The only electrical work to complete is to wire up the three cables which protrude from the casing as described shortly. If this sounds daunting, an amateur could fix

the consumer unit in place, clip the cables securely and get an electrician to make the final connections. Either way, it is less expensive than having the complete job done professionally.

However, if you follow the DIY approach, when everything is finished, you **must** have the installation checked by a qualified NICEIC member **before** the system is connected to the mains and put to use. A contractor holding membership of the National Inspection Council for Electrical Installation Contracting (NICEIC) will be able to issue a Completion Certificate and a signed Inspection Certificate after everything has been checked and tested.

Period check-ups are recommended as well, and certification provides written verification that the 'van has met all safety standards, an important point when a the caravan is sold at a later date.

When wiring up a caravan, two main components need to be installed and these are discussed in in the next two Sections.

Fitting a recessed input socket

The type of input socket which is supplied in an enclosure is suitably protected from road dirt. Its box is fairly easy to fit into a caravan which has sandwich construction side walls; this is shown in the accompanying sequence photographs. Older caravans with hollow walls need a different approach and the guidance on the work involved is discussed in Chapter 5.

Firstly you must decide on the position for the socket. It will receive most protection on a side wall, but since it is going to make a small intrusion inside the 'van, check that it is neither obstructed nor visually intrusive. Select a location as close as possible to the intended position

Six-photograph sequence showing a recessed input socket being installed in a caravan with sandwich wall construction.

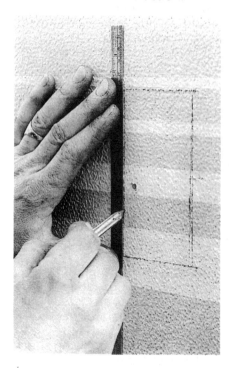

i) Firstly the size of the aperture is carefully marked out.

ii) The corners of the aperture are drilled through to the interior.

iii) The aluminium skin is penetrated using a sharp cutting knife.

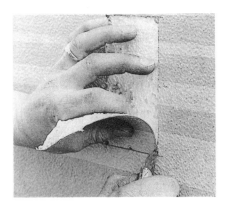

iv) Aluminium is peeled away from the scored area.

v) Foam insulant is removed before cutting away the inner ply.

vi) When the socket is wired, the casing is finally offered up to the aperture.

of the Consumer Unit. For reasons given earlier in this chapter, the cable connecting these items needs to be short and must be positioned where damage is highly unlikely.

The sequence photographs show a box being fitted. The use of a sharp cutting knife produces a clean edge when removing the aluminium skin, although some installers prefer to work with a speed controllable jigsaw. If you prefer using a jigsaw, affix masking tape around the aperture to protect the paintwork. Remember that a standard length blade is likely to rip through the ply inner skin at the same time.

When the box is finally offered up, a neoprene gasket provides

a weatherproof installation. However, it is worth applying some exterior grade silicone sealant around the perimeter as well.

Fitting a Residual Current Device (RCD) & Consumer Unit

Recognising that interior wall boarding and furniture panels are only made from thin plywood, you will need to carry out some strengthening work **before** fitting a Consumer Unit. This can be achieved using a piece of 9 mm ($^3/_8$ in) plywood, cut slightly larger than the case of the RCD, and fixed with an impact adhesive (e.g. Evo-Stik).

In some installations the reinforcement can be fixed inconspicuously on the **reverse** side of the panel. When adopting this approach, screws inserted through the base of the unit will pass firstly through the 3 mm ply of the cupboard side, and then into the 9 mm plywood behind. This effectively sandwiches the weakest material between the robust plastic of the casing and the 9 mm strengthening plywood.

With the cover removed, a pre-wired Powerpart Consumer Unit is screwed to a plywood base of suitable thickness.

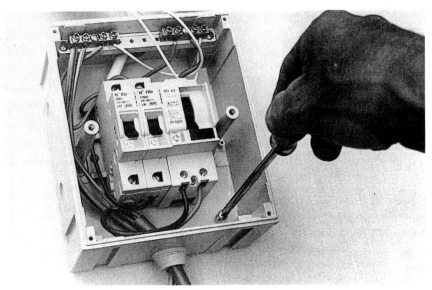

Inside the Powerpart consumer unit, the residual current trip switch and check button is on the right; miniature circuit breakers to serve two separate circuits are on the left.

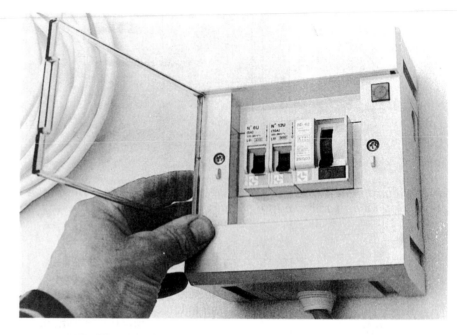

Consumer Units must be earthed to the caravan chassis. A green covered earth wire in the Powerpart kits is already supplied with an earthing eye (arrowed).

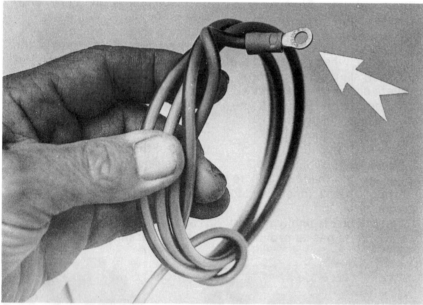

As regards electrical connections inside the casing of an RCD and Consumer Unit, the installation leaflets in a wiring kit usually make everything perfectly clear. However, many DIY kits are pre-wired, leaving tails outside the casing as described in the Section entitled *Installing a mains system – methods of approach.*

When dealing with the earth wire which is covered in green sheathing, this must be routed through to the chassis and bolted on to a convenient point. Any paint on the chassis should be removed to produce a sound connection, and this is essential for the correct operation of the RCD. A warning tag must be attached to this earth point and metal labels stamped with the words, 'SAFETY ELECTRICAL CONNECTION DO NOT REMOVE' are available from any electrical specialists. It is unfortunate that some caravan wiring kits provide all the parts *except* this important warning tag.

The earth wire should be taken through the floor and fitted to an existing hole on a caravan chassis member which has been cleaned to produce a good electrical contact.

"SAFETY ELECTRICAL CONNECTION DO NOT REMOVE" When the chassis earth connection is made, it is essential to fit a warning safety tag of approved design.

As regards the cable leading from the RCD to the 13 amp sockets, this should be routed appropriately, clipped frequently and hidden wherever possible. In exceptional circumstances, cable can be taken under the floor, but make sure that it is securely fixed and located where accidental snagging is unlikely.

Connections in the sockets follow normal wiring procedure. The earth point will be marked in the moulding; so, too, will the polarity for the positive and negative feeds. It is crucial that these connections are made correctly.

If the kit supplies flexible cable, the colour coding on the insulation is:

Brown wire = positive
Blue wire = negative
Striped green and yellow
   wire = earth
If, on the other hand, grey sheathed twin and earth cable is supplied:

Red wire = positive
Black = negative
Bare copper wire = earth

This bare earth should then be covered with a green insulation sleeve where it connects into the rear of the 13 amp sockets. Sleeving is available from any electrical supplier. Irrespective

Wiring a 13 amp socket is no more difficult than wiring a 13 amp plug; the live, neutral and earth terminals are clearly marked.

of the type of cable supplied, it **must** be fixed permanently using electrical clips.

The Kestrel KT3 integrated control unit

Now that the installation of a mains supply is a popular requirement, several innovative products have appeared. The Kestrel KT3 from Plug-in-Systems Ltd is a good example.

The Kestrel is unusual because it integrates the control

The Kestrel 3 Unit from Plug-in-Systems Ltd is unusual because it combines the 12 v fused distribution system within the same housing as a 240 v RCD/Consumer Unit.

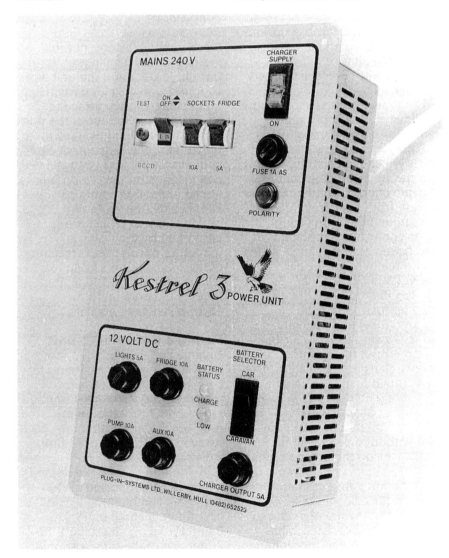

of **all** electrical systems, both 240 volts AC and 12 volts DC, within **one** master unit. For instance it features a Residual Current Device and has to be linked to an approved mains input socket. Secondly it includes a mains operated battery charger. Thirdly it features a 12v fused distribution unit for low voltage circuits. All the control items and safety devices discussed in Chapters 7 are 8 are thus incorporated in one casing.

The facia is clearly labelled and divided into two sections. The upper section is concerned with mains control and has the RCD, a miniature circuit breaker for the fridge supply, a miniature circuit breaker for other electrical appliances, a reversed polarity warning lamp, a cut-out test button, and an illuminated control switch for the 5 amp automatically controlled battery charger.

The low voltage section below includes a 12v supply source switch with an isolating 'off' position, and battery status lights which indicate high or low charge condition. This means you can choose whether to draw current from the caravan or the towcar, and the monitoring lights confirm the condition of the chosen battery. There is also fusing to cover four separate low voltage circuits, namely lighting (5 amp fuse), fridge (10 amp fuse), water pump (10 amp fuse) and auxiliary items (10 amp fuse). A further 5 amp output fuse affords battery charging protection. The glass tubed fuses are held in turn-screw holders which enable an individual supply to be switched off by removing the fuse without disconnecting appliances on the other circuits.

The Kestrel has been fitted by Carlight into some of their models. It's also an ideal product for anyone planning to upgrade a caravan which has neither a controlled low voltage

The rear of the Kestrel 3 includes a clearly marked connection block for all 12v DC connections.

fused supply system, nor a mains system. The instruction booklet is clear and the unit is supplied with a trailing mains input cable already attached.

In addition, the rear of the unit is labelled so that it is easy to understand the function of each connection. All low voltage connections on the wiring blocks are labelled. On the mains supply side, there are two outlets, both of which are controlled by their own miniature circuit breakers. One of the mains outlets is exclusively for the fridge; the other is to serve up to three 13 amp switched sockets.

Fitting a Kestrel KT3 unit
Given a suitable location, a Kestrel unit is easy to fit and to connect up. Procedures for making a cut-out were described in Chapter 7 together with methods for strengthening caravan furniture prior to fitting a distribution unit.

In addition to this, the Kestrel needs to be supported at the rear. This can be done by making up a small plinth in 9 mm (3/8 in) ply to support the underside of the unit. It should

be designed so that there is no loss of ventilation via the slots in the underside of the aluminium casing.

In use, the Kestrel unit can get warm, particularly when the battery charging facility is in operation. The instruction booklet gives information on ventilation to prevent overheating.

Once the mechanical fixing is complete, the connections can then be made to each supply circuit. Details about wire size needed for 12v DC low voltage supplies were given in the previous chapter. Making mains connections to 13 amp sockets together with the need for checking by an NICEIC specialist were discussed earlier in this chapter.

Fitting other integrated battery chargers
There are several control units offering a low voltage fused distribution system together with an integrated mains charger as well. Examples can be found in the Zig range manufactured by P. Everard Ltd. Unlike the Kestrel KT3, however, these products are for low voltage distribution and do not include the RCD or MCB protection afforded by a Consumer unit supplying 240v circuits.

As with the Kestrel unit described above, the installation of these products requires a sound surface, support for the unit, together with adequate ventilation. Installation procedure is detailed in Chapter 7.

Scott Power SP225/12 electrical system
Different yet again is a system from Scott Halleys Ltd. which comprises a Residual Current Device/ Consumer Unit mounted on a special board alongside a Mains Operated Battery Charger. This has been developed in conjunction with Plug-In

Systems Ltd. and is intended for installation by a competent handyperson.

The key units are already wired-up on the power panel although the system presumes that a battery charger will be situated somewhere in the caravan. However, this can be remotely located. Once fitted, final checking must be undertaken by a qualified electrician.

The Powerpart Mobile Supply unit
Previous sections have emphasised that installing a mains supply system is **not** something to be taken lightly.

A Powerpart Mobile supply unit provides three fully protected 13 amp sockets in a casing with RCD/MCB protection, together with a 20 metre hook up lead and plug.

Whichever product is chosen for DIY installation, a final check should be carried out by a qualified electrician. The Powerpart Mobile Unit, however, is an exception because it's a self-contained supply system.

Undoubtedly the majority of purchasers of this portable unit are campers. On the other hand it is ideal for use in a caravan awning because it has clips on the rear for attaching to a vertical pole; it can also be suspended using a metal handle on the top.

But the Powerpart Mobile can also be used inside a caravan where the owner doesn't want to spend time or money fitting a permanent installation. This may be the case when a caravan is likely to be sold in the near future, recognising that the Powerpart product can be merely transferred to the replacement 'van.

The Powerpart Mobile Supply unit comprises a Residual Current Device with test button, two Miniature Circuit Breakers, a polarity reversal indicator light, three 13 amp sockets and a 20 m hook-up lead with plug. The hook-up lead is permanently connected to the unit and all electrical items are housed within the plastic casing.

Like caravan electrical kits, the Powerpart Mobile Unit is tested to meet British Standards. But unlike the other systems described in this chapter, it has many other uses. One of its applications, for example, is to act as a protection device when using power tools outdoors.

Portable generators
An alternative method of providing a mains supply is via a portable generator. Several models are available which are relatively quiet and conveniently compact. They look light as well, but this is deceptive. For instance, the Honda EX650 is listed at 23 kg (50 lb) before the addition of fuel.

Depending on the number of appliances in use, a leisure generator will run on a full tank of petrol for 3 to 4 hours.

Unlike their large industrial counterparts, these models are enclosed in smart casings with built-in tool compartments and featuring a host of fail safe systems. Some models have a special take-off point for 12v battery charging as well as a standard 13 amp socket for supplying the mains system. However, to use this socket you will need an adaptor because the caravan hook up lead will be fitted with a blue industrial plug.

Modern leisure generators are a compact source of portable power; they are ideal for touring caravanners who prefer remoter sites which are not equipped with hook-ups.

The leisure generator is small enough to stow in the boot of a tow car although it's likely to be heavier than it appears at first sight.

Used sensitively and in situations where low decibel noise levels are unlikely to annoy caravan neighbours, a portable generator is a great asset. However, the output from these machines is not notable. For instance the rated output at 50Hz on the Honda EX650 is 450 watts; the quiet Yamaha RF600 has a rated output of 400 watts. Compared to site hook ups which typically offer around 1200 watts, the output from a generator will operate far fewer appliances.

However, the real problem occurs in respect of microwave ovens which are becoming popular in caravans. Caravanners are often puzzled why a microwave oven rated as a 500 watt model cannot be operated by one of these smaller leisure generators. The reason is that the quoted 500 watts refers to the **output** of the microwave appliance and not the required **input** to make it operate.

As a rough rule of thumb, the output figure (e.g. 500 watts) should be doubled, and then a margin of approximately 10% added to establish the size of generator needed to operate the appliance. In other words a 500 watt microwave oven will need a generator whose output is 1050 watts or more. A model

A generator like the Kawasaki GA1400A, which produces a 1200 watt output, is able to operate many types of microwave oven.

like the Kawasaki GA1400A produces around 1200 watts and will certainly operate a microwave oven without problem. This presumes, of course, that there are no other high consumption appliances in use at the same time. But the GA1400A, like other makes of a similar size and capacity, is relatively noisier in operation. On many caravan sites, they are too noisy if neighbouring pitches are a matter of metres away. Meantime the ultra quiet generators which are less intrusive are unable to produce the power needed by a microwave oven.

Inverters
Another method of providing 240v AC power is to use an inverter. This is a device which is connected to a 12v DC source and which converts the supply to 240v AC. The idea sounds good but it has to be recognised that an inverter may draw as much as 10 amps from the battery, even more than a fridge operating on battery power. In other words a battery will rapidly become discharged if the inverter is used for long.

Small inverters are used to produce a supply for a 240v electric razor, like the Lab-Craft Razor socket. Other models produce around 80 watts, just

Several manufacturers produce small inverters which convert a 12v DC input to a 240v AC supply but the Tornado range includes models with unusually high outputs.

enough to operate two 40 watt light bulbs. But you cannot gain 'something for nothing' and the penalty is undoubtedly the significant load that an inverter places on your battery.

Conclusion
Mains electricity systems in caravans are now commonplace. Many developments are occurring as well, such as the production of modular units for installing in a purpose made locker enclosure. For example a modular product from Plug-in Systems Ltd, allows a caravan manufacturer to fit the complete system as a unit on the production line.

Recognising that most new caravans are now fitted with mains electrics, the sale of fitting kits will gradually diminish. But even if mains supply systems become universally accepted, the potential dangers of a 240 volt supply must never be underestimated – regardless of whether the supply comes from a site hook up, a generator, or an inverter.

Chapter 9

WATER SUPPLY SERVICES

The days when water was collected in an enamel jug are long past. In the 1960s and 1970s, caravans were fitted with a pump, a supply hose and a delivery tube over the sink called a 'faucet'. The pumps were either operated by foot or by a hand lever.

More recent caravans are fitted with electrically operated pumps which require a 12v supply. There are also taps at sinks instead of faucets. Hot water systems are popular and a large number of caravans have a shower.

Many changes have taken place in water supply systems whereas the arrangements for removing waste water are primitive. This chapter looks at both areas of attention, recognising that a wide range of products are currently in use.

Manual pumps

In spite of the popularity of pumps driven by an electric motor, it would be wrong to overlook the repair and maintenance of manual units. There are still caravanners who dislike a system which is reliant on a battery and they recognise the reliability of manual pumps. Moreover, the availability of service kits for several types of manual pump enables an owner to keep one in full working order.

But there are disadvantages too. For example if a caravan has a hot water system and a shower, an electric pump is essential. In summary, both types have their merits and both receive attention in this chapter.

Hand operated models

One of the leading suppliers and manufacturers of pumps is Munster Simms Engineering Ltd. The products are specifically designed for caravanners and carry the 'Whale' trade mark. All types of pump are available including hand operated models. For instance the Flipper pump features a 'to and fro' lever action whereas the Whale V pump is operated by withdrawing and lowering a plunger which forms part of the central pillar. Each model has a similar maximum output of 6.8 litres per minute (1½ gallons per minute) and the model chosen is usually determined by the amount of space available.

Taking the Flipper pump as an example, this comprises a swivelling outlet pipe to the sink and its operating lever permits a fine control of water discharged. To fit the Flipper you merely need to form a 51 mm (2 in) diameter opening in the work top to accommodate its moulded feed at the base of the unit.

The 51 mm aperture can be cut using a hand brace and an expansive drill bit. This kind of drill has an adjustable cutter to create larger-than-usual holes. Alternatively the job can be done with a hole saw which is fitted into an electric drill. Hole saws are regularly stocked in DIY stores.

If you have access to neither device, a large hole can be formed by marking the aperture in pencil and then drilling a series of small pilot holes all around the perimeter. When there are enough holes, the central core is pushed out completely and the rough edges are tidied up with a wood rasp.

Like all Whale pumps, the

Flipper is designed to accept a 13 mm (½ in) supply hose. It is also supported by a service kit whose components fit both the latest Mk 4 model and its Mk 3 predecessor as well.

If space around the edge of a sink is limited, there might not be enough room for the base plate of the Flipper; equally, there might not be enough room for the to and fro action of its operating lever. In this situation, the Whale 'V' pump is likely to be more suitable.

Installation is especially easy and this model, merely requires a 25 mm (1 in) hole in the work top. As regards maintenance, a service kit is available.

Foot-operated models

A useful feature of foot-operated pumps is the fact that the operator's hands are left free. Whereas hand pumps incorporate their own outlet pipe, a foot pump has to have a faucet fitted on the sink. Unlike a tap which arrests the flow of water, a 'faucet' is simply a curved metal or plastic outlet which is angled towards a sink or basin. There are fixed, fold away and telescopic faucets, all of which are easy to fit.

Three foot pumps are manufactured by Munster Simms and each differs in design. The Whale Tiptoe model is fixed through the floor and many older caravans are fitted with this pump. When in use, the plunger projects above the floor surface although the main casing is attached underneath the 'van. One of its attractive features is the manner in which the plunger can be locked flush with the floor. Once it has been depressed, a twist of the foot ensures that it is held captive in the down position.

The output from a Tiptoe (7 litres per minute/1.5 gallons per minute) is slightly less than the other models mentioned although water is delivered on each stroke. On account of its

floor location, the unit is more exposed to road dirt as well as being susceptible to frost damage. However, where internal space is limited e.g. in smaller caravans, its compact design is an important advantage.

To install a Tiptoe pump, the instruction leaflet shows that you have to form a 75 mm (3 in) cut-out in the floor. However, before starting work it is obviously important to check that there are no obstructions; chassis members **cannot** be moved whereas service pipes can usually be re-situated.

On an older caravan with a solid plywood floor, the flange of the Tiptoe is secured using three countersunk wood screws. However, on caravans with a sandwich construction floor, long narrow bolts produce a better fixing. But you must also check that the thickness of a composite floor doesn't obscure

the outlet tube on the side of the casing.

The Whale GP51 foot pump and its smaller partner the Baby Foot Pump Mk2 are designed for floor mounting **inside** the caravan. Both models have a single domed diaphragm which is pushed down with the foot. An internal spring then returns the diaphragm to its original position, sucking water into the pump chamber ready for the next discharge stroke.

Since the design of these pumps places the top of the diaphragm at least 70 mm (2¾ in) above the floor, they are often fitted in a floor level

The Whale GP51 is often fitted in the bottom of a cupboard; the dimensions in the drawing indicate how much space is needed to accommodate the unit.

(courtesy of Munster Simms Engineering Ltd)

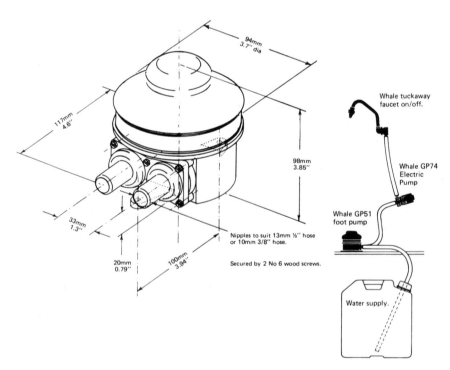

Whale GP5I Foot Pump/Specification

MODEL	CODE	STROKE	OVERALL LENGTH	OVERALL WIDTH	HT ABOVE FLOOR	HOSE BORE	WEIGHT	OUTPUT (Max)
GP51 FOOT PUMP	GP5150	7/8'' 22mm	4 5/8'' 117mm	3¾'' 94mm	3 7/8'' 98mm	½'' 13mm	12½ oz 35kg	1.2 g.p.m. 5.5 l.p.m.

Materials: acetal copolymer resin, synthetic rubber, plated mild steel, brass.

cupboard. The output for the Baby foot pump is 8.0 litres per minute (1.76 gallons per minute), whereas the GP51 delivers 10.1 litres per minute (2.22 gallons per minute). Service kits are available to replace rubber components and by noting the instructions enclosed with a Whale pump or repair kit, overhaul procedure is straightforward.

The largest output foot pump from Whale is the Gusher Galley Pump. (16.4 litres per minute/3.6 gallons per minute) The neat design of the casing means that the unit can be fixed to either vertical or horizontal surfaces. Moreover, the fact that its operating pedal projects forward of the casing means that it can be hidden from sight with only the lever being visible.

The Gusher Galley Pump has a smooth double action which can be accurately controlled by varying foot pressure. However, the leverage can impose rather more strain on the body of the pump than on other models. Hence to prevent the casing from deflecting on its mountings, it is better to fix it in place using bolts rather than screws.

Manual pumps paired with electrical units

In some water systems, you will find that a manual pump has been installed in conjuction with an electric pump. This is because certain designs of electric pump have an impeller to push water through the unit and these designs have to be primed before they can start pumping water. Priming requires that water has to be introduced into the casing and one way to achieve this is to put the water supply container high enough to provide a gravity feed. But this is usually difficult to arrange and a more convenient solution is to fit a foot pump in the system. As soon as this has fed water into

the electric pump, its job has been fulfilled. However, an advantage of this arrangement is that if a flat battery prevents the electric pump from operating, the foot pump can be used as a backup arrangement. The pairing of pumps is discussed more fully in the Section called *Inboard centrifugal pumps*.

Electrically operated pumps – general description

Nearly all modern caravans are equipped with an electric pump. In the previous section, however, it was mentioned that some types of electric pump have an impeller inside and need to be primed. These are called centrifugal pumps and inboard versions like the Whale GP74 are usually fitted in a kitchen unit somewhere under the sink.

Strictly speaking, the submersible pump is a centrifugal pump, too. But this is usually used outside the caravan. Whereas submersible pumps are popular in mid priced caravans, more expensive models are usually equipped with a diaphragm pump. Inside one of these models there are small pistons which move up and down and operate a valve assembly inside the housing.

Most centrifugal pumps are not self-priming and have to be primed, i.e. filled with water, before pumping can take place. This is always necessary if air has entered the system, e.g. when the supply has been disconnected prior to towing. It will also occur if a water container is allowed to run out completely and air is pumped into the system. But it isn't normally necessary to precede *every* operation by priming; once the case is full of water, it will retain its state of prime unless there is some way in which the water drains out of the pump or air makes an entry.

However, in the case of a

submersible pump, priming is achieved as soon as it is dropped into the water. If it fails to deliver water, this is usually caused because there is air still trapped in the casing. The cure is to tap it against the bottom of the water container; this dislodges the air bubbles and the problem is then solved.

Whatever type of electric pump is fitted, a 12v power supply is an essential element. In spite of the fact that a pump only operates intermittently, it places a considerable load on the battery and a typical current draw is around 4–5 amps. In consequence, a separate caravan battery is recommended because it would be unwise to risk discharging the towcar's battery.

A switching system for the pump is also needed. The simplest arrangement would be to fit a Whale foot switch; alternatively this can be installed on a vertical surface so that you operate it with your knee. However, the usual method of controlling an electric pump is to incorporate a microswitch in the tap itself. When the tap is turned on, the motor springs into life and water is duly delivered to the sink or basin.

In practice, the total system is rather more elaborate because many caravans have taps at both a sink *and* a washbasin. There may be a shower as well. This means that you cannot use faucets to accompany a simple switch because as soon as the motor is switched into action, water would be delivered at *every* outlet simultaneously. Whenever there are several outlets, taps have to be fitted with an internal closure device. Taps are discussed later in the Section called *Switching systems for pumps*.

Submersible pumps

One of the cheapest ways to provide electrically pumped water is to fit a submersible

...

pump. Unfortunately, however, these are probably the least reliable of all electrical caravan pumps and cannot usually be repaired. For this reason, it is always wise to take a spare on holiday.

Cracked casings are a common problem on cheap models; more expensive types are undoubtedly more robust and worth the extra cost. Some are cleverly designed like the Crystal Water System from Carver; this incorporates a double core 'fold flat' hose and a stowage compartment which is fitted into the wall of the caravan. The pump is permanently connected up to the interior pipework via its folding hose. So, too, is the cable to feed the motor, although this is routed through a separate core within the flexible pipe. Another innovative feature of the Crystal unit is its replaceable water filter which is an integral part of the moulded storage box.

The Crystal storage box is built with an integral water filter cartridge which is replaced by unscrewing it from the housing.

On arrival at a site, the Carver Crystal system is quick to set into action. If the water seems reluctant to flow, this is a sign that there's air trapped in the casing of the pump. Knocking it against the bottom of the water container usually dislodges any trapped air bubbles.

Apart from the Crystal System, most submersible pumps have to be plugged into the side of the 'van on arrival at a site. This means that both the water feed **and** an electrical feed have to be coupled. A neat coupling arrangement has been manufactured by Whale called the 'dual connector' and when the moulded fitting on the feed hose is offered up to the socket and pushed into place, electrical pins are connected at the same time as the water freeway is formed.

The Whale 'Dual Connector' is a neat coupling arrangement for a submersible pump, with connections for both the hose and the electrical feeds.

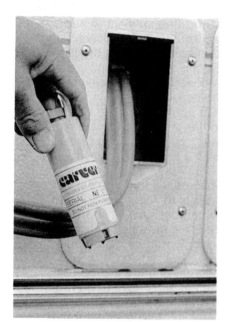

Speed and convenience is one of the attractions of the Crystal system; the hose and pump are permanently 'plumbed-in' and merely need lifting out of the box.

Provided the submersible pump is shaken when it is inserted in the water container to release air bubbles, it can be relied upon to work efficiently.

When fitting a submersible pump on a caravan previously served with a different system, the first job is to establish the correct height above the ground for the input.

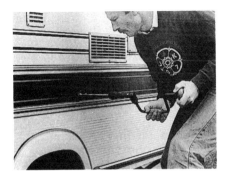

An expansive bit on a hand drill is effective in scoring a deep circle in the surface of the caravan's aluminium skin.

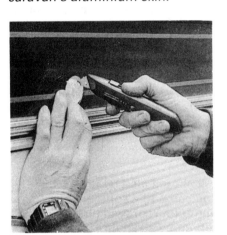

A woodworking knife fitted with a sharp blade can be used to incise around the scored line intended for a Whale Dual Connector.

Once all connections are formed, the Whale Dual Connector is finally offered up, using a bedding sealant to ensure a weather-proof installation.

The Whale Watermaster System includes many excellent design features; it is an ideal product for equipping an older caravan with an electrically pumped water system.

A development on this theme is the Whale Watermaster system which was introduced in 1992. This includes many excellent design features e.g. the non-return valve incorporated in the wall socket which prevents water flowing out of the system whenever the plug is removed. The plug itself features a sturdy shroud which protects the hose and wire connections when the caravanner wants to disconnected the pump. Moreover, when the water container needs refilling and the submersible pump is withdrawn, you can park the hose in a groove on the wall plug so that

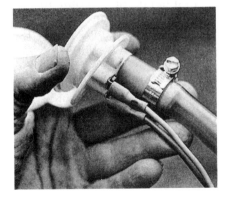

The Whale Dual Connector should be wired up and connected to the internal feed hose before inserting it into the aperture prepared in a caravan wall.

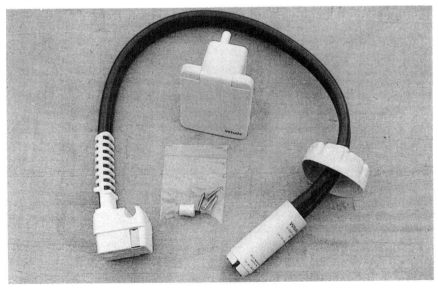

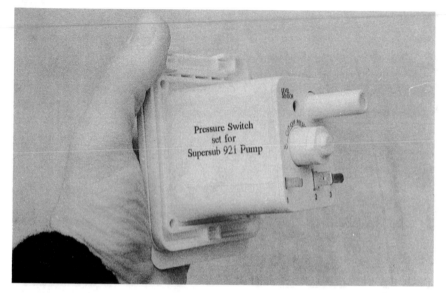

The wall unit on the Watermaster system incorporates a pressure switch set for the Supersub 921 and a non-return valve.

the pump doesn't drag on the ground.

Anyone wishing to add an electrically pumped water system to an older caravan would undoubtedly find the Watermaster product ideal for the purpose. However, if the walls are hollow, it will be necessary to line the aperture with a core of softwood so that a secure fixing point is produced.

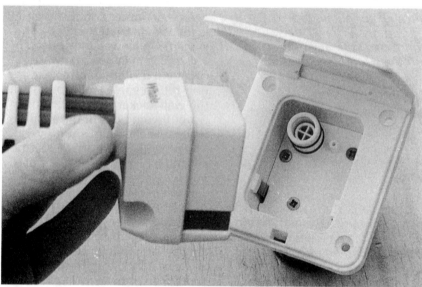

The Watermaster plug includes a sturdy shroud which protects the wires and hose from damage whenever the unit is connected or disconnected.

It should also be noted that you can add a submersible pump to a caravan already served by a Whale Tiptoe pump, a Jupiter Jet, a Gusher Galley foot pump, or a Whale handpump. This gives the best of both worlds. With the electric pump in operation, the water will pass freely through the valves and pump chambers of the manual pump en route to the sink. On the other hand, if the supply battery fails you can operate the manual pump instead because water will flow freely through the submersible unit.

The advantage of having both types of pump in circuit is clear; but remember that you cannot mix and match all types of pump in this way.

When the water container needs refilling, you can park the Watermaster hose in a groove to prevent the pump from dragging on the ground.

Inboard centrifugal pumps

Since they are not submersed in water, centrifugal pumps which are fitted *inside* a caravan are usually more reliable. A model like the Whale GP74 is sufficiently light (245 grams/8 oz) to be suspended by the coupled feed pipes; alternatively its fixing bracket can be used to anchor it to a solid base. The only problem is the fact that the base can act like a sounding board, amplifying the noise of the motor. However, if it is unpleasantly noisy, it is acceptable to cover the unit in sponge foam.

The GP74 Mk 5 has a maximum output of 11 litres per minute (2.42 gallons per minute). Provided the supply battery is in good condition, this pump is capable of firing up a Rinnai instantaneous water heater and delivering hot water to a shower rose fixed at head height.

If the flow needs to be boosted further, a second electric pump like the Whale GP99 in-line model can be installed as well. This is wired up so that it switches into action at the same time, and with the two pumps working in series, the pressure is considerably improved.

Since the GP74 is a centrifugal pump with an impeller inside the casing, it needs to receive an initial prime as discussed previously. This is usually achieved by pairing it with a foot pump like the Whale GP51. The priming pump has to be installed in the water supply hose somewhere *between* the entry point on the exterior of the caravan and the GP74 electric

A Whale GP74 centrifugal electric pump is often matched with a Whale GP51 foot pump which provides the prime. But watch out for a kinked hose as shown here to spoil the system's efficiency.

pump. As explained earlier, this also enables the system to be operated using the foot pump on its own, a useful back-up facility if the battery loses its charge.

The pairing of pumps was used by several manufacturers in the 1980s (e.g. Elddis). Similarly it is not difficult to install this arrangement in an older caravan which is being refurbished. The Whale literature from Munster Simms Engineering gives full instructional guidance including diagrams showing pipe layouts and wiring requirements.

Improved output with an inline pump

In a tight space, a Whale Superline 99 pump can be used instead of the GP74. It has a maximum output of 12.3 litres (2.7 galls) per minute and is extremely compact. Once again, it isn't a self-priming pump and most installers would match it with a foot pump like the GP51.

In addition to its asset as a space saver, this pump can also be used as a booster in systems which have a poor flow rate. But before taking this step, it's important to check there are no kinks in any of the water hoses because this is a common cause of poor performance.

In the previous section, it was reported that the Superline 99 can boost the output of a GP74 pump. It can also boost the performance of a submersible pump by installing it in the main supply pipe. Wires which activate the submersible merely have to be extended to the connections on the Superline 99 so that both units come into operation at once.

Diaphragm self-priming pumps

High specification caravans are usually fitted with a self-priming diaphragm pump. These units are engineered to a high standard and can be expected to last for many years. They are also backed by a strong after-sales service.

There are three main ranges of diaphragm pumps used in the caravan industry. These are the Fiamma range made in Italy, Shurflo models from the United States and Evenflow pumps which are made in Britain and marketed under the Whale tradename.

The Shurflo has been installed in caravans for a number of years and is supported by a good service back-up. If you do not wish to repair a Shurflo pump yourself, you can send it to the British distributor in

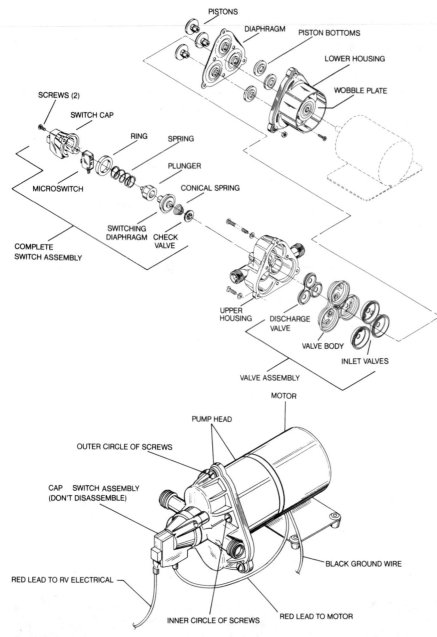

PISTONS
DIAPHRAGM
PISTON BOTTOMS
LOWER HOUSING
WOBBLE PLATE
SCREWS (2)
SWITCH CAP
RING
SPRING
PLUNGER
CONICAL SPRING
MICROSWITCH
SWITCHING
DIAPHRAGM
CHECK
VALVE
COMPLETE
SWITCH ASSEMBLY
UPPER
HOUSING
DISCHARGE
VALVE
VALVE BODY
INLET VALVES
VALVE ASSEMBLY
MOTOR
PUMP HEAD
OUTER CIRCLE OF SCREWS
CAP   SWITCH ASSEMBLY
(DON'T DISASSEMBLE)
RED LEAD TO RV ELECTRICAL
BLACK GROUND WIRE
INNER CIRCLE OF SCREWS
RED LEAD TO MOTOR

All major parts are available to repair a Shurflo pump and the manual gives exploded diagrams and part number listings.
(courtesy of Leisure Accessories Ltd)

Norwich for overhaul, testing, and servicing. Alternatively, all major parts are available for the do-it-yourselfer, and exploded diagrams indicate which part numbers need to be quoted on an order form. A similar service is also offered by Munster

Simms to support the Whale Evenflow diaphragm pumps.

These pumps are sophisticated in design and most models can deliver water to a heater, a shower, and two sinks. When the motor is in motion it turns a 'wobble plate' which in turn operates a piston. In most models, however, there are three pistons attached to rubber diaphragms. Their reciprocating movement yields a stroke which may be as short as 3 mm ($\frac{1}{8}$ in), and thus it is essential that **no** solid matter is

drawn into the mechanism. In consequence a filter is an essential item and this usually forms part of the inlet.

Diaphragm pumps are notable in several respects. For instance, the Whale Evenflow 600 and 1000 models are self-priming from 2 m (6 ft 6$\frac{3}{4}$ in). Another feature is the motor switching operation which works on a pressure principle using sensors built-into the pump itself. As soon as a tap is opened, pressure in the system falls and the motor immediately starts to operate. Obviously the success of this switching system is dependent on sound joints; a small leak might cause the motor to cut-in. For this reason, it is also necessary to fit an additional isolating switch in the power wire to the pump.

Another benefit of many diaphragm pumps is the fact that the motor can be left running by accident; even if the pump is dry it will not be damaged. This is not normally the case with centrifugal pumps.

There is, however, a disadvantage with an electric diaphragm pump. As explained previously, it is not normally possible to install one in conjunction with a foot pump to provide a manual back-up system. Unlike a centrifugal pump, water is unable to pass freely through the pump mechanism when the motor is inoperative. This means that if the supply battery becomes discharged, the caravanner will have to carry water to the sink in a saucepan.

Installing a diaphragm pump

Installing a diaphragm pump in an existing system is extremely easy. Whilst a horizontal position is recommended, several models can be mounted vertically, horizontally, or upside down.

On some models, the inlets and outlets are threaded to receive $\frac{1}{2}$ inch BSP couplings,

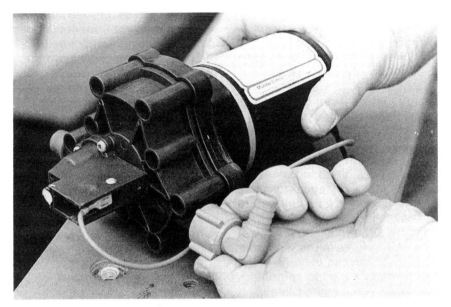

Whereas the Evenflow pump's inlets and outlets are threaded for ¹/₂ in BSP couplings, most caravanners will fit the hose connectors.

though barbed hose adaptors are usually supplied as well. In most British caravans, purpose made flexible hose is used for the water supply system and this is pushed on to the barbed nozzles and secured with a hose clip. When routing hoses to and from the pump, it is important to check that no kinks form.

A problem with many diaphragm pumps is motor noise and for this reason they are supplied with four rubber mountings. When screwed down to a base, it is important to ensure that these feet are not over-compressed.

Installation instructions also make clear specifications about the wire which has to be fitted. For example the minimum gauge of wire recommended for Evenflow 12v pumps is 2.5 mm square (cross sectional area) and this achieves an approximate continuous current rating of 21.5 amps. This matter was discussed in detail in Chapter 7 and wire of the required gauge can be purchased at an auto electricians.

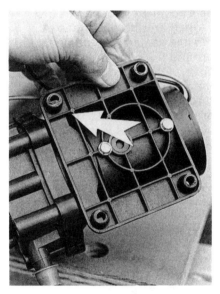

The Evenflow motor is mounted on a base plate with rubber feet (arrowed); do not screw down too hard or the sound deadening effect will be reduced.

Other appliances in a caravan are likely to be served by a narrower gauge wire and it is strongly recommended that the wire serving the pump is kept separate. A disabling switch located in a convenient position should be fitted on the positive feed and the supply should also be fused. The installation instructions are likely to recommend a 10 amp fuse.

Switching systems for pumps

Whereas diaphragm pumps are manufactured with their own automatic pressure switch, most pumps need a separate switching arrangement. In the simplest set-up where a caravan has one sink and a faucet rather than a tap, you could fit any simple electrical switch on the positive feed to the pump. The Whale button switch (Cat. Ref BS7204) or the foot switch (Cat. Ref FS7210) would be ideal.

Most caravans, however, have a wash basin as well as a sink; if faucets (i.e. open tubular outlets) were fitted, both the basin **and** sink would fill whenever the pump started to operate. To solve this, taps are fitted so that the outflow of water is controllable. For example, if you turn on the tap at the sink, water won't be delivered at a washroom basin or at a shower head as well.

Setting the pump in operation can be done in two ways. One approach is to fit an in-line pressure sensing switch which works like the units fitted in a diaphragm pump. The Whale Pressure Switch Mk2 would be suitable but this type of switch only works satisfactorily if joints in the water supply pipes are **totally** sound. It should be fitted as close as possible to the pump on the **output** side. In addition, a filter strainer must be fitted as near as possible to the water input point so that grit cannot get into the mechanism.

Recognising that systems are susceptible to changing conditions and fluctuations in battery voltages, the Whale Pressure Switch Mk 2 has a setting knob to adjust cut-out pressures within the working range of 5 to 25 p.s.i. (0.4–1.7 bar). It also has an integral non-return valve. The switch is normally screwed to a horizontal or vertical surface and two spade terminals are fitted for making the electrical connections within the positive feed to the pump.

Pressure sensitive switching is ingenious but a more common option is to have a mechanical switch embodied into the tap unit itself. Pump operation coincides with the opening of a tap and the switching principle isn't dependent on having completely air-tight hose connections.

Since space is limited, a tiny microswitch is usually fitted within the tap assembly. Unfortunately, a microswitch can give trouble if damp gets into the casing. It is therefore wise to carry a spare; in some instances, however, you can clean out the mechanism yourself and this is explained in the next Section.

When refurbishing a caravan, it is certainly advisable to choose taps which offer easy access so that a microswitch can

Whale Modular taps are made so that the microswitch is fitted externally (as arrowed); this means that if a switch gives trouble, it can be changed in a matter of seconds.

be hastily removed and replaced. Earlier models from Whale were far from easy to dismantle as shown in the next Section. But the more recent 'Modular' and 'Elegance' designs afford immediate access to the microswitch and are available in tuckaway versions, single units and mixer taps. Using a 'remote' conversion kit, it is also possible to fit the water outlet at some distance from the operating knobs, a useful feature if space is limited.

Fitting a Modular tap involves little work. Holes in the work top need to be formed to accommodate the tap spindle assembly. A flat cover plate is also provided and this is useful as a cover-up if the holes are ragged around the edges. A flexible sealant should be used around the edge of this coverplate to prevent water on the work surface from leaking through into the cupboard or the area below the sink. This will also ensure that water doesn't work its way down the cut-out and damage the microswitch. The tap knobs are a push fit on to the receiving spindle and can

be quite hard to remove at a later date. As with previous switches described above, it is the positive feed cable from the battery to the pump which should be routed via the tap.

Routine maintenance merely involves a replacement of parts which are likely to sustain wear over a long period of time. For example all rubber components are included in the Whale Service Kits. Unlike some types of tap, the Modular unit is quite easy to dismantle. There are some products which cannot be taken apart or serviced at all.

Microswitch repair and replacement

Recognising that microswitches can give trouble in the steamy atmosphere of a caravan kitchen or shower room, it isn't suprising that replacements are stocked at caravan accessory shops.

But this is little help when you're holidaying abroad and have forgotten to take a spare. The repair shown in the accompanying photographs was carried out for this reason. In this instance the switch was faulty and the water pump started operating intermittently of its own accord.

This problem is not unusual and it occurs when an accumulation of dampness and condensation causes corrosion around the contacts in the microswitch. The gap between the contacts is always very small, and any further reduction caused by a corrosive deposit can cause current to leak across this gap.

To carry out the repair, the tap must be removed from its location. This involves disconnecting both the water pipe feed **below** the short tail of flexible tubing and the accompanying twin core flex. You must also disconnect the screw which passes through the base plate and holds the complete assembly to the work top.

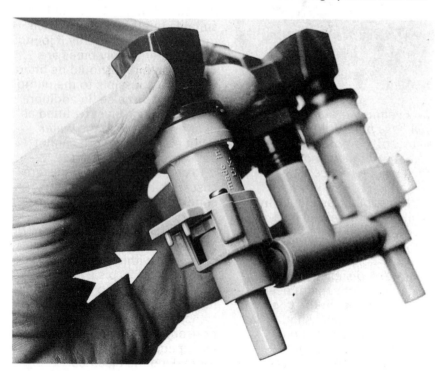

Whether it is a mixer tap or a single unit, a damaged tap assembly must first be unscrewed from the worktop.

Sequence of eight photographs on repairing a microswitch on an older pattern of Whale tap.

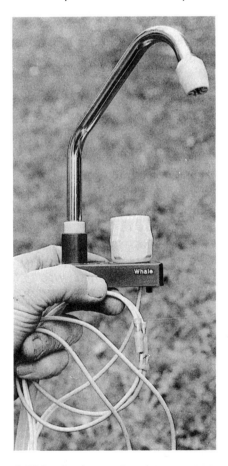

i) This single tap from a caravan offering cold water only, had a problem with a microswitch which sent the pump into action automatically and unexpectedly.

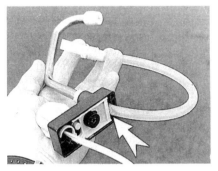

ii) Underneath it will be noted that water flow is arrested when a clamp (arrowed) squeezes tightly against a short length of flexible pipe.

iii) To dismantle the assembly, the first job is to prise off a rubber bush which holds the clamp in place.

iv) With the bush removed, the sliding clamp is lifted clear of the pump base; note the curved spring on the right of the clamp.

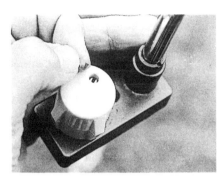

v) With the help of a very fine electrical screwdriver, the red or blue (hot or cold) pin must be withdrawn from the tap top.

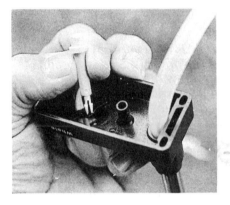

vi) In order to release the tap top, the control pin must also be withdrawn from underneath.

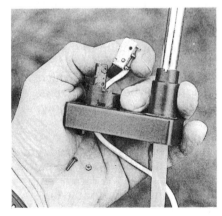

vii) As soon as the tap top has been lifted clear, it becomes possible to unscrew the microswitch from its mounting.

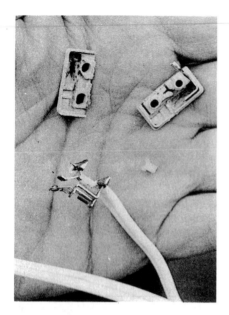

viii) Using a very small screwdriver, it is now possible to unscrew the casing of the microswitch; this usually reveals a damp interior.

On this older type of tap, which is fitted to many caravans still in use, the flow of water is arrested when a clamp plate presses against the flexible polythene tubing connected to the outlet. The plate is slid back and forth by an eccentric pin and stabilised by a curved spring. It must be removed from its location by prising off a rubber bush. You can then see the route taken by the electrical flex.

Turning attention to the tap knob, you must next remove the red or blue plastic plug which designates whether the tap is linked to a hot or cold supply. The plug requires patient probing with a small screwdriver. Once removed, you will then see the top of the peg which activates the movement of the clamp. This should be disconnected from underneath so that the tap top can be pulled off to reveal the microswitch.

Once the microswitch has been unscrewed from its mounting, complete with its trailing wires, it can be dismantled. A very small

screwdriver is needed; also patience. Poor eyesight and fumbling fingers are a distinct handicap. It is not a job to carry out over grass or a gravel drive; drop the tiny screw or the spring and the part is lost for ever.

The electrical portion of a microswitch resembles the contact breaker points on a car distributor, albeit in miniature. These often collect a deposit of carbon which must be removed. So, too, must any accumulation of moisture in the casing or around the tap top. Absorbent toilet tissue does the job well.

Finally, the opening and closing action of the contacts should be checked when pressing the plastic button on the side of the microswitch casing, watching that the components do not fall from their seating. Reassembly is unlikely to cause problems.

Water supply systems
If the designs of taps and pumps have progressed at pace, caravan plumbing as a whole remains pretty primitive. Flexible hose rather than rigid pipe is used in nearly all production caravans and this is usually 13 mm ($\frac{1}{2}$ in) in diameter. A narrower 10 mm ($\frac{3}{8}$ in) hose is far less common although a few pumps and taps are supplied with adaptor sleeves so they can be coupled up to the smaller gauge product.

Clear plastic hose is less commonly available nowadays. In its place, opaque blue hose is preferred because it prevents light from entering the system, thus discouraging the growth of green algae inside the pipes. Appropriately a hot water system is served by a reinforced red hose which is specially manufactured to withstand the temperatures of water delivered from a heating unit.

An advantage of flexible hose is that it can be quickly routed to each component needed in a supply system. In winter,

residual water left in the system is likely to freeze at some stage, but flexible plastic hose can accommodate the expanding ice without fracturing. But there are disadvantages, too.

If you inspect your system carefully, it isn't unusual to find a kink in one of the pipes. This often develops at the point where a hose passes through the floor of the caravan; typically the pipe run is required to negotiate a fairly sharp bend at this point. But any deformed section seriously affects the flow of water and if a kink is long established, the length of hose may need replacing completely. If it's difficult to reduce a sharp angle in a pipe run, it is better to fit an angle connector; most caravan accessory shops will keep these couplings in stock. But this introduces two further joints in the system and herein is another weakness when hose is used.

Even when a clip is fitted, push fit hose connections are not reliable. You also need a lot of them. For instance, a typical hot and cold water system with a shower, wash basin and sink is likely to require no fewer than 28 clipped coupling points. Add a water filter and a non-return valve and there are more than 30 joints.

In previous Sections, it was explained that if a water system operates with pressure sensitive switching, airtight joints are essential; a loss of pressure caused by a faulty coupling will activate the pump. Needless to say, a system with over thirty pipe clips calls for good workmanship at the time of assembly, and regular checks to confirm the integrity of the connections.

When repairing, replacing or extending a water supply system it is strongly advisable to use the best type of hose clips available. Worm driven clips bearing the 'Jubilee' trade name are robust, but if overtightened, the drive mechanism can get damaged.

If work is carried out when it's cold, the hose is surprisingly inflexible. Before making a join, it is recommended to immerse the ends in a cup of very hot water. Alternatively a hot air gun can be used, but care must be taken not to melt the material. Both strategies make the plastic more pliable, easier to slip onto a connection, and more likely to bed down when a hose clip is tightened.

In spite of taking these steps, hose systems can still give problems. As an alternative, semi-rigid plastic tubing with purpose-made couplings is a much better answer. Some couplings employ compression fittings which are similar in principle to those used in domestic plumbing. A few manufacturers have recognised the merits of rigid tubing; for example, Abbey incorporated this system in the 1992 County and Spectrum ranges.

Qest Qicktite by Leisure Accessories is one example of this system and the product has been available for several years. It employs a semi rigid polybutylene tube measuring 10 mm (³/₈ in) internal diameter and 13 mm (¹/₂ in) external diameter. This is supported by elbows, T couplings, drain valves and pipe clamps. Hose coupling adaptors are also included so that connections **can** be made with other items designed for a hose and clip arrangement. Qest products can be ordered through caravan accessory specialists.

More recently introduced is the Whale 'System 12 Semi Rigid Pipework System'. This was announced in 1992 and Bailey first used the Whale system in 1993 models. Unlike the Qest product, this semi rigid system employs push fit couplings. No tools are needed other than a pipe cutter which ensures the 12 mm (outside

diameter) tubing is cut cleanly. Blue and red pipe is available and an advantage of the system is the fact that by applying pressure on a collet held in the couplings, connections can be disconnected and the couplings re-used.

To support the Whale product, around twenty five fittings are available to meet the needs of all kinds of installation and the system represents an obvious way to improve a caravan's plumbing system. Without doubt, hose and clip systems are long due for an update.

Fresh water layout alterations

Once a fresh water supply arrangement is understood, it is easy to cure problems or to upgrade the system completely. The orginal design can often be improved; for example some manufacturers situate input and output sockets alongside each other. A more hygienic arrangement is to locate the fresh water input at a considerable distance from a waste water outlet.

When improving a fresh water system, you might decide to fit a non-return valve in the supply hose. This in-line fitting should be installed as close to the fresh water inlet socket as possible. Its purpose is to prevent water in

the pipes from draining back into the supply container whenever the pump is not in use. When this happens, air can enter the system and this causes problems with some types of electric pump.

It should be recognised, however, that a non-return valve will mean that water is always kept captive in the pipes. During a winter lay-up period, frost might cause damage, particularly at the joints. Furthermore, on the first outing the following year, the system should be allowed to run for a short spell in order to purge the system of stale water. The alternative is to disconnect the non-return valve at the end of the caravanning season in order to drain the system.

Inboard tanks

Another upgrading project might be to fit an inboard fresh water tank. Regular winter caravanners sometimes fit an inboard container in an internal locker box, situating it as near to the axle as possible.

For cold weather caravanning, it is sometimes advantageous to fit an inboard tank like the Fiamma product; this has a wide access point to clean out the interior.

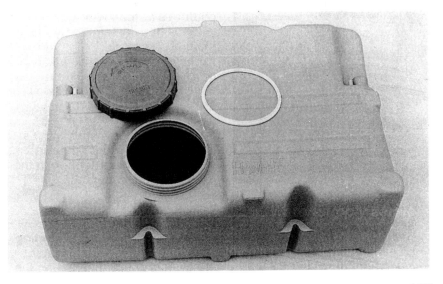

A 70 litre water tank is available from Fiamma and this has a large screw cap for easy cleaning. There are also tanks available from CAK, and a bespoke service is offered so that a container can be made to a particular pattern and capacity.

Obviously the weight of water can be significant in the loading of a caravan and a built-in tank should only be filled with a minimal quantity for en-route drinks. The surge of water in a tank can also affect handling, particularly when the outfit is being braked.

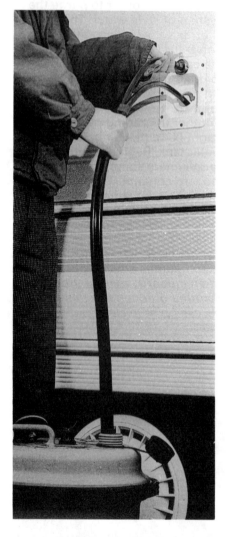

A way of filling an inboard water tank without moving a caravan to a water tap is to use a water barrel in conjunction with the Whale 'Filler Pump'.

Re-filling an empty tank can be a chore once a caravan is sited and a collapsible hose or a Whale Filler pump are important accessories. In summary, although an integral water tank has benefits, it is an accessory more appropriate for motor caravans.

Water treatment and filtration

Concern with water quality in the home is an issue which currently attracts considerable interest. Several products are made to improve the water quality in caravans, too, and these are fairly easy to install.

At the simplest, a filter which acts as a strainer is a desirable addition and the importance of preventing solid matter from damaging pump mechanisms has already been mentioned. With regard to the improvement of taste, an in-line charcoal filter is often used and several of these are manufactured for caravan systems. Logically these are best positioned as close to the tap as possible. Another example is the filter which forms part of the Carver Crystal water system; this is housed in the box which provides storage for the submersible water pump.

Provided a charcoal filter is changed periodically, it will certainly improve water taste. This is very desirable in the countries abroad where tap water is heavily tainted by the taste of chemicals.

Rather more expensive products are also available which will purify water as well as make the taste more palatable. Some types are relatively easy to install and it's likely that products of this kind will receive more attention in the future. (See Chapter 14)

Waste water system improvement

On most caravans, the plumbing arrangements for waste water are even more primitive than the

hose and clip system for fresh water. Modern caravans are usually connected with 19 mm ($^3/_4$ in) opaque coloured hose which is convoluted, i.e. it has moulded ribbing around the outside. Older 'vans were fitted with clear hose without the ribbing. Both types are larger in diameter than fresh water hose although neither are particularly good at discharging waste.

Underneath a caravan, it's not unusual to see this hose sagging between the clips which secure it against the floor. These sagging sections often harbour food remnants together with residual water. Since there's no trap under a caravan sink outlet, odours can easily rise into the 'van through the sink waste.

With a relatively small investment of time and money, a caravan waste system can be greatly improved using the rigid ABS (acrylonitrile butadiene styrene) pipe used in the building trade. It is made under a number of trade names, e.g. Osma, and can be purchased in various diameters.

Rigid 32 mm (1$^1/_4$ in) pipe is ideal for a waste system on a touring caravan. Leaflets on ABS waste systems can be obtained from any builders' or plumbers' merchant and these list junctions, bends, support brackets and so on.

Before upgrading the waste system, look critically at the original layout, especially the outlet point. For example, if the outlet was at one end of the 'van, it might be better to reduce the pipe run by selecting a side outlet. However, this shouldn't be on the same side as the door since it would place the outlet within an awning.

If the new system is planned with care, it should be possible to fit the pipe in such a way that it has a gentle fall, i.e. slope, continuing to the point where it discharges into the waste water container. This will be effective as long as the caravan is sited level on its pitch.

When fitting the pipe, a fall is produced by placing wooden blocks under the floor to coincide with the fixing points for the pipe clips. These must vary in thickness to create a gradual slope along the pipe run.

When purchasing 'T' pieces for junctions in the system, look for connectors which incorporate a gentle curved course just near the point where the joining pipe enters the run at right angles. This helps to ensure that water joining the main trunkway from a branch pipe is steered towards the point of outflow.

The system is also likely to need 135 degree angle connectors for steering the pipe runs in the required direction. If two of these connectors are coupled together, they can be twisted in such a way as to increase or decrease horizontal alignment as well. This can be helpful if it is necessary to make slight directional alterations to negotiate a chassis member. Before finally glueing-up the system, twisting these connectors can also help to 'fine tune' the fall.

Overall the system should be assembled in a dry state first. When creating the fall, advantage should be taken of apertures in the main chassis members. Pipe can be cut to length with a hacksaw and burrs removed with glasspaper. In addition, the joining surfaces of pipes should be roughened with glasspaper.

The proprietary adhesive for these products is sold in a tin which includes a brush in the lid. All you have to do is to coat both joining surfaces, offer up the components, give a small twist back and forth, and then

When building a waste system, it often helps to check sections by assembling them as separate units in a dry state.

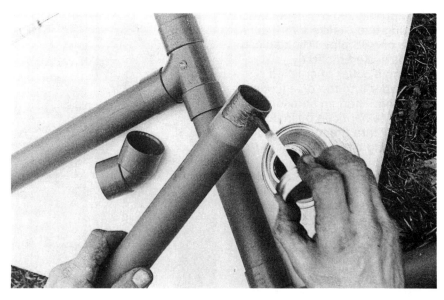

The adhesive intended for uPVC waste water pipes is supplied in a tin with a convenient brush in the lid.

hold the pieces for 20 to 30 seconds. Surplus adhesive may ooze from the joint and can be removed with an old rag. After three or four minutes, the welded sections will be fairly strong although full strength and a resistance to water will not be attained for around four hours. If the pipe layout has been carefully planned, some

sections can be prefabricated before finally offering them up and making the connections underneath the 'van.

When fitting a large bore waste system, the ideal arrangement would be to connect up to a matching outlet at the sink. However, unless the sink is being changed to a domestic type, such as an Optimus Mini Kitchen model, you will need to make a suitable junction of old and new. This can be done by retaining a short length of original hose under the

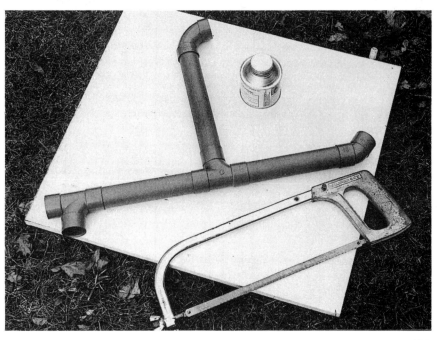

sink (approx. 200 mm/8 in) and inserting this ***inside*** a vertical length of ABS pipe. The gap can then be sealed by firstly pressing a collar of crushed newspaper into the pipe to act as a bung. Then an aerosol can of foam sealant can be injected sparingly into the top.

Retaining a short length of the original outlet hose means there's a small restriction in the overall pipe run, but since this only extends for 200 mm (8 in) in the vertical drop from the sink, it represents little reduction to the efficiency of the system as a whole.

At the outflow point, a smart finish can be achieved if you fit a threaded collar to the end of the pipe which can then be closed off with a screw-on cap. Being able to fix a cap will seal off the pipes, ensuring that neither insects nor vermin enter the system when the 'van is in storage. In addition, the termination of the outlet with a threaded collar enables you to fit a purpose-made spout when the caravan is in use.

A spout can be made using another screw-on cap. Firstly its centre should be removed using a sharp woodworking knife or by drilling a pilot hole large enough

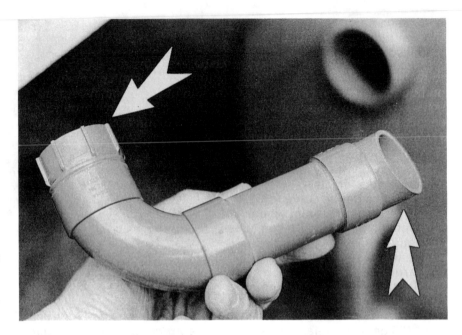

The outflow piece is formed from a modified threaded collar (left arrow) and a 135° bend section which is shaped to direct the flow into a waste container.

to receive the blade of a coping saw. When forming the hole, care should be taken not to damage the threads on the inside. Having done this, a suitable angle piece should be welded in place with ABS adhesive, followed by a short length of pipe so that the

outflow will be directed into the waste receptacle. This entails forming a butt joint between the modified cap and the angle piece, but the bonding qualities of this adhesive are first class.

Alternatively, a short length of car radiator hose of suitable diameter can be sleeved over the outlet on arrival at the site. Either way, the finished conversion will produce a far more efficient waste water system than the original run of sagging hosepipe.

Chapter 10

GAS SUPPLY

Safety first

Liquefied Petroleum Gas, or LPG as it is usually called, is heavier than air. This can have serious implications if a leak develops in a pipe fitting or connection. If this occurs, the escaping gas will sink to the lowest point, which is usually at floor level. This is one reason why a caravan is constructed with a number of low level ventilators. These must *never* be covered because they provide the escape route for leaking gas. Low level ventilators are equally important in an exterior locker designed to accommodate gas cylinders.

In water craft e.g. canal boats and cabin cruisers, the situation is much more severe. Unbeknown to the occupants, leaking gas might sink into the bilges, accumulate, and have no escape route. This represents a severe hazard as soon as a naked flame is used elsewhere in the vessel.

It is most important, therefore, that all gas connections are sound. If there are any doubts about their integrity, checks should be made using a leak detection fluid. Under no circumstances should a naked flame be used to search for a gas escape. If doubts *still* persist, a specialist repairer must be asked to carry out a pressure test on the entire gas system.

Recognising that leaks *can* occur, and since LPG has no natural smell, the suppliers add what is known as a 'stenching agent'. This gives good warning of a leak and the unpleasant smell leads many people to believe that the gas is poisonous. But this is not the case.

Fortunately gas explosions are a rare occurrence in caravans. It is equally fortunate that compression joints used in a gas supply system are easy to form and if a coupling is made correctly, it is unlikely to fail. On the other hand, nothing must be left to chance and the British Standard Publication relating to gas installations is very clear in its prescription. When dealing with gas appliances, it states categorically that all types of gas connection must be made by a 'competent person' working to the Gas Safety (Installation and Use) Regulations, 1984.

This statement is made in the interests of everyone's safety, which includes both the present owners of a caravan, together with any future owners as well. Arguably the term 'competent person' may be difficult to define, but the position is clear in respect of an inexperienced do-it-yourself enthusiast.

Needless to say, an amateur proficient in woodwork could fit an oven, a fridge or heater as far as the carpentry work is concerned and these tasks are discussed in later chapters. But when it comes to completing the work by coupling up to a gas supply, this part of the installation should be undertaken by an experienced gas fitter.

The supply source

There are two types of LPG and both are supplied in purpose-made steel cylinders. The majority of caravanners use butane which is ideal for caravanning in warm weather.

However, in colder seasons of the year, propane is more suitable.

Both gases are supplied in a liquefied state. As long as the temperature is warmer than 0 degrees centigrade (32 degrees fahrenheit), butane is able to change from liquid form into a vapour. But the gas fails to vapourise, when it gets colder. In contrast, propane vapourises at much lower temperatures. In fact it can be used at temperatures as low as minus 40 degrees centigrade – hence propane is the choice of the winter caravanner.

In Britain, both types of LPG are readily available; in addition, the type of regulators needed to suit butane and propane respectively are stocked in any well-equipped caravan accessory shop. But this is not always the case abroad. For example, in some Continental countries it is not unusual for LPG cylinders to contain a mixture of propane *and* butane.

In modern caravans, gas operated appliances may be manufactured to operate from either type of gas. But it is absolutely essential that the regulator fitted on the flexible hose is the right kind to suit the gas; the vapour pressure of propane is around *five times* that of butane.

Some caravanners use a regulator in conjunction with an inbuilt automatic switch-over device. This is for use with a twin cylinder supply. When one cylinder is empty, the device automatically switches over so that the alternative supply cylinder is brought into operation. It should be noted, however, that some pressure-sensitive automatic switch-over systems will only operate with propane gas.

As a general rule, manufacturers who supply both types of LPG use containers of distinctive colours. In the case of Calor Gas, for example, propane

The Gaslow automatic switching unit for Propane incorporates pressure sensitive switching; when one cylinder empties, the other takes over and an indicator verifies which one is ready for changing.

is always supplied in a bright red cylinder; butane is supplied in a blue cylinder. Turning to Camping Gaz products, all cylinders are blue and these always contain butane.

As regards the size of containers, this varies considerably. Typically a larger container will provide the owner with gas at a cheaper rate per kilogram than gas supplied in a small container. But a cautionary note is needed for touring caravanners who are tempted to obtain a large gas cylinder. Recognising that the valve devices on top of gas cylinders sometimes develop a leak, the containers must *always* be kept upright. For this reason, you must *never* stow a cylinder on its side when towing from site to site. Escaping gas in its liquid state will automatically convert to a very substantial volume of gas; in fact there is approximately a two hundred times increase.

In Britain, Calor Gas is one of the best known products. In the

first instance, a Calor Gas cylinder must be obtained on a hiring agreement. When its contents are exhausted, this will then be exchanged for a full replacement with the price covering the cost of the gas. Alternatively a refund of up to 70% of the hire charge will be given to a customer if a cylinder is returned with the Calor Hire agreement form. When looking at Camping Gaz, which is available throughout most European countries, this is sold in a different manner because a cylinder has to be purchased outright rather than hired.

Most caravanners touring in Britain prefer to use Calor Gas rather than its Continental counterpart because it is available in larger cylinders. This can be more convenient if substantial quantities of gas are required. Moreover, when using larger cylinders there are price saving implications as well. But regrettably, Calor Gas isn't available abroad.

Calor cylinders used by caravanners are available in the following sizes:

3.9 kg (8.6 lb) Propane
4.5 kg (10 lb) Butane
7 kg (15.4 lb) Butane
13 kg (28.7 lb) Propane
15 kg (33 lb) Butane

As regards the external sizes of Calor Gas cylinders, it is useful to note that a 3.9 kg Calor propane cylinder is the same size as a 4.5 kg butane cylinder. Moreover, a 13 kg Calor propane cylinder is the same size as a 15 kg butane cylinder. The reason for different 'fills' in cylinders of equivalent sizes is that propane is 'lighter' than butane. Therefore a given size of cylinder will hold less propane (by weight) compared with butane.

On many occasions, caravanners have suggested that Calor Gas Ltd. should introduce a propane version of the 7 kg butane cylinder (which

The 4.5 kg Calor Gas butane cylinder (or its 3.9 kg propane equivalent) fits easily into all caravan drawbar locker boxes.

A 19 kg cylinder is normally too large for caravanners, except for the winter enthusiast who intends to remain on a pitch for a week or more in cold conditions.

There are Gaslow gauges to suit most Calor cylinders; this example is fitted to the smallest butane cylinder.

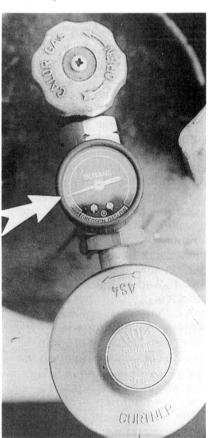

The needle in the yellow section of this Gaslow gauge is a warning that the supply is beginning to get low.

would effectively contain 6 kg of propane gas). Several approaches have been made and the Company claimed it would use market research to establish the economic viability of the proposed product. In 1991, however, it was stated that 'in the present difficult trading conditions, Calor will not be introducing a 6 kg propane cylinder.' This decision is viewed with great disappointment, especially by caravanners who tour in the winter months.

Larger capacity cylinders than those listed above are less suitable for touring on account of their size and weight. Admittedly, a large 19 kg propane cylinder is sometimes used by winter sports enthusiasts if a caravan is going to remain on the same pitch for an extended period and when heating is needed throughout the stay. But difficulties arise if the cylinder isn't exhausted by the end of the holiday, remembering that it must **not** be transported home in a horizontal position for reasons stated earlier.

In contrast, Camping Gaz is only available in smaller cylinders, the largest of which is 2.72 kg (6 lb). The two smaller sizes (1.81 kg (4 lb) and 0.45 kg (1 lb)) hold insufficient gas to meet the normal requirements of caravan appliances.

Irrespective of the gas or type of cylinder, caravanners are often faced with the problem of wanting to know how close a gas cylinder is to exhaustion. There are a number of products on the market designed to provide the answer. These include: i) devices for weighing the cylinder, ii) graduated strips containing a chemical crystal which are stuck on the **outside** of the cylinder.

Particularly popular are gauges manufactured by Gaslow and several types are available to suit different gas cylinders. However, to be strictly accurate, a Gaslow gauge doesn't indicate how much gas is remaining in a cylinder once it has been disconnected. Reference to the gauge should be made when everything is connected and in operation. With gas appliances in use, the needle on the gauge will point to coloured 'traffic light' bands. If the needle points to the green zone when appliances are in use, the supply is in good condition. The yellow zone, however, indicates that the supply is far from full, whereas the red zone gives a warning that the cylinder cannot sustain the needs of the appliances for very much longer.

The Gaslow gauges thus provide a useful means of monitoring supply and demand, and are available through any good accessory shop. A warning of a dwindling supply is especially useful when a meal is being prepared.

The supply system

Unfortunately, the connections on gas cylinders vary in design. The large 15 kg Calor Gas cylinder employs a switch-on type of coupling whereas smaller cylinders are made with a hand wheel on/off control and a threaded coupling. This has a left-handed thread and many caravanners purchase a Calor open-ended spanner for tightening or loosening the brass nut which forms part of the regulator. Inside the nut assembly on a butane regulator, a washer ensures that the coupling is leakproof. However, the washer needs changing periodically and replacements are stocked by Calor Gas stockists.

A different arrangement is employed with propane cylinders. These incorporate a female connection point on the cylinder whereas the regulator is made with a male nozzle to create the union.

Yet another system is needed for coupling up to a Camping Gaz cylinder. An adaptor is required which includes an on/off tap and a threaded connector to match the coupling nut on the regulator.

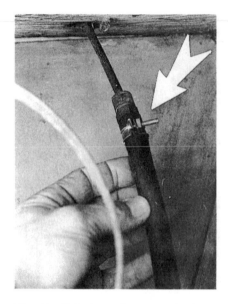

The flexible hose in a gas locker is made from a special material which should be replaced regularly; always check it is connected to the pipe connecting union with a hose clip (arrowed).

After passing through a regulator, gas is taken via a short length of flexible hose to the copper pipe which serves the rest of the system. The hose is made specially to suit LPG; it is not rubber because this would be unsuitable. It should be replaced periodically and it's a good idea to make this a routine task at the start of every season.

Hose clips must be fitted at either end to provide a firm grip on the coupling nozzles. When attaching clips, care should be exercised to avoid undertightening, which could lead to leaks, and overtightening, which could cause the hose to crack. It should be recognised that flexible hose must **never** be used in any other part of the supply.

Elsewhere the system will be made with copper feed pipes. These can be purchased in several diameters and the usual designation for main feeds and branches is:

5 mm ($^3/_{16}$ in) outside diameter (OD) = feed to a gas lamp
6 mm ($^1/_4$ in) OD = feed to most types of appliance e.g. fridge
8 mm ($^5/_{16}$ in) OD = main trunk feed in a touring caravan, including heaters
10 mm ($^3/_8$ in) OD = main trunk feed in a residential caravan

The recommendation of this manual is to leave repairs and alterations to the competent gas fitter, although it is useful if the

Underneath the caravan and throughout the interior, the entire gas supply system must be made with rigid purpose-made pipe.

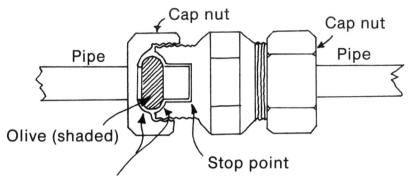

Cap nut

Pipe

Cap nut

Pipe

Olive (shaded)

Stop point

Sloping surfaces on the fitting which cause the olive to be squeezed inwards when cap nut is tightened

The way in which a compression joint achieves a gas-tight connection is clearly shown in this cut-away drawing.

caravan owner is aware of the way that compression joints are made. To understand the principle of operation, reference should be made to the olive and cap nut shown in the accompanying drawing.

The cap nut is a machined brass fitment which is threaded to match the threaded section of a connector, a 'T' junction, or a tap assembly. This is the first

When a compression joint is formed, the cap nut is fitted to the pipe first; the olive (arrowed) is slid on to the pipe next.

component to be slipped on to the end of a section of pipe. The olive is added next and this is a loose collar which fits snugly around the copper pipe. Some fitters then smear the olive with a jointing compound that has been specially formulated to suit LPG systems. However, the *Dealer Information Booklet* published by Calor Gas clearly points out that jointing compounds should ***not*** be used with compression fittings.

The end of the prepared pipe is inserted fully into the fitting as shown in the exploded drawing. When the cap nut is then tightened, its sloping inner surfaces bear against the olive and have the effect of compressing it. On account of its

soft, malleable material, the olive is thus forced inwards towards the pipe creating a close register.

The experienced fitter will know how tight to make the joint. Too few turns on the cap nut mean that the olive will not grip the pipe tightly, the pipe might even dislocate completely from the fitting. On the other hand, overtightening causes too much distortion and the pipe starts to buckle.

When an installation is finished, the fitter will then test the integrity of each joint in turn. Special leak detecting products are available although many installers use washing up fluid. Once a gas cylinder has been connected, the soap fluid is squeezed around the fitting and held in place with the fingers. Even the slightest leak of gas will then be revealed when bubbles start to form. As a rule, the cure for a leak is to tighten up the cap nut a fraction more. This usually remedies the problem, although over-tightening will distort the pipe and lead to further difficulty. A more rigorous procedure is to use a pressure test and a specialist installer will check to see that the system fulfils the requirement to work at a pressure of 150 mbars.

Other points of importance when fitting a supply are shown in the accompanying photographs. For instance when pipe has been cut to length, it is always important to clean up the ends. Any burrs on the outside can be quickly removed with a file; a rough edge on the inner surface can be tidied using a de-burring tool. A cross head screwdriver can be used as a make-shift alternative. Either way, it is important to ensure that all swarf is removed from the pipes.

Another important requirement is that support is given to a coupling by a spanner or wrench when the cap nuts are

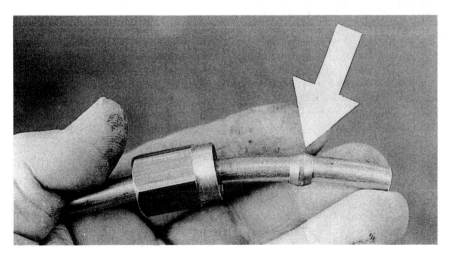

When fitting a gas supply
system, copper pipe of the
appropriate size can be cut to
length with a hacksaw.

To ensure that no leaks are likely
in a compression joint, a gas
engineer is meticulous in
removing any burrs from around
the cut section of pipe.

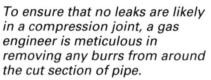

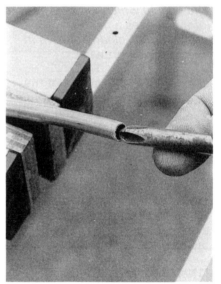

Copper remnants left inside a
cut length of tubing can be
easily removed by inserting a
large cross head screwdriver.

When forming a compression
joint, it is important to support
fittings while a cap nut is being
tightened up.

The integrity of coupling joints within a feed pipe is maintained by using clips positioned closely on either side of the fitting.

being tightened. This is shown in the photographs. Lastly, the runs of copper pipe should be clipped at regular intervals, making sure they're no further apart than 0.5 m (19 ⅝ in) centres, especially below the floor. Where a 'T' piece has been fitted, clips should be used on all three outlet pipes to provide full support.

Where the supply pipes branch off to feed an appliance, on/off gas taps will be fitted so that the supply can be isolated if necessary.

Special regulator systems
Reference has already been made in the previous section to gauges and control products which are marketed by Gaslow. Another interesting range of products is also available from Carver Engineers Ltd.

One particularly useful item is a gas regulator which incorporates a pressure gauge. Versions are available for **both** butane and propane gas and the important feature of the gauge is the fact that it will indicate if there's a leak in the system.

Another product of interest is the Carver GSD shut-off valve. The device incorporates a remote control facility so that the gas supply can be switched on or off from inside the caravan. The supply is controlled from a small box which is fitted with electrical-type rocker switches. The GSD shut-off valve is connected into the system between the regulator and the copper supply pipes.

Where propane is being used, an even more elaborate control system is called the 'De-luxe Duomatic regulator kit'. This includes two regulators for coupling up to a twin cylinder supply. The purpose of the Duomatic regulator is to ensure there's an uninterrupted flow of gas. For instance, as soon as the supply cylinder approaches exhaustion, gas then starts to be drawn from the back-up cylinder. A situation in which **both** cylinders are contributing gas continues until the original cylinder is finally emptied. At this point the back-up cylinder is now the sole provider, which means that the exhausted cylinder can be disconnected and replaced without disturbing the supply.

In addition, the Carver De-Luxe Duomatic system also incorporates a special control panel which is mounted **inside** the caravan. This offers remote control switching and there are

also light emitting diodes which indicate which cylinder is providing the gas. It means you can check if a cylinder has been exhausted without having to go outside.

A leak detecting gauge mentioned earlier is also included in the system. So, too, is a de-icer which has a heating element operated by a 12v supply. This prevents the formation of ice in the regulator, thereby ensuring an uninterrupted flow of propane even in the coldest conditions.

Overall, the gas supply system in a caravan can be fairly simple. On the other hand, the kind of products available from specialists like Carver, Gaslow and Gimeg UK enable the caravanner to enjoy benefits more usually associated with LPG supplies in domestic premises. Undoubtedly this provision adds a further dimension to the quest for caravanning comfort.

Chapter 11

INSTALLING SPACE HEATERS AND WATER HEATERS

Fitting gas appliances

In the previous chapter, it was emphasised that gas supply systems should be installed by a competent gas engineer working to the Gas Safety (Installation and Use) Regulations, 1984. The same applies when a gas operated appliance is fitted. Tasks like connecting the appliance to the supply, installing a flue, conducting a leak test and verifying that everything is safely operational are jobs which *must* be undertaken by a competent gas engineer.

Furthermore, any appliance fitted in a caravan should have either been certified to British Standards or have been approved by a recognised test house. If you have any doubts when looking at appliances for your caravan, seek the advice of a specialist gas supplier.

These cautionary notes concern the supply of gas and, where necessary, the construction of a flue. However, when an appliance is installed, part of the work involves woodwork and this element could be undertaken by a do-it-yourselfer who is competent at carpentry. It is essential, of course, that the manufacturer's installation instructions are meticulously followed. For instance any requirements regarding clearance distances must be strictly observed.

Clearances are laid down to ensure that adjacent surfaces do not overheat. In addition, appliances which are not room sealed e.g. instantaneous water heaters, require air for the combustion process and ventilation must also be adequate.

When installing an appliance, it is usual that a large part of the work is unrelated to the gas safety element. The kind of work involved might include preparing a suitable location, modifying nearby furniture and then fitting the appliance so that it is fixed securely.

Examples of appliances which an owner might wish to install are shown in the subsequent sections. The products featured have been used for several years in the author's own caravans and have given good service. When a report on one of the projects appeared in a national journal, the distributor of the appliance arranged reprints and issued them as a supplement to the installation instructions.

The case histories include three space heating systems; these have proved very efficent when caravanning in winter. Water heaters are featured, too. However, the two appliances described represent completely different methods of providing hot water.

Fitting a Riviera underfloor space heater

The accompanying photographs show the work involved when a Riviera underfloor space heater was installed in a 1972 caravan. This heater is ideal in small touring caravans when there's insufficient wall space to accommodate a conventional wall-mounted heater. In addition, the Riviera is very suitable in folding caravans.

Like the other space heating appliances discussed in this chapter, the Riviera doesn't have naked flames. Furthermore, it doesn't permit the products of combustion to enter the living space. This provides a high level of safety; it also helps to minimise the problem of condensation inside the living space.

During the process of combustion, liquefied petroleum gas (LPG) is a known creator of humidity. In consequence, older types of gas fire with an open burner aggravate the problem of condensation. Fitting a heater with a sealed unit is much better, although this won't completely cure a condensation problem. Some vapour originates from the hob; a kettle and steaming saucepans are contributors as well.

The Riviera's principle of operation involves a heat exchanger and a balanced flue. The flue system means that the **input** of air needed for gas burning is carefully balanced with the **output** of exhaust fumes. In addition, the Rivera De Luxe has Piezo ignition and a flame failure device which ensures that the gas supply is cut off automatically if the burner extinguishes by accident. A small inspection port also confirms that the burner is alight.

The top of the appliance is covered with a chromium plated grille which is sufficiently robust to withstand the weight of anyone walking over it. When the heater is not in operation, the unit can be covered with a metal shield; alternatively a piece of plywood covered with an offcut of the floor covering material is even neater.

Before fitting a Riviera heater, careful thought must be given to location. Bearing in mind that the heater needs adequate ground clearance, a central position is advisable. If situated near the ends of a caravan, the pitch and toss of towing is more likely to lead to grounding. The position must also be related to the chassis members.

The installation shown here was carried out on a 1972

The full depth of the casing should be checked and related to the proposed position underneath the caravan.

Lynton Javelin caravan built with a traditional ply-on-joist floor. Chassis members didn't cause problems when looking for a suitable location, but the wooden joists supporting the floor were unavoidable. It was therefore necessary to remove a section of one of the joists and to substitute a timber framework around the intended floor aperture. This in turn was fixed firmly into the exposed ends of the severed joists so that the overall integrity of the structure was preserved.

The cut-out in the floor ply was made with an electric jig saw; this gave better access to the joist underneath and a section was then removed with a panel saw. The edges of the opening in the floor were then tidied and squared-up with a wood rasp. In some installations it might also be necessary to re-route wires and service pipes to create space for the heater unit.

To protect the floor ply from the heat of the metal casing, a protective framework has to be fitted and four lengths of pre-drilled aluminium bracket were supplied to line the aperture.

Once the location is confirmed and marked out, it is a simple matter cutting an aperture in the floor.

As regards the balanced flue, this is attached to the side of the casing and the installation instructions state that the flue opening must **not** face forwards. Disregarding this would mean that road dust and spray could be driven into the flue when the caravan is being towed. On the installation shown here, the flue faced the side of the caravan and this also fulfilled a further requirement that a minimum of 100 mm (4 in) of free space is available so that nothing impedes the inflow and outflow.

Before the appliance can be lowered into the cut out from inside the 'van, the flue section has to be removed. This is a simple operation because the

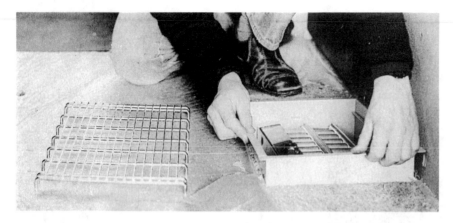

A side mounted balanced flue unit must be unscrewed from the casing before the appliance can be lowered into position.

unit is attached by two self-tapping screws. Once the heater is in place, the flue section should then be replaced from underneath the floor. It is important to ensure that it is not inverted by accident and this can be verified by looking at the outlet and inlet holes. The ones protruding outwards are for escaping exhaust fumes and should be uppermost.

As regards the gas connection, a qualified gas installer will connect an 8 mm ($^5/_{16}$ in) supply pipe to the coupling point on the side of the casing in accordance with the instructions. All new joints will then be tested for leaks before the heater is put into commission. Moreover, when lit for the first time, fumes may rise from the heater briefly while the new components 'burn-in'.

When the installation was complete, the Riviera heater operated efficiently, providing good heat whatever the outside temperatures. Technical details of the product are as follows:

The Riviera underfloor space heater is a room sealed appliance which takes up no wall space for its installation.

Dimensions (approximate)
Length – 365 mm (14$^3/_8$ in)
Width – 270 mm (10$^5/_8$ in)
Depth – 215 mm (8$^1/_2$ in)
Maximum floor thickness –
    54 mm (2$^1/_8$ in)
Weight – 9 kgs (19.8 lb)

Other technical data
Cap input – 6800 BTU max, 2400 BTU min.
Consumption – Min 0.7 CFH, Max 1.73 CFH
Fuel – Butane 280 mm (11 in), Propane 356 mm (14 in)
Ignition – Piezo spark activated by push button. A remote control version is also available.

Fitting a Carver High Output Space Heater
Irrespective of the size of caravan, Carver (Engineers) Ltd is certain to manufacture a suitable heater. Carver gas appliances have been prominent in the caravan industry for many years and the project reported here focuses on the installation of a high output model. Known as the SLP 3002, the model has been used as standard equipment in many large deluxe caravans manufactured in the 1980s. It is also available with a Truma blown air facility which is dealt with in the next Section.

More recently, the SLP3002 has been replaced by the 3000 model which has a redesigned casing; this later version is being installed in many 1990s caravans. However, the manner in which the new unit is fitted is little different from its predecessor. Hence the photographs and descriptions which follow can be regarded as equally applicable to the kind of work involved if a newer model is fitted.

Although the project here shows a high output model being fitted, there are many other heaters in the Carver range. Moreover, the catalogue clearly explains the intended application for each model. To guide the owner who wants a new heater, the output of different appliances is related to

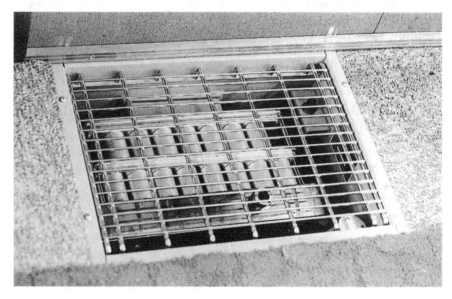

The Carver SL3002 is a high output model that can be operated alone or in conjunction with a Truma blown air system.

the interior length of a caravan. For example, the Carver 1800 model has a 1.64 kW maximum output and is suitable for heating caravans up to 5 m (16 ft) in Spring, Summer, Autumn and mild Winter conditions. At the other end of the range, the Carver 5000 Auto has a maximum heat output of 5.55 kW and is intended for mobile homes, very large caravans and site offices.

Like the Riviera heater described in the first Section of this chapter, all Carver appliances are 'room sealed'. This means that the gas burning process is kept entirely separate from the caravan interior. All air needed for combustion is drawn from the outside so that no oxygen is extracted from the living space.

The gas burners operate in a chamber which is totally sealed from the living area. Heat produced by the burners travels around a large finned aluminium chamber called a heat exchanger. Air around this

exchanger is then warmed and convected, or blown with a Truma fan, into the living space. Fumes from the combustion process are vented to the outside via a flue. Within this system, the cast aluminium heat exchanger is the key to the excellent heat transfer for which

Inside the casing, heat from the burners travels around a large finned aluminium enclosure called a heat exchanger.

Carver appliances are renowned.

When comparing the different models fitted to 1980s caravans, it will be noted that several types of flue system were used. Perhaps the best arrangement is to vent the waste gases above roof level, but an inconspicuous route to take a flue pipe from the heater and through the ceiling is not always easy to find.

With this in mind, one appliance – the SW 1800 – was manufactured with a side wall flue. It also featured a wall air intake which was especially useful if chassis members restricted the space underneath. In addition there were models like the SB 1800 which avoided both roof **and** wall flues. Instead the exhaust fumes were expelled **under** the 'van. This arrangement avoids cutting through the roof or wall panels, although certain constraints apply if there are bed box air vents in close proximity. The same underfloor flue arrangement was adopted in the replacement model, the 1800, which was introduced in 1990.

When considering the implications of installing one of these appliances, Carver heaters have to be built into a shallow recess. This means that a panel is needed which is free of

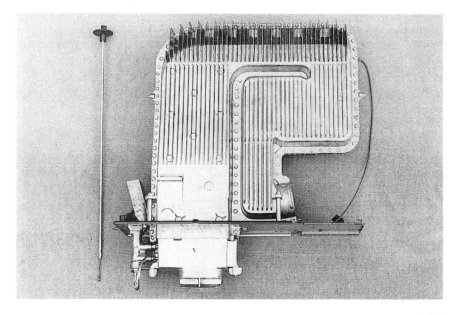

obstructions to the rear of the fire. In reality, the encroachment is modest, for instance the 1800, 2000 and 3000 models intrude no more than 110 mm (4⁵/₁₆ in).

When selecting a location, it is also important to check for obstructions underneath the caravan. The need for clearance will vary from heater to heater and some models require space for both the air intake and the flue assembly. Whilst a small degree of adaptation is possible with wooden floors, no alterations can be made to chassis members.

Having selected the location for an appliance, the installer will then embark on some straightforward woodwork. It is only when gas and flue connections have to be made that Carver insists that the final work is given to an experienced gas engineer.

When fitting the SLP 3002 model, the first task was to make cut-outs in both floor and wall mounting surfaces using the template provided. With this particular model, the floor

When fitting the appliance, cut-outs in both floor and wall mounting surfaces are made using templates supplied with the unit.

aperture is quite small - 205 x 100 mm (8 x 4 in). Just in case this coincides with a chassis member, the appliance is reversible so that the cut-out for the air intake could be made at either end. To confirm there were no problems, pilot holes were initially drilled in each corner of the proposed aperture before making the final cut-out.

The wall panel also had to be cut to accommodate the reflective metal installation box. The requisite aperture measured 485 x 485 mm (19¹/₈ x 19¹/₈ in). Recognising that caravan furniture plywood is around 3 mm thick, it is possible to make a clean cut using a sharp woodworking knife and a steel rule. The knife will need to be passed over the surface several times, but the result of the effort will be a sharp edged aperture.

When fitting a space heater, any carpet has to be removed in the vicinity of the fire and the template gives precise details about the cutting position of the aperture. In addition, two 8 mm holes were also needed for anchoring the unit, and these were also printed on the template to ensure accurate drilling. A cut-out in the floor can be made with a jigsaw or padsaw. If you own neither, make the cut-out by drilling a

number of holes around the perimeter. Then join these up using a hand-held hacksaw blade. A wood rasp and some coarse glasspaper can then be used finally to tidy up any ragged edges.

The sides of the aperture must also be protected, and a metal collar was assembled using two pre-formed sections provided in the kit. The collar was held in place when the heater was offered up. Meantime a hole had to be made in the side of the installation box through which the exhaust would pass. Knock-out pieces were provided on both right and left sides and you merely needed to punch out the one appropriate for the particular installation. This recognises that the heat exchanger is made to fit either way round.

Glass covered flame inspection ports are fitted on both sides of the appliance.

If it is necessary to reverse a heat exchanger, it will be noted that glass covered flame inspection ports are fitted on both sides of the unit. Only one small adjustment is necessary before reversing the fitting. The thermostat phial must be remounted so that it will appear

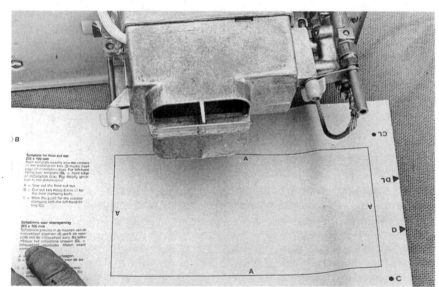

on the forward face. Bolting the unit to the floor using the metal straps is clearly explained in the instructions, although when carrying this out, it is advisable to add two woodscrews through the baseplate holes to improve anchorage.

Together with the work of making the final gas connections, work on the flue is another task which should be entrusted to a competent fitter. A mistake here could again have serious repercussions. For example, the flue serving the SL 3002 model has to be fed through the caravan roof, and it is crucial that it has **no** downturns between the appliance and the final outlet.

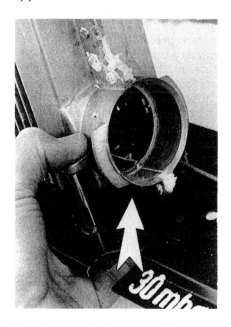

The flue outlet (arrowed) is situated on the side of the heat exchanger unit; its connections should be carried out by a competent gas engineer.

This is because rain might be driven into the roof cowl in a particularly bad storm. Rainwater entering the flue would then start to pool in the down turn, thereby creating a water seal and preventing the escape of exhaust gases. If the flue is correctly mounted in vertical alignment, the ingress of

The best flue system is one in which the waste gases discharge above roof level; this is the rain-proof cowl fitted with the SL3002 heater.

snow or rainwater isn't a problem because the appliance is manufactured with a built-in drain hole.

Bearing in mind that a flue gets hot, the Carver systems comprise a concentric arrangement of a pipe within a pipe. The outer stainless steel flexible duct which protects the caravan fabric has to be clipped in position at regular intervals.

At the roof, the fitter will form a 60 mm (2³/₈ in) hole to accept the cowl. A sharp cutting knife is often used to penetrate the sheet aluminium. A metal collar is then inserted in the hole for reinforcement prior to the introduction of the cowl from the outside. The cowl's weatherproof seal comprises a rubber washer, a tightening nut, and a horizontally mounted tightening screw which functions as a pinch bolt.

Once the flue is correctly coupled, the installation finally involves fitting the control knobs, linking up a wire to connect the piezo ignition, and clipping the outer casing over

the heat exchanger and burner assembly.

Technical Specification SLP and SL 3002
Heat Output:
Max. 3.2 kW. Min. 0.5 kW
Gas Consumption:
Max. 270 g/h (9.5oz/h)
Min. 40 g/h (1.4 oz/h)
Efficiency (Gross):
86% (Nett 95%)
Gas Supply Required:
Butane 28 mbar (11" W.G.)
Propane 37 mbar (14" W.G.)
Mixtures 30 mbar (300 mm W.G.)
Gas feed pipe size: 8 mm O/D
Smallest permissible supply pipe to heater: 6 mm O/D
Approximate weight:
10.6 kg (23.4 lb)

Truma blown air heating
The SL 3002 is one of Carver's appliances which can be matched with a Truma heat distribution sustem. So, too, are the more recent models such as the 1800, 2000, and 3000 heaters. The Truma system comprises an electric fan which is bolted to the rear of the appliance and a series of heat ducts and outlets distributed throughout the interior. Whereas some of the heat from the appliance emerges through the grill on the front of the casing,

Outlets can be fitted with a terminal unit which features a flip-over air control flap.

With some Carver space heaters, a blown air system can be installed by adding a Truma electric fan to the rear of the casing.

heat is also blown through the ducting system by means of the fan at the back. Both 12v and 240v are fans available to suit the owner's preference.

The SL 3002 is designed to accept a Truma fan, and a knock-out hole on the rear casing has to be removed before mounting the unit. The ducting arrangement is then left to the installer to plan.

Wherever possible, ducting will be routed through bed boxes and similar enclosures. However, if a section of ducting cannot be discreetly hidden inside the 'van, it is possible to fit an insulated and reinforced waterproof duct underneath the floor. However, this should be as short as possible to minimise heat loss.

Carver ducting is easy to cut using a sharp knife. Junctions, terminals, and outlets are available to create individual branches from the main trunkway. Outlets made with a

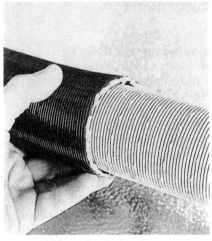

If necessary, the warm air ducting can be taken under the floor of the 'van using special reinforced double-skin trunking pipe.

flip-over flap allow the caravanner to control heat output in different parts of the interior.

The fan operation is controlled by a three point main control switch which can - (a) switch off the fan completely, (b) place it in manual operation in accompaniment with a heat setting scale, or (c) place it in automatic mode. On the

automatic setting, an electronic thermostat (thermister) in the unit, sets the motor speed to match the amount of heat available. For instance when the heater is first ignited, the control system prevents the fan from blowing cold air around the caravan. But as temperature increases around the heat exchanger, the fan starts to operate, blade speeds are matched accordingly and the heat is distributed.

When fitting a 12v Truma fan, a fuse protected power source must be fed into the control unit. Having removed the cover on the back, you will note the labelled terminal block.

Overall the installation is straightforward, but if problems are encountered, there are around three hundred Carver dealers in the UK who can provide assistance.

Technical Data
Power Supply: 12v DC
Consumption: 0.2 amp to
   1.0 amp
Delivery: Up to 170,000 litres of
   air per hour.

Fitting a Carver E1800
In contrast with the previous space heater, the E1800 has a built in blower system. It is also extremely compact, making it ideal in a caravan which lacks space for a wall mounted heater. Unusually, the E1800 can be

The Carver E1800 blown air heater is compact and has a thermostatic remote control unit; like all Carver heaters it is room sealed and can be left operating at night.

fitted in a bed box or in the bottom of a wardrobe, from which point air can be ducted around the caravan.

The case design is also unusual, and the plastic enclosure gives no clue that the interior houses a heat exchanger. One of the openings has to be connected up to a balanced flue and like the other space heaters mentioned in this chapter, the entire combustion process is kept separate from the living space. Air for combustion is drawn from outside; waste gases are similarly returned to the caravan exterior.

When the E1800 heater is mounted in a bed locker box, the casing may get slightly warm but there's no risk of damage to blankets. Moreover, this heater can be left in operation throughout the night, making it eminently suitable for winter caravanning. All control is

carried out from a small panel which can be fitted wherever it is easily accessible.

Heating levels operate with thermostatic monitoring via the wheel selector on the panel. In addition, a switch activates the automatic ignition. It is also possible to select a 'half' flame setting for gas economy.

In addition to its suitability for motor and touring caravans, the E1800 heater is used in the cabs of long distance lorries. There are three models in all and the numerical designation depicts their outputs in kilowatts. The E1800 pictured here is the smallest with a 1.8 kW output and this is suitable for the smaller caravan.

On account of its design, the E1800 is one of the easiest heaters to install. A caravan owner should find no difficulty in mounting the unit, locating the accompanying central control system, and then fitting the control panel. Similarly the construction of ducting routeways only involves simple carpentry. The ducting itself is the same as the kind described in the previous Section for Truma blown air systems.

Before starting work, careful thought must be given to location. It is necessary to consider the position of the flue outlet, the siting for an air input pipe, and the likely route for warm air ducting and output points.

Having chosen a place, small metal lugs then have to be fitted to special recesses in the casing. These act as supports on which the appliance will be suspended, and fixing screws have to be inserted through the lugs and into a vertical surface in the caravan. Obviously the mounting material needs to be suffiently strong to carry the weight of the unit. For example, 3 mm plywood often used for caravan furniture should be firmed up by fitting an additional layer of plywood using an impact adhesive.

Before fitting the E1800 into this bed box, small metal attachment lugs had to be screwed into the casing.

In addition to the heater unit and its accompanying ductwork, the E1800 includes a black box containing electronic control components. This is the master control unit and the instructions describe how it is wired up to the heater. In addition, a 12v permanent live feed has to be provided for the internal fan. This would normally be taken via a fused distribution box in the caravan.

There is also the switching box referred to earlier which is little larger than a matchbox.

The control unit allows the selection of air recirculation in summer, and either half flame or full flame operation in winter; output temperature is thermostatically controlled.

This has to be fitted in a convenient place so that occupants can switch on the appliance, observe the operation of red and green warning lights, and set the temperature control wheel. This switching unit has to be connected up with the control box, and you should choose a suitable route for the wires so that they are neatly out of sight.

The warm air supply system is assembled using Carver's purpose-made lightweight ducting. This was discussed in the previous Section in connection with Truma blown air systems. However, in this installation, a special duct is also needed to draw air from the caravan **into** the appliance. On the outlet side, warm air vents can be situated wherever they are needed in the living space.

Notwithstanding the ease of installation, final connections to both the gas supply and the flue system should be made by a qualified gas fitter. Even though the manufacturer's fitting instructions are clearly presented and the connection work is straightforward, Carver's technical staff make a special point that this part of the installation must **not** be tackled by an amateur.

The flue outlet is made of a cast alloy material and is supplied complete with a moulded rubber washer. This ensures that the outlet fits snugly against the exterior wall of the caravan and that the component is completely weatherproof. Overall the E1800 units from Carver are easy to fit, easy to operate, and particularly efficient in use.

The external flue outlet is a neat fitment on a caravan wall; a moulded rubber washer ensures that it is completely weather-tight.

Technical Specifications E1800

Dimensions: 380 x 254 x 120 mm (15 x 10 x 4.7 in)
Weight: 4.5 kg (9.92 lb)
Fuel: Butane or Propane
Working pressure:
 37 Mbar (Alternative working pressure: 50 Mbar)
Heat Input: 1.9 kW
Heat Output: 1.8 kW
Gas Consumption:
 Full speed 150 g/h
 Half speed 75 g/h
Current consumption:
 12v Full speed 1.1 amp
 12v Half speed 0.6 amp
Fan capacity:
 Full speed 100 cubic metres per hour
 Half speed 56 cubic metres per hour

Water heaters – general points

The development of hot water systems has been a most welcome advance in caravanning comfort. At the sink, it is always a nuisance having to produce washing up water by the kettle-full; taking a shower isn't fun when the water's cold. It is no surprise that water heaters have become so popular.

However, these appliances are relatively recent and are usually only fitted to more expensive models. At the same time, it isn't difficult for a competent do-it-yourselfer to fit a water heater as part of an upgrading exercise. Without exception, the final task of connecting up the gas feed should be left to a qualified gas fitter, but the preceding jobs are often undertaken successfully by a practically minded owner.

Before embarking on an installation project, it's important to realise that a water heater can only be fitted in a caravan which has an electrically pumped water supply. This also means that the 'van should have its own 12v battery and low voltage supply system for activating the pump, a point dealt with in Chapter Nine.

A further point to recognise is that there are two different types of water heater, both of which have their advantages and disadvantages.

At present, the majority of touring caravans are fitted with a storage heater. There are several appliances of this type on the market although the Carver Cascade 2 is the model most frequently fitted. After its debut in the 1980s, a second version called the GE model was added in 1990 and this operates from both gas and 240v mains electricity.

The Cascade models have many good features. The appliance fits discreetly in a bed box, making no intrusion into the living space. It is also a room sealed appliance with a balanced flue. Operation is easy via a switch panel which is often situated remotely at a considerable distance from the appliance itself. Whenever you want to light the gas burner, this is fulfilled by the flick of a switch.

The Carver Cascade 2 requires a 12v supply for its operation and if the caravan battery loses its charge, a red warning light will appear on the panel to indicate that its electronic control system is unable to operate. In practice, this doesn't happen often because only a modest amount of current is required.

Among the disadvantages of the storage type of water heater is the fact that it cannot produce hot water quickly when it's initially switched on. Information describing the Carver Cascade 2 indicates that water at 55–60 deg C will be available after 30 minutes when starting from cold. In practice, however, a **small** quantity of warm water may be available after ten minutes.

In the case of a Carver Cascade 2 GE, hot water can be produced slightly more quickly

if a 240v mains supply is available. The heating process is speeded up by operating both the mains immersion heater and gas burner at the same time. Technical data for the GE model states that some water at 55–60 deg C will be available after 20 minutes from cold, ten minutes quicker than the standard model. However, this doesn't help on a roadside picnic stop unless you have a portable generator sufficient to meet the 660 watt consumption requirement of the Cascade GE.

Another disadvantage of storage heaters is their limited supply of hot water. The Carver Cascade 2 models have a capacity of 9 litres (2 gallons) and the water may reach a maximum temperature of 70 deg C. Water at this temperature will be too hot for a shower and by the time cold water is added, the quantity available would exceed 9 litres quite substantially. Nonetheless, if all members of a family want to take a shower before an 'evening out', the storage limitation might become evident.

Recognising the problems, caravanners learn to plan their events and switch on a system from cold well before the hot water is needed. Moreover, on arrival at a site, many caravanners leave the heater in operation because the Cascade 2 has external venting and a full complement of safety features. In addition, the efficient insulation of the casing means that once the cylinder water is hot, gas consumption is minimal because the heat loss is only around 3 deg C per hour.

Instantaneous water heaters – advantages and disadvantages

An instantaneous water heater is different in all sorts of ways. To begin with, this type of appliance lives up to its name and produces hot water without

a moment's delay. This is useful when you pull into a lay-by for a hasty soup and a sandwich and want to wash the dirty dishes before returning to the road again. Another benefit is the fact that hot water can flow unceasingly until either the supply of cold water is exhausted or you run out of gas.

Presuming that the gas supply is plentiful, the only limit is the size of the water container. Recognising that one water barrel on the market holds around 31.8 litres (7 galls), a significant quantity of hot water is available on tap. In addition, if someone is charged with the job of replenishing the container, every member of the family can enjoy a hot shower.

Looking at the disadvantages, an instantaneous heater cannot be hidden out of sight like the Carver Cascade. It also takes up wall space.

On a practical note, the burners of an instantaneous water heater fire up automatically when water is pumped rapidly through the appliance. This means that if the water flow becomes sluggish on account of a tired battery, the gas burners in the water heater are not going to ignite.

The power of the pump is another point to check. It has been found that there are no firing-up problems using diaphragm pumps in the Shurflo, Whale Evenflow and Fiamma ranges. Similarly, some of the more powerful centrifugal pumps such as the Whale GP74 will have a sufficient output to trigger off the main burners in an instantaneous water heater. These products are discussed in more detail in Chapter 9.

It is also appropriate to recognise that modern instantaneous water heaters, like the Rinnai, are designed with an electronically operated pilot burner. This means that matches are not needed to light the pilot which was an unappealing feature of older instantaneous heaters. In fact with the Rinnai, there's no need to keep the pilot flame permanently alight. You merely push the electronic ignitor switch when hot water is required and then press the extinguishing button after use. In other words there's no waste of gas when the system is not in operation.

Some instantaneous water heaters require a minimum of 600mm (24 in) of flue pipe to remove the products of combustion effectively. This has implications for the siting of an appliance and a competent gas engineer can advise on this matter. The Rinnai heater can be supplied with a flue kit and to conform with BS 5546/1990 this is necessary where the appliance is going to be in continuous operation for more than 5 minutes. However, for briefer periods of operation a deflector supplied with the product can be mounted above the appliance to deflect warm air away from the ceiling.

Ventilation is another important issue. Since this type of appliance is not usually 'room sealed', additional ventilation will be required at high and low level. The precise amount required will depend on the gas consumption of an appliance and whether it is flued or unflued. British Standard 5601:Pt.1 gives details of ventilation requirements and a competent gas engineer must be consulted regarding the size and location of these ventilators. Furthermore, when the gas connection is made by a gas engineer, the operating effectiveness of the ventilators should be checked, together with the efficiency of the flue.

It must be made clear that when delivering hot water, an instantaneous water heater creates a large quantity of heat. The National Caravan Council (NCC) is fully aware that this type of water heater **must** be

correctly installed and a potential purchaser might want to consult the technical department of the NCC for supplementary advice.

Having focused on the 'plus' and 'minus' points of the two appliances, the owner should then decide whether to ask a caravan dealer to fit the preferred type of heater or whether to complete the woodworking element of the installation themselves. Either way, the gas connection and checking must be carried out by a competent gas engineer as explained at the beginning of the Chapter.

Fitting a Carver Cascade 2 Water Heater

A confident do-it-youselfer should have no difficulty fitting a Carver Cascade. The instructions provided with the appliance are clear and templates are provided so that the aperture in the caravan wall can be cut accurately.

Prior to purchasing a Cascade water heater, it is important to check its dimensions and to decide on a location. It was mentioned in a previous Section that most Cascades are fitted into a blanket locker underneath a bed. This location requires a front-to-back depth of at least 560 mm (22 in) measured from the exterior face of the caravan wall to the vertical forward edge of the locker box. Most caravan lockers fulfil this requirement although you should also be able to reach the location from above.

In most caravans there will usually be several locker boxes which could accommodate the unit. However, when comparing locations, look for a position where the hot water feed between the Cascade heater and the final outlet points is kept as short as possible. A long feed means that hot water left in the run is wasted; it also means that a tap will need to operate for

several moments before hot water starts to appear at a sink, shower or basin. In addition, to reduce heat loss, it is desirable that all hot water feeds are fitted *within* the caravan.

The accompanying sequence photographs show the chief tasks involved when installing a Carver Cascade 2. Nothing is particularly complicated although an owner may feel apprehensive about cutting a large aperture in the wall of a caravan. But this is not difficult, especially in a modern caravan which has sandwich construction walls. Before tackling this part of the job, it would be advisable to look at the descriptions of different types of caravan structure in Chapter 5.

With regard to the gas connections, the point is emphasised again that this must be carried out by a competent gas engineer as stated at the beginning of the Chapter.

Sequential photographs showing the installation of a Carver Cascade 2 Water Heater. (Produced by courtesy of Tony Bradford, former Editor of Caravan Magazine, who fitted the water heater in a 1988 Bailey Maru caravan).

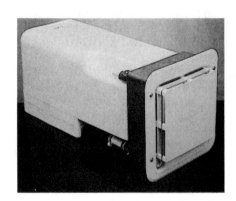

i) Whereas only a small part of the heater is seen externally, the appliance is designed to fit in a bed box and is enshrouded in polystyrene insulation. (Courtesy Carver (Engineers) Ltd)

ii) An electric jigsaw is useful for cutting the aperture; alternatively a sharp woodworking knife can be used to cut the aluminium skin, followed by a padsaw.

iii) When the aperture has been cut, sufficient polystyrene insulation should be cut away from the top and sides so that timber fillets can be inserted to accept the fixing screws.

iv) Special red, reinforced hot water hose is needed, together with pipe clips. There must be sufficient slack in the pipes to insert or withdraw the heater externally.

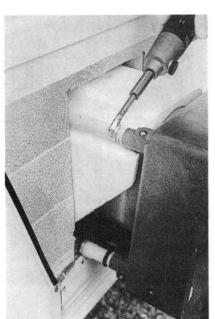

v) Before the appliance is pushed into place from outside, silicone mastic is applied around the flange; fixing screws must then be tightened in the order shown in the instructions.

vi) In accordance with normal procedures, an in-line gas tap is fitted in the supply pipe to the appliance.

vii) Both a positive and negative supply has to be brought through to the control unit; this should be fitted with a fuse as described in the instructions.

viii) From the outside, the appliance is neatly finished. However, on this installation, the metal trim piece has to be shortened to make space for its outer frame.

Fitting a Rinnai Instantaneous Water Heater

Prior to purchasing this type of appliance, it is important to consult with a gas engineer to ensure that it would be suitable in your particular caravan. Some of the requirements have been described previously, particularly the provision of additional ventilation and flue facilities.

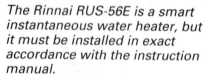

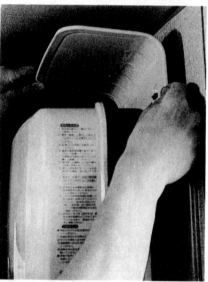

The Rinnai RUS-56E is a smart instantaneous water heater, but it must be installed in exact accordance with the instruction manual.

Recognising that a substantial amount of heat is emitted from an instantaneous heater, the manufacturer will specify strict clearance distances from other furniture, and items like roof level lockers. An installation should only proceed if it is possible to comply with all these stipulations.

Once a suitable location has been selected, two main tasks have to be undertaken. Firstly the unit has to be fixed permanently to the wall and secondly the water connections have to be made.

One matter which has to be resolved concerns the wall fixing. Like most water heaters, the Rinnai is supplied with a single fixing point near the top of the casing and two fastening points at the bottom. This provision is sufficient in a domestic installation where the

A heat deflecting plate is provided with the unit, but in some installations the optional flue is preferable; consult a gas engineer or the distributor to establish what is best for your type of caravan.

appliance is being fixed to solid masonry. But in a caravan, the walls are usually made of a slender lining of 3 mm decorative plywood.

If the appliance relied on three self tapping screws driven into the thin plywood, it would soon be shaken from the wall when the 'van is being towed. Much thicker material is needed to

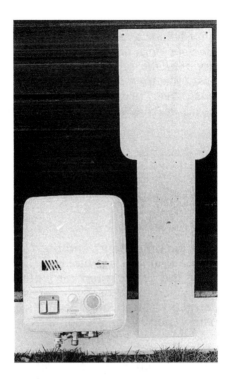

To ensure a firm fixing for the unit and its feed pipes, a backing panel of 9 mm (³/₈ in) ply was cut to shape and then screwed and glued to the interior wall of the caravan.

receive the fixings and the accompanying photographs show how this can be achieved.

You are advised to purchase a piece of 9 mm (³/₈ in) plywood which should be cut to the same shape as the casing, but slightly smaller so that it will not be visible later. An electric jigsaw is an ideal tool for cutting the plywood. In the installation shown here, the plywood also projected below the water heater casing so that it could rest on top of a cupboard for extra support.

This backing piece was fixed to the wall of the caravan using Evo-Stik impact adhesive. In addition, a generous number of screws were used as well. The result is a firm backing board which adds up to a total of 12 mm (¹/₂ in) and providing plenty of 'meat' to accept the three screws for holding the appliance in place.

Once the heater is fixed to the wall, the water connections can be made. The appliance's inlets and outlets have threaded ¹/₂ in BSP nozzles and these have to be fitted with hose adaptors. If adaptors are not included with the unit, the UK Distributor should be approached for advice about a supplier because these items are not always stocked by plumbers' merchants.

The adaptors allow standard caravan hot and cold hose to be pushed on to the barbed end of the fittings, and tightened with a hose clip. If you are converting a caravan to a hot water supply

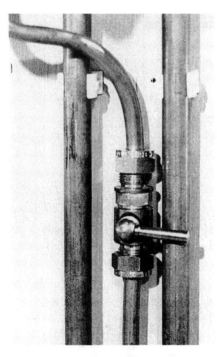

In keeping with normal practice, a separate stop cock is connected up in the gas supply line to the water heater.

for the first time, diagrams showing pipe connections are given in Whale water pump catalogues. This was discussed in Chapter Nine.

When the caravan is taken to a gas fitter for completion, the gas supply will be made using 8 mm (⁵/₁₆ in) copper pipe. This will be connected into the existing system via a 'T' piece. The

instructions also recommend that a standard caravan in-line gas valve is fitted so that the appliance can be isolated if servicing work is necessary. The gas engineer will then finally check the supply for leaks before the appliance is put into commission. The engineer must also be asked to check if the addition of this appliance would merit the need for further fresh air ventilators to serve the caravan living space. It was mentioned earlier that British Standard 5601:Pt.1. details the requirements of ventilation.

Finally, as regards the ignition system on the Rinnai Water Heater, this is operated by a dry cell battery which is included with the appliance. The battery is placed in a plastic container situated underneath the casing. Operation is very efficient and it is not unusual for the battery to operate for more than two years before needing replacement.

Having installed two Rinnai heaters in his own caravans, the author has found them to be exceptionally efficient and utterly reliable.

Servicing and routine maintenance to water heaters

All gas heaters should be serviced annually and it is recommended that this is carried out at the commencement of each caravan season. This makes certain that spiders and other intruders are removed before an appliance is put back into commission.

However, this is not a DIY job. For instance if you remove the casing of any type of water heater, it will immediately be obvious that the appliance is extremely complex. An instantaneous heater is particularly complicated in its design. The message to the unqualified person is therefore clear; servicing is **not** a matter for an inexperienced person to tackle.

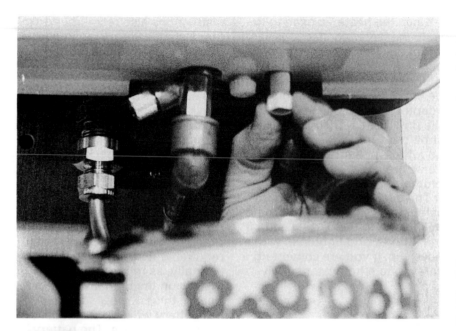

Whereas regular maintenance must be undertaken by a gas specialist, draining down the Rinnai heater before the onset of frosty weather is a task which must never be overlooked.

On the other hand, end-of-season draining is a vital task which the owner **must** carry out as directed in the user instructions. Both storage and instantaneous heaters contain residual water and if this is allowed to freeze, the appliance could be irreparably damaged. The accompanying illustrations show draining procedures for both the Carver Cascade 2 and the Rinnai appliances.

Hot water is an undoubted asset in a caravan; to allow this provision to sustain frost damage through lack of vigilance would be most regrettable.

On a Carver Cascade 2 water heater, the drain plug for removing all stored water prior to frosty weather is situated on the bottom left side of the exterior casing.

Chapter 12

REFRIGERATORS

Introduction

A refrigerator is one of the most useful appliances in a modern caravan. It is also one of the most reliable. However, this does not mean that it will provide unceasing service. Periodically a fridge has to be disconnected and taken out completely from the 'van so that certain parts can be cleaned and adjusted. After a winter lay-up in particular, fridge operation should be checked several days before setting off on a holiday.

Fortunately the routine maintenance work needed on a refrigerator can be carried out by any practically minded owner. In addition, fitting a new model in place of an older appliance, isn't too difficult either. Apart from making the connection to the gas supply, previous experience of refrigerator installations isn't important.

If the space is available, it is

To carry out maintenance work, a competent owner should not find it difficult to disconnect and remove a refrigerator.

usually possible to add a fridge in an older caravan. Modifications to the kitchen furniture may be necessary and apertures will have to be formed in the wall for the ventilation system and the flue. But many do-it-yourselfers have done this using the instructions and illustrations contained in an Electrolux Installation Leaflet.

Whereas routine maintenance

work and fridge installation are explained in this chapter, the chemistry of refrigeration processes is not discussed. Similarly, if the cooling unit breaks down, repair work would undoubtedly be beyond the scope of DIY self-help. Fortunately this is very unlikely; as we stated at the beginning, modern fridges are extremely reliable.

Fitting a refrigerator in a caravan normally involves the modification of kitchen units to create space.

Older models and their problems

Refrigerators were not introduced in many caravans until the early 1970s. Even then, a refrigerator was usually only available in a de luxe model. To give an example, a Morphy Richards Astral model was fitted in the Lynton Javelin 'Executive' range of caravans around 1972. However, by modern standards this was a primitive appliance; for instance the burner had to be lit with a match from outside the 'van. In wet and windy weather, this was most inconvenient.

The Astral was built to operate from either gas or a 12v supply, but the selection wasn't made on an internal facia panel. Access to the switch involved opening a hatch on the outside wall. Again this lacked the simplicity of a modern fridge where everything is controlled from indoors.

The operation of the Astral was good, but problems often occurred after a long lay-up period because the chemicals

had separated. This can still be a problem with modern fridges, although improved designs rarely lead to the difficulties experienced twenty years ago. If you own an older model and find that in spite of being able to light the burner, cooling doesn't take place, then chemical separation is likely to be the cause.

The cure for this problem is to remove the fridge from the 'van and to invert it for a period of 12–24 hours. The fridge is then turned back up the right way and re-installed, whereupon its performance should return to normal. This remedy may sound unusual, but it is an approved procedure.

Modern models

Nearly all present day caravans are fitted with a fridge manufactured by Electrolux, although two refrigerator models are also made under the Camping Gaz brand name. As regards the features on these modern appliances, a number of innovations have helped to make their operation easy.

Most casings are rectangular in design but in order to make the best use of space, one of the current Electrolux models is designed to fit around a caravan wheel arch. This provides storage space right down to floor level.

Modes of operation

Many modern fridges operate from LPG gas (butane or propane), mains 240v electricity, or a 12v DC battery supply. The 240v option, however, is not normally available on older refrigerators; nor is it fitted on

the Electrolux RM122 model. However, the manufacturer does sell kits to complete a conversion to mains electricity.

On site, the appliance would be operated from either a gas supply or from a mains hook-up, provided the caravan has been wired up to IEE safety standards. The purpose of the 12v option is to keep a refrigerator operating when the 'van is being towed; in this operating mode, however, there is no control of cooling. It is true that a gas flame can often remain alight when a caravan is on the road, but this is an extrememly dangerous practice. The risk of a petrol explosion is a serious matter and for obvious reasons it is an offence to enter a garage forecourt with any gas appliance in operation.

Under 12v operation, the drain on a car battery is substantial (minimum 8 amps) and the fridge should only use this supply when the engine is running. To achieve this automatically, the supply must be wired with an electrically operated switch known as a relay; this is explained in Chapter 3. Suitable relays are the Lucas SRB 630 and the Hella Single Relay Kit, Part No. 4RA 003 LGE-141. These devices automatically create the link with the 12v car battery as soon as the ignition is turned on. With the engine running, the towcar's

By fitting an ignition controlled relay switch, there is no risk of a towcar battery being discharged accidentally by the fridge.
(courtesy Electrolux Leisure Appliances)

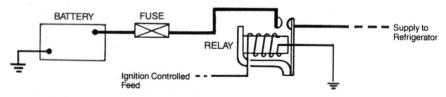

DIAGRAM SHOWING AN IGNITION CONTROLLED RELAY IN THE WIRING TO THE REFRIGERATOR

alternator or dynamo is able to prevent a serious battery discharge. As soon as the ignition is switched off, the relay then automatically disconnects the feed.

When wiring up the feed from the relay in the towcar to the appliance in the caravan, it is important to ensure that there is a minimal loss of current by using wire of sufficient thickness. To achieve this, wire of 2.5 mm square cross sectional area (21.5 amps continuous current rating) is supplied in the relay kits available from Hella. This more than meets the requirements given in Electrolux installation instructions which state that wire with a minimum cross section area of 2 mm square must be used. This achieves an approximate continuous current rating of 17.5 amps. Automotive cable made to this specification will be made up of copper strands measuring 0.30 mm and there will be 28 strands in total. The subject of 12v supply and cable suitability is discussed in detail in Chapter 3 and Chapter 7.

The complete arrangement needed to produce 12 v operation from a towing vehicle is easily understood when seen diagrammatically.

(courtesy Electrolux Leisure Appliances)

As regards the supply to the appliance inside the caravan, it is again important to observe the manufacturer's recommendations. Thinner wire must **not** be used. Irrespective of whether the supply feed is taken via a 12v fused distribution unit in the caravan, you should make certain that throughout its **entire** length, the feed is made with automotive wire of at least 2 mm square cross sectional area.

Notwithstanding this requirement, the point was made in Chapter 3 that the red wire inside grey multicore cable used to wire up to the 12S plug and socket is only 1.5 mm square in cross sectional area, i.e. it is made up of 21 strands and achieves a continuous current rating around 13 amps. Herein is an element of modern caravan practice which might be worthy of revision since this represents a 'weak link' in the 'car to fridge' supply line. Electrolux acknowledges this 'weak link in the chain' and recommends that the length of grey multicore cable forming the part of the feed connected to the 12S plug and the 12S socket should **not** exceed 2.5 metres. If it can be shorter, so much the better. Moreover, the Electrolux heater element presumes that **some** drop in voltage will occur and is designed accordingly.

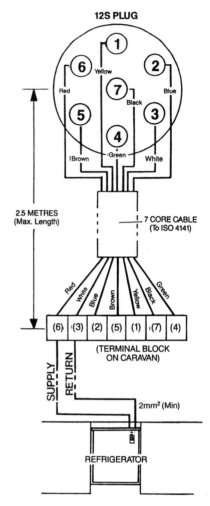

To avoid voltage drop, Electrolux recommends that no more than 2.5 metres of grey multicore cable is used between the 12S socket and the terminal block inside a caravan.

(courtesy Electrolux Leisure Appliances)

Car   Caravan

12V WIRING ARRANGEMENT

The refrigerator flue

There is no need for the caravanner to understand refrigeration processes, except to say that cooling is paradoxically produced as a result of a heating process. Where this involves a gas burner, the flame at the rear of a refrigerator requires a properly constructed flue which can efficiently discharge all the exhaust products to the outside of the caravan. Typically the tubing which forms the flue is diverted towards the side of the 'van via a connector shaped like the letter 'T', albeit with a sloping top. This is often

The flue kit which is supplied with an Electrolux refrigerator comprises four main components.

(courtesy Electrolux Leisure Appliances)

referred to in instruction manuals as the 'lazy T'.

Inevitably the flue pipe itself will get quite warm when the burner is alight, and it is therefore important to see that when it passes through the side wall of the caravan, no damage is caused to the surrounding fabric. The tube should be wrapped in mineral wool or other non-combustible material as a safety precaution. Meanwhile on the outside of the 'van, the point where the flue terminates is covered with a square metal plate. In operation, this usually gets warm. On models manufactured in the UK, there used to be a small rubber flap fitted just behind the coverplate which was to help prevent downdraughts from extinguishing the flame. However, this provision was withdrawn in mid 1988 to

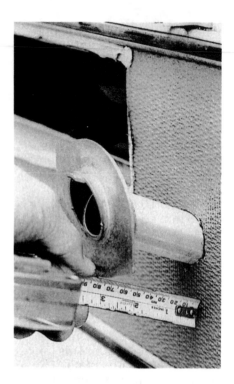

The length of a flue is critical; in this DIY installation, the excess is measured and trimmed to finish flush with the side of the caravan.

conform with European Regulations and the latest flue kits do not have this component.

When installing a refrigerator, it is most important not to extend the flue pipe in any way. This might cause an imbalance in the gas/air mixture; poor combustion could occur as a result and this might be dangerous.

In many refrigerators, the flue is an entirely separate component with its own outlet and cover plate on the side of the caravan. However, in 1990, Electrolux introduced the A1609 combined flue and ventilator grille as an alternative to earlier systems. Several manufacturers started to fit this new component to their 1991 caravans and the Electrolux installation instructions were revised in the same year to describe how to fit this integrated flue and ventilator cover.

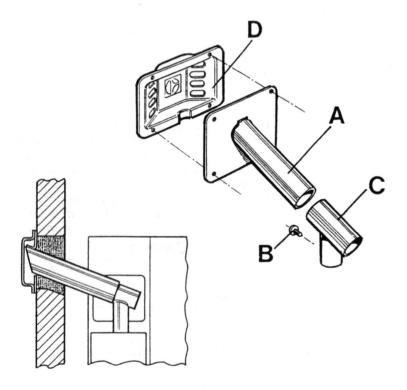

A Exhaust Tube.
B Screw — Self Tapping No. 6 × ¼ in.
C Flue Top Complete
D Flue Outlet Cover Plate

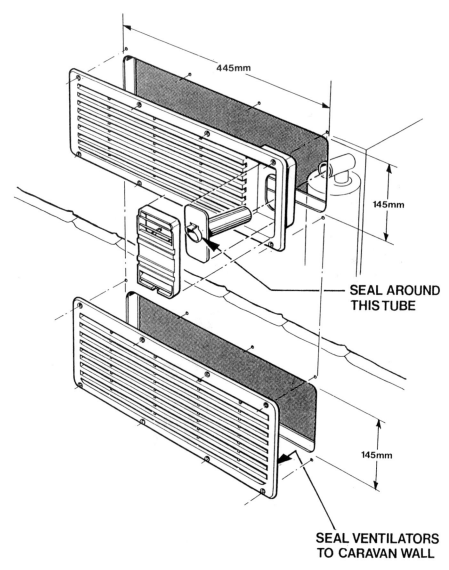

445mm

145mm

—— SEAL AROUND
THIS TUBE

145mm

SEAL VENTILATORS
TO CARAVAN WALL

*The combined flue and
ventilator grill has been fitted to
many caravans since its
introduction in 1990.
(courtesy Electrolux Leisure
Appliances)*

Ventilation

Whether servicing an existing
fridge, or fitting a new model, it
is essential that the system of
ventilation is not confused with
the flue system already
described. The systems are
entirely separate.

For a fridge to operate
correctly, the appliance must
receive a constant movement of
air over the cooling unit on the
rear of the casing. In
consequence, ventilators are
fitted as part of the installation.
But construction of the routeway
which provides a throughput of
air is entirely separate from the
flue arrangement. When you
compare different caravans, it
will be evident, however, that
there are variations in the way in
which ventilation is provided.
Broadly speaking, there are two
systems, external ventilation
and internal ventilation.

External ventilation

Without question, external
ventilation is far more efficient
than a system involving internal
ventilation. For this reason,
Electrolux no longer approves
the internal arrangement for
fridges whose capacity exceeds
1 cubic foot. For maximum
efficiency, a through-way for air
is constructed across the back of
the casing so that it is **totally**
sealed from the interior of the
caravan. Equally this zone of
ventilation behind the fridge
should be entirely separate from
any sections of neighbouring
kitchen units.

The input point for air
travelling along this through-
way can either be a vent-
covered aperture in the caravan
wall in line with the lowest part
of the appliance, **or** a similar
aperture in the floor. If a floor
level vent is fitted, it should
always be situated as far from
the burner as possible. In either
case, the size of the aperture
must yield the correct amount of
air space recommended by the
manufacturer, and this will
relate to the choice of model. To
quote an example, the Electrolux
RM2200 model is required to
have a ventilator whose free air
space yields at least 240 cm. sq.
(37 sq. in.).

As regards the upper
ventilator, this has to be fitted
into an external wall so that the
lowest part of the opening is in
line with the uppermost part of
the refrigerator casing. This will
facilitate the best possible flow
of air. In reality, the upper
aperture will still provide a
measure of ventilation if it is
slightly lower. Nevertheless the
uppermost side of the ventilator
must never be lower than the
top of the control panel on the
front of the fridge. In addition, a
deflector plate should be fitted
above the top of the refrigerator
condenser to direct air towards
the top vent as shown in the
accompanying diagrams. In
many caravan installations this
is formed from a piece of
aluminium sheet and the
amateur should be able to
obtain a suitable offcut from any
caravan workshop concerned
with body repairs. Alternatively
a special kit (Part no. IK1) is
available through Electrolux

Viewed from underneath a sink unit, a deflector made from aluminium sheet has been fitted to direct warm air from the fridge condenser towards the upper vent.

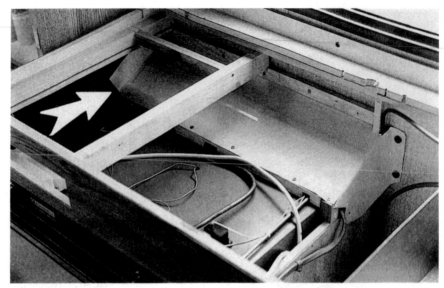

Installation requirements for an Electrolux refrigerator are shown in this diagram, including alternative methods of providing ventilation.

(courtesy Electrolux Leisure Appliances)

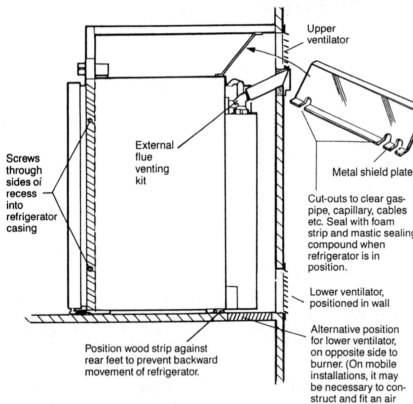

Screws through sides of recess into refrigerator casing

External flue venting kit

Upper ventilator

Metal shield plate

Cut-outs to clear gas-pipe, capillary, cables etc. Seal with foam strip and mastic sealing compound when refrigerator is in position.

Lower ventilator, positioned in wall

Alternative position for lower ventilator, on opposite side to burner. (On mobile installations, it may be necessary to construct and fit an air deflector below.

Position wood strip against rear feet to prevent backward movement of refrigerator.

In this installation, the ventilation area to the rear of the refrigerator is sealed at the sides from the rest of the caravan using a sheet of galvanised steel.

dealers for use with five of the most popular refrigerators.

Even though these requirements are clearly laid down in the Electrolux installation instructions, it is most regrettable that several caravan manufacturers disregard some of the recommendations. For instance, it is not unusual to find that the

ventilating zone has not been properly isolated from adjacent cupboard units. There are even caravans where a breeze blowing into the upper vent causes draughts in the living quarters. This is unpleasant for the occupants when the weather is cold and impairs fridge efficiency when the weather is hot.

Internal ventilation

An alternative method for ventilating the cooling unit is to draw air from *inside* the 'van via a routeway underneath the fridge. This air is then passed over the cooling unit and returned to the interior of the 'van either via an outlet directly above the rear casing or via an outlet situated just above the facia control panel. A number of older caravans are still in use with this ventilation arrangement and it avoided the need to cut apertures in the side walls. However, with the exception of the RM122 and 123 models, Electrolux ceased to recommend this ventilation option in 1989.

The shortcoming of internal ventilation is the fact that warmed air which has passed over the back of the appliance is returned to the living quarters. In the summer, this not only adds unwanted heat to the interior, it progressively worsens the opportunity for the cooling unit to receive adequate ventilation. Hence at a time of year when the caravan can easily become intolerably hot, the fridge falls well below its normal level of efficiency.

Installation considerations
Installation details given in the previous section enable an owner to check if a fridge was correctly installed when the caravan was originally built. In hot locations, some caravanners complain that their fridge has failed to cool the contents very effectively. Invariably a contributor to this poor performance is the fact that the installation has been incorrectly carried out, but it is usually the fridge which gets the blame.

Caravan manufacturers only provide an 'Operation Handbook' in a new 'van. Since installation manuals for individual appliances are not supplied, a purchaser is unable to verify that the correct methods of fitting have been carried out.

As regards the ventilation enclosure around the rear of a fridge, owners of a caravan can often improve on a poor factory finish. Equally, anyone fitting a fridge from scratch can get it right in the first place!

Attaching and removing a fridge
To carry out regular servicing work on a fridge means that it has to be removed. Herein lies another problem. Quite often, caravan manufacturers fit a fridge first and then build kitchen units around it

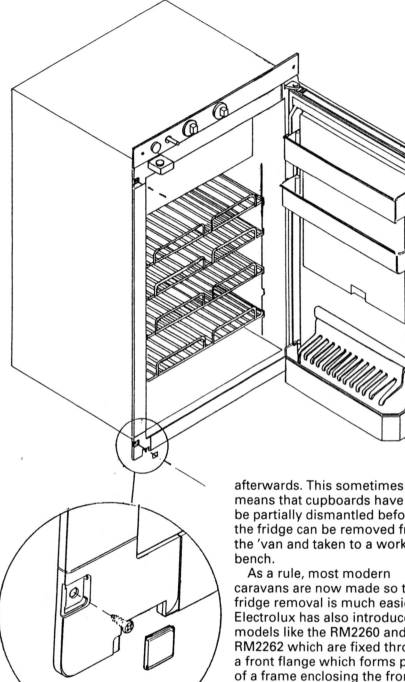

As an alternative to driving screws into the sides of a refrigerator, more recent Electrolux models have a front flange to produce a firm fixing.
(courtesy Electrolux Leisure Appliances)

afterwards. This sometimes means that cupboards have to be partially dismantled before the fridge can be removed from the 'van and taken to a work bench.

As a rule, most modern caravans are now made so that fridge removal is much easier. Electrolux has also introduced models like the RM2260 and RM2262 which are fixed through a front flange which forms part of a frame enclosing the front of the appliance. This greatly facilitates both the removal and the fixing of the unit. However, other models are less easy to deal with. Another problem for the home maintenance enthusiast is the fact that few owner handbooks explain how to remove a fridge and the first job is to work out how the appliance is anchored in place.

Methods vary although one of

the most common procedures is to drive sturdy self-tapping screws through the sides of adjacent furniture, directly into the metal casing of the fridge itself. This is acceptable as long as the screw isn't too long. If you are fitting a fridge yourself, you have to be careful that the screws do not penetrate the casing by more than 12 mm (1/2 in). Longer screws may pass completely through the insulant and then penetrate the interior plastic lining. If carried out properly, the fitted fridge should be held in a truly horizontal position whenever the 'van itself is parked on a level site.

When preparing to remove a fridge for the first time, it may help to lift it cautiously in order to get an idea of the position of fixings. Since the gas piping is still attached this must be done gently. A variety of fixing ideas are used. For instance in one well-known marque, the projecting door hinge at the front is drilled so that an angled screw can be driven into a timber batten below. You may also find that the metal control facia directly above the door has been used for additional anchorage.

Disconnecting gas and electricity feeds

Before finally withdrawing an appliance, it is necessary to disconnect the gas feed pipe. Obviously the mains and low voltage connections don't have the same measure of rigidity and should include some slack in the feed wiring.

Before going any further, be meticulous in your approach and check that:
★ the gas supply has been disconnected and the bottle removed
★ the 12v supplies from both the car and inboard batteries have been disconnected
★ the mains supply has been disconnected at the input plug

The point where supplies are linked to the fridge is usually on top of the appliance. However, there may be alternative places where you can disconnect the feeds, particularly in the case of the mains cable. For example it may be easier to disconnect the three core flex at a nearby junction box, thus leaving a trailing lead still attached to the appliance. Sometimes it will be fitted with a 13 amp plug. However, in the case of the gas connection, this usually involves undoing a securing nut situated behind the facia panel.

Gaining access to the top of a fridge may again involve some ingenuity. Sometimes the connections are made accessible by taking out a drawer. Or perhaps the fridge is situated beneath a draining board and access is improved by removing the entire sink and drainer.

Once the objective is in sight, it will be straightforward to disconnect the 12v feed wires at a joint block and to loosen the cap nut which forms part of the gas connection.

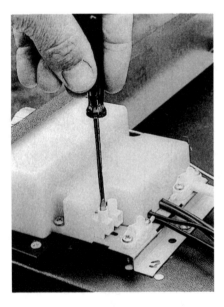

Gas, mains electricity and 12v supply sources are usually connected up to a refrigerator behind the front fascia panel.

Abbreviated recess

The only other point where a fridge may be attached is at the rear of the casing. If the original installation complied with the manufacurer's recommendations, a sealed ventilation zone at the rear will have been formed. This is often created from sheet aluminium and an enclosure which has been constructed around the rear of the appliance in this way is known as an abbreviated recess.

Where an abbreviated recess has been specially fabricated, it is more than likely that it will be screwed to both the inside surface of the caravan wall **and** to the casing of the fridge. Where this strategy has been adopted, there will probably be several self tapping screws to remove before the fridge can be finally released.

Improving the means of attachment

A few fridges are quite difficult to remove. Bearing this in mind, it is often possible to find ways of improving a method of attachment so that future releasing operations can be carried out much more quickly. For instance small adaptations to the surrounding kitchen units can make it possible to insert a screwdriver through a discreetly drilled access hole in order to reach the heads of more obscure fixings.

Gas escape provision

When working in reverse and fitting a fridge for the first time, the installation requirements call for many features which haven't been mentioned so far. For example it may be necessary to create a special low level vent for dispersing leaking gas, although this depends on the method adopted for ventilating the rear of the appliance.

Where a fridge has been fitted at floor level and with wholly internal ventilation, a 40 mm

(2¹/₈ in) diameter hole must be formed in the floor underneath the casing on the side opposite the burner. Remembering that caravan gas is heavier than air, this means that if a leak occurs, the gas can escape to the outside. This outlet is ***most*** important.

If an internally ventilated fridge is mounted ***above*** the floor level of the caravan, the hole in the shelf on which it sits should then have a 40 mm (2¹/₈ in) relief pipe connected to the floor escape outlet.

The provision for gas escape is not needed on an externally ventilated fridge, as long as the lowest louvre of the grille is situated ***below*** the installation level of the appliance.

Where a gas escape vent is made in the floor, it is usual to fit a small aluminium shield underneath the 'van to prevent dirt being thrown up from the road. This should be attached on the forward edge so that spray cannot be scooped into the vent aperture as the caravan is being towed. The shield can easily be cut from a small piece of aluminium sheet, although purpose-made covers are sometimes obtainable.

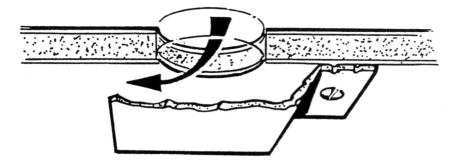

An aluminium shield should be fitted beneath a gas escape hole in order to deflect road dirt away from the opening.
(courtesy Electrolux Leisure Appliances)

Gas connection

For safety reasons, making a gas connection to a fridge should

only be carried out by a person who has experience in fitting gas appliances. This point is clearly stated in the general chapter on gas and is based on recommendations set out in British Standard documentation on LPG appliances. Hence to make the final coupling, a caravan should be taken to a servicing specialist so that the work can be carried out by a skilled fitter.

In practice, coupling up a fridge is very straight forward. On most modern appliances the input point is behind the facia panel and the appropriate coupling is obtainable at any well-stocked accessory shop.

As regards the supply itself, this ***must*** be made using approved copper pipe and compression joints. Under no circumstances should flexible hose and push-on connectors be used because a refrigerator is a permanent installation and not simply a portable appliance. In addition, all threaded joints should be sealed with a proprietary LPG jointing compound such as Calor-Tite. If a thread to thread joint is involved, Calor-Tite is inclined to be messy and some fitters use

PTFE jointing tape instead. But this practice is no longer recommended because PTFE tape can get bunched up, thus failing to get locked into the threads as intended.

If the supply to the fridge involves the use of compression fittings, Calor Gas makes it clear that these should be formed

without the use of a jointing compound. (*Dealer Information*, published by Calor Gas Ref: Safety 301, Reprint 1987, Page 30.)

When viewing the supply as a whole, it is also important to fit an in-line gas tap so that the feed to the refrigerator can be cut-off easily and conveniently.

If the supply has been thoughtfully planned, it will also include an easy way to uncouple the gas feed so that the appliance is easily removeable for servicing. For example it can be helpful to have a short run of feed pipe attached across the top of the fridge, terminating in an easily accessible connection. This is worth adding so that there is every incentive to remove a fridge periodically for maintenance.

As described in the Chapter on gas installations, all connections have to be tested to confirm there are no gas leaks. A naked flame must ***not*** be used, and proprietary test liquids are available which reveal leaky joints. Alternatively, washing up fluid can be diluted with water and smeared around each joint in turn. This is inclined to run away from the test point and it is usually necessary to cup the fluid close to the joint surfaces with the fingers. If the connection is suspect, bubbles will appear as soon as the gas is turned on. A faulty joint can often be improved by tightening; alternatively, it should be re-formed.

Routine servicing work

To help the owner carry out simple servicing work, Electrolux sells packs of items such as a special flue brush and replacement jets. There are small differences from model to model, but the broad principles described and illustrated here are much the same.

In all appliances, it is the burning process which creates sooty deposits and these need to be removed. Moreover, the all-important jet can get clogged with dust, especially if the 'van is stored for several months. This means that the burner isn't going to operate properly.

Before starting the routine servicing work, the fridge must be emptied and the ice tray removed from the freezer compartment. Gas bottles should be disconnected and the power supply from a caravan inboard battery should also be switched off. Finally the entire appliance should be lifted out of the 'van as described above and transferred to a work bench.

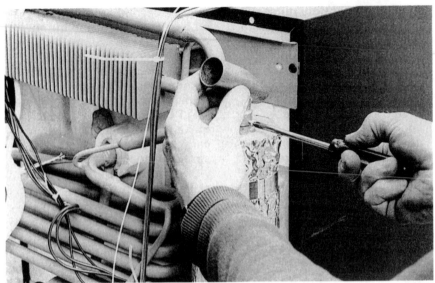

Once all feeds and fixings are disconnected, a refrigerator should be lifted out of the 'van and transferred to a work bench for routine servicing.

Disconnecting the flue and baffle

The 'lazy T' piece on top of the vertical flue tube should be lifted clear. This may involve loosening a small fixing screw on the side of the aluminium casting, although some caravan manufacturers rely on a push fit. Earlier illustrations indicate how the flue is linked to the outlet in the wall.

It may be necessary to loosen a self-tapping screw to remove the 'lazy T' from the top of the vertical flue tube.

The vertical flue tube attached to the casing is padded with an insulant and encased in silver foil. There is also a baffle down the central pipe which comprises a length of wire and a twisted piece of sheet metal attached at the bottom. This is an important component which concentrates the heat from the burner in the lower part of the flue tube.

In order to perform correctly, the lower point of the baffle should be situated 75 mm (3 in) above the bottom of this padded tube. This position is adopted automatically provided the baffle isn't caught when inserted and as long as the suspension wire is seated correctly at the top. When removed from the tube, it will be sooty and should be put to one side in readiness for cleaning. The fridge should now be tipped forward on to its door in order to give better access to the burner assembly.

Provided the baffle suspension wire rests correctly at the top of the burner tube, the baffle will hang in the correct position.

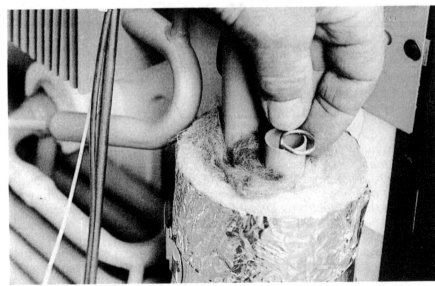

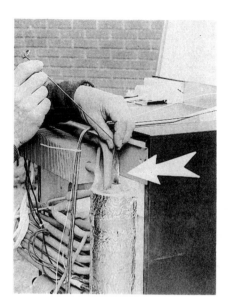

The flue baffle (arrowed) and its support wire are lifted clear from the top of the burner tube for cleaning.

Prior to cleaning the flue, the complete burner assembly should be unscrewed and bent to one side.

A purpose-made brush for cleaning the flue in the burner tube is obtainable from any caravan dealer who stocks Electrolux products.

Removing the burner using the RM212 model as an example

Looking at the foot of the flue tube, you will notice that the burner is protected by a metal enclosure. This has to be removed by releasing its fixing screws. When this has been put to one side, two self-tapping screws should be removed in order to detach the burner assembly. Having removed the screws, the burner is then disconnected by withdrawing it from a keyhole cut-out in its mounting plate. With its feed pipe still connected, it can be carefully bent to one side away from the flue tube. The fridge can now be stood up once again in its normal position.

Other models of fridge such as the Electrolux RM122 and the 2200 have slightly different burners, but the broad principle of attachment is similar and removal is along similar lines.

To inspect the burner, its metal enclosure must be unscrewed and removed.

Cleaning the flue

Cleaning the flue should not be done with the burner in situ because dislodged deposits can fall into the jet. With the burner removed as described in the previous section, it is an easy matter to carry out the cleaning work. A long handled brush which reaches the full length of the burner tube can be purchased from an Electrolux dealer under Part No 151404. Once it has been inserted down the centre of the flue, only a few strokes will be needed to shift all the deposits.

Cleaning the burner and renewing the jet

Sooty deposits should also be removed from the burner. On the RM212 and certain older fridges (e.g. the 120, RAM10, RAM 23 and RAM24 models) you will find that there is also a wire gauze directly above the jet. All components other than the jet itself can be cleaned with a brush, although it is also worth finishing the job by wiping the assembly with a cloth dipped in methylated spirits.

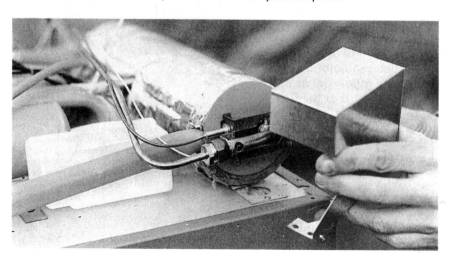

Two spanners are needed when the gas supply pipe to the burner is disconnected to gain access to the jet.

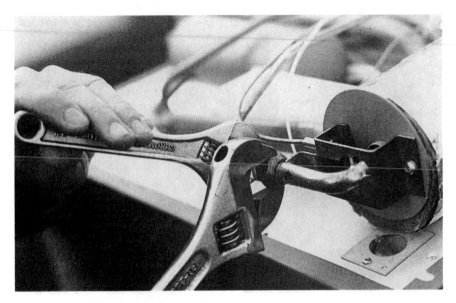

As regards the jet itself, this can sometimes be cleaned using methylated spirits. However, it is strongly recommended that the jet is renewed using an Electrolux replacement. Under no circumstances should metal be poked into the aperture of the jet. The tiny hole is carefully machined and its internal size has been manufactured to critical tolerances. Any attempt to clean this with a filament of wire stands the risk of enlarging the aperture, and even the smallest degree of abrasion can upset the fine tolerances.

Once the gas supply pipe has been disconnected, the burner jet can be easily removed from its housing.

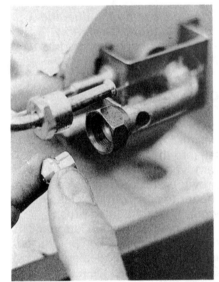

When purchasing a replacement burner, there is no problem obtaining the appropriate unit for fridges in British built 'vans. On a 'van manufactured abroad, however, there may be a jet of a slightly different size. This is matched to the type of gas regulator which is also different on many caravans of foreign origin. For example, those fitted in Germany, Austria and Switzerland are different from the British regulators. Dutch regulators follow either the British standard or the German systems. If in doubt, you must consult your dealer, providing full details about your 'van and the model of fridge.

The hole in the jet is so tiny that cleaning is extremely difficult; it's better to fit a complete replacement.

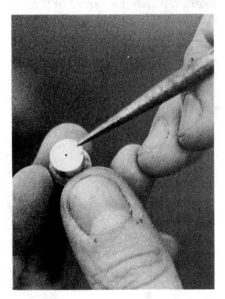

Using the Electrolux RM212 as an example, removing the jet requires two open ended spanners or wrenches. One is to support the cap nut on the burner assembly, the other is to fit on the jet itself. When replacing the jet, it is important to insert the narrow collar into its housing first. Start by tightening the jet with your fingers in order to check that the components haven't been cross threaded and then finish the job with spanners.

Ignition check
Before replacing the fridge, check that the ignition system is operating properly. In the case of models which have piezo ignition, you should depress the button on the facia panel while looking at the quality of spark. If there's any doubt about its power, the electrode tip should be bent very carefully to re-direct the route taken by the spark. Make sure that the screw which holds the electrode in place hasn't worked loose. For best performance, a gap of 3 mm ($\frac{1}{8}$ in) is recommended between the tip of the electrode and the burner.

If there is no spark at all, check the other end of the ignition wire behind the facia panel to see that it hasn't come loose by

Check the small nut for tightness where the thermocouple is connected at the rear of the control facia.

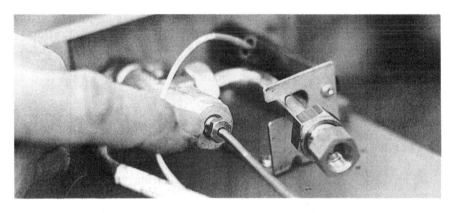

accident. Check that the small earthing screw is fully tightened.

Many modern fridges have an electronic ignition system rather than the piezo igniter. Since 1986, this has become more and more popular. Power to operate this is normally taken from the 12 volt caravan system and the igniter uses a negligible amount of current. Electronic ignition is unlikely to fail and if you find that the system isn't operating, rig up a temporary 12 volt DC supply and check to see that the feed wires haven't become accidentally disconnected when the fridge was removed. If this isn't the reason for failure, repair of an electronic system is not a job for an amateur to tackle.

All Electrolux electronic igniter components are available as spares, but repair work is not for the amateur to tackle
(courtesy Electrolux Leisure Appliances)

Re-assembly
A final task is to clean the glass covered inspection port. On fridges with a port for confirming a burner is alight, the inspection point is in the bottom corner of the cooling compartment. Having cleaned the glass, the burner assembly can be reinstated, making sure that the baffle is replaced in the flue tube as well.

The fridge can now be reinstalled. If the ventilating grilles have been disturbed on the outside of the 'van, these need re-bedding with new sealant. Sealing tape made by W4 Caravan Specialists provides a suitable bedding compound and if there are any doubts about weatherproofing, a silicone sealant can then be applied around the perimeter afterwards. As a word of

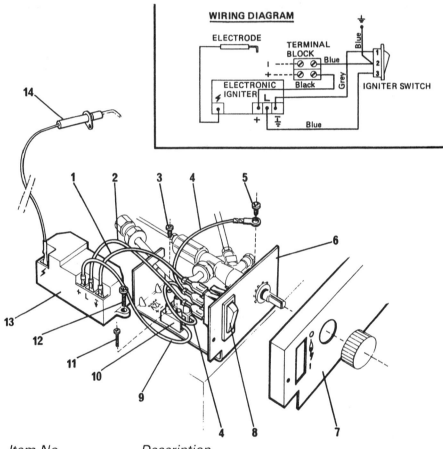

Item No.	Description
1	Lead complete, grey, switch to igniter
2	Lead complete, blue, switch to igniter
3	Screw, Flange Hd., $^5/_{16}$" No. 6
4	Lead complete, blue, switch to terminal block and earth
5	Screw, Pan Hd., $^1/_2$" No. 8
6	Bracket
7	Facia Panel
8	Igniter Switch
9	Lead complete, igniter to terminal block
10	Terminal Block, 2-way
11	Screw, Rd. Hd., $^5/_8$" No. 4, for terminal block
12	Screw, Pan Washer Hd., $^1/_2$" No. 6
13	Electronic Igniter
14	Electrode, with lead

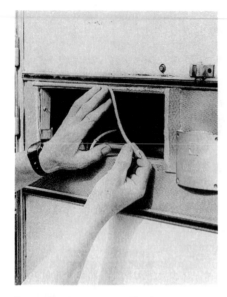

In order to ensure that a ventilation aperture is suitably weatherproofed, sealant is placed around the opening to ensure that the grilles are seated properly.

warning, make sure that the screws holding the grilles in place are not overtightened. If they are old, the plastic grilles may be brittle and an overtightened screw can cause the framework to crack. Admittedly replacements are easy to obtain, but they are not particularly cheap.

A final maintenance task is to clean out the inside of the freezing compartment. A recommended cleaner is Milton sterilising agent which can be applied on a cloth. This is available from chemists and is better known as a product for cleaning baby bottles.

In summary, fitting a new fridge or maintaining an existing one demands patience rather than skill. Only the work coupling up a gas connection would be regarded as an operation more appropriately undertaken by a qualified gas fitter.

If there are problems, this trouble shooting guide is useful for tracking down the fault.

If problems are encountered, the accompanying fault finding guide may provide the answer. In addition, the following customer guide is important to note:

Electrolux Caravan refrigerators: helpful hints

1. Defrosting should be carried out regularly.
2. The refrigerator door should be left open when it is not to be used for some time.
3. Liquid or items with a strong odour should be well packaged.
4. Ensure the ventilation openings are unobstructed.
5. The door is secured by means of the travel catch when the caravan is on the move.
6. Ensure only one mode of operation is used to run the refrigerator at any one time.
7. If the refrigerator fails to work on gas check that:
   i) The gas bottle is not empty.
   ii) The LP gas valves are open.
8. If the refrigerator fails to work on 12v check that:
   i) The 12v supply is connected to the refrigerator.
   ii) The fuse on the 12v supply is intact.
   iii) That the 12v switch is on.
9. If the refrigerator fails to work on 240v check that:
   i) The 240v supply is connected to the refrigerator.
   ii) The fuse is intact if a 13 amp plug is fitted.
   iii) That the 240v switch is on.
10. It is recommended that a service engineer checks the refrigerator once a year. There is a nation wide network of Electrolux service specialists.

(Reproduced courtesy of Electrolux Ltd)

In conclusion, Electrolux is noted for its keen interest in the needs of the caravanner. Any written enquiries sent to the Company are dealt with by expert technical staff.

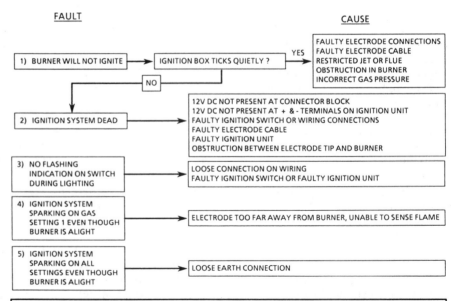

Chapter 13

COOKERS, GRILLS AND HOBS

Kitchen design

A successfully designed caravan kitchen is both functional and attractive. However, the level of provision varies; for instance, imported models don't always include a grill. Similarly, some caravanners consider an oven to be unimportant; on holiday, elaborately cooked meals are seldom served.

'Fast food' is often the order of the day and microwave ovens are becoming increasingly popular. But we all have different priorities and if our caravan lacks certain appliances there's no reason why they shouldn't be added. This chapter explains what is involved.

Safety

Since many cooking appliances are operated by gas, it is essential to read the information here in conjunction with the safety points given in Chapter 10.

In practice, the major part of most projects requires woodworking skills. Owners who are confident in this work would have little difficulty

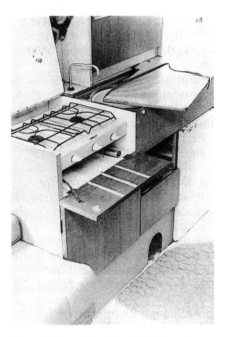

The kitchen in this 1972 Lynton Javelin caravan was due for a re-fit; the hob smoked badly and the grill failed to operate because of rust.

undertaking modifications and installations. Needless to say, all instructions given by the manufacturers of appliances must be observed strictly.

But when it comes to making gas connections, this part of an installation must be carried out by a competent gas engineer as detailed in Chapter 10.

Re-building a kitchen – general principles

Kitchen improvement work relates closely with topics dealt with in other parts of this manual. Where appropriate, reference should be made to the chapters which deal with:

Furniture construction (Chapter 6)
Fresh and waste water systems (Chapter 9)
Gas supply systems (Chapter 10)
Water heaters (Chapter 11) and Refrigerators (Chapter 12)

Acknowledging that many kitchen appliances are heavy, it is unwise to make radical alterations to an interior layout. For instance it was explained in Chapter 4 that a modern chassis is constructed in accordance with the position that the caravan's designer selected for the kitchen. In consequence it would be quite unwise to build a new 'end kitchen' if the original caravan was manufactured with a central kitchen over the axle.

Further problems about 'end kitchens' and body stress were discussed in Chapter 5. Noting that problems have occurred in several caravans recently, it would be unwise to install **additional** heavy appliances (e.g. an oven) in an end kitchen layout. However, it's unlikely that this would cause problems in a **central** kitchen.

A number of manufacturers specialise in kitchen equipment and products can be ordered from a caravan accessory shop. For example, Camping Gaz (GB) market the Mini Kitchen, having taken over the product from Optimus in 1988. There are also attractive enamelled sink and hob products available from Alde International (UK).

Many caravans built in the 1980s were fitted with sinks, drainers, hobs and ovens manufactured by S. & J.E. Fellows. However, Primus-Sievert (UK) acquired the manufacturing, marketing and distribution rights of these appliances in 1989.

Other products will be shown in Joy & King and Burdens Wholesale Catalogues and most caravan dealers can get a prompt delivery of these items.

Having obtained the products required, fitting them is unlikely to be a major undertaking; the following sections give details of three similar projects in which a sink, drainer and hob were fitted.

Fitting the Mini Kitchen – main materials
Both the Mini Kitchen from Camping Gaz (GB) and the units from Alde International (UK) add colour to a kitchen. In the latest caravans, there has been a move away from stainless steel sink and drainer units and products like the ones shown here are justifiably popular. These products are not difficult to fit and the illustrations here are

Several modern kitchen systems are available. The Mini Kitchen is an attractive system featuring colourful enamelled units.

taken from three refurbishment projects in which Mini Kitchens were fitted.

A preliminary job is to level the caravan, this means that if a worktop is fitted later, it can be checked with a spirit level. Water and gas services must be disconnected next and the orginal units removed.

The removal of an old sink and drainer gives a good opportunity to inspect the waste water hose, the fresh water supply, and the general condition of kitchen furniture.

It was decided to mount the replacement units in 18 mm ($^3/_4$ in) plastic laminated chipboard. Normally, this material is too heavy in a caravan but here is an exception. When the cut-outs have been made in the board, the remaining structure amounts to such a small amount of material that the weight is insignificant.

Preparing the top
Plastic laminated chipboard from a DIY Superstore was measured and cut to size. To avoid chipping the veneer, cutting lines were deeply scored by passing a woodworking knife along a steel rule and a fine tooth tenon saw was used to

make clean cuts. The exposed edges were then planed square and covered with matching laminated strip.

Marking the cut-outs for the sink, drainer and hob is less critical because each unit has a substantial lip. Since the lip is likely to hide any minor chipping, the apertures can be cut using an electric jigsaw.

As work progresses, the skeleton framework of the chipboard panel will become increasingly fragile. It must therefore be supported on good trestles and handled with care. Then at the earliest possible opportunity, battens of approximately 25 x 13 mm thickness (1 x $^1/_2$ in) should be screwed around the apertures on the underside to strengthen the structure. As work proceeds, the board should be periodically offered up to the cabinets to confirm there are no obstructions.

When fixing batten supports around the apertures, it must be remembered that space is needed for the metal tags on the units which fasten them to the work top. These have to grasp on the underside of the apertures, hence the need for adequate clearance.

The forward edge of the chipboard top can be finished in matching plastic strips, or a hardwood lipping. In one of the projects shown here, the

With the Mini-kitchen units inverted, the position of each unit was marked with a pencil.

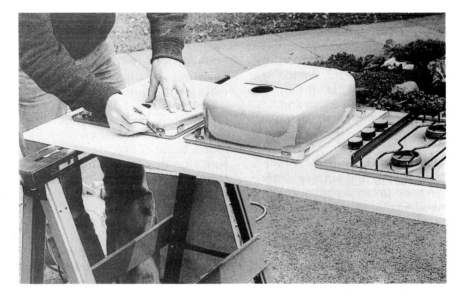

Apertures can be cut with an electric jigsaw; any minor chipping around the edge will be hidden by the lip around the units.

At the earliest opportunity, battens should be fixed in place around each aperture to strengthen the chipboard.

The grill enclosure should be made from aluminium sheeting and fixed to the underside of the work surface directly below the aperture made for the hob.

manufactured edge veneer was retained and a narrow length of chipboard was fixed underneath so that the completed structure resembled a box lid. When placed on top of the kitchen cupboards, it slid down and enclosed the uppermost edges of the units.

Attaching the units

Recognising that surface water can seep under a sink or drainer, the kit includes some sticky backed foam strips. This is cut into lengths and stuck around the perimeter of the cut-outs.

Four claw grips then have to be attached to special lugs on the underside of the sink, drainer and hob. These can be swung out of the way when the units are lowered through the aperture, and then repositioned before tightening.

Damage to the surface glaze on the units will occur if these claw grips are tightened too much. Scrunching sounds are a sure sign that the enamel is starting to craze, and the screw must immediately be loosened-off.

Waste outlets and taps

The Mini Kitchen is supplied complete with waste outlets and rubber washers. A large washer

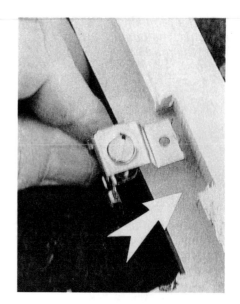

Cut-outs in the support battens around each aperture (arrowed) may be needed in order to accommodate the metal clips which hold the units in place.

provides a water-tight seal underneath and the chrome grille on top is held to the underside outlet by a central bolt. The waste pipe fitted to the outlet should be secured with a hose clip.

Taps serving the sink will be mounted on the laminated top and it's often easier to fit these **before** the completed assembly is finally installed. As a general rule, large holes are needed to

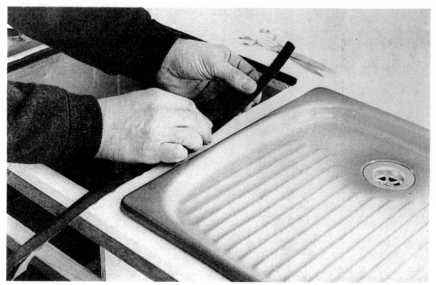

The units are supplied with foam rubber strips which help to prevent water from seeping under the edges of the sink.

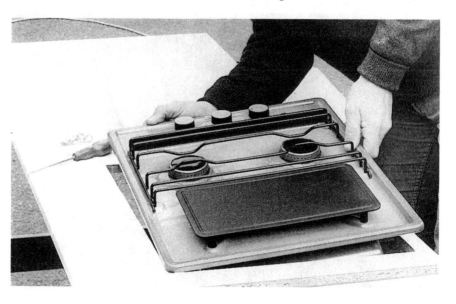

The hob and grill are offered up to the aperture in order to check the fitting.

accept the taps. These can be cut using an electric drill and a high speed 'flat bit'. Where the point is expected to penetrate, cramp a piece of waste timber to the underside of the chipboard; these drill bits can split laminated materials unmercifully when they penetrate the face underneath.

Grill enclosure

Installation instructions must be noted carefully with regard to the grill compartment. The heat under a gas grill is quite considerable and the entire enclosure must be lined with reflective aluminium sheeting. Suitable off-cuts are usually available from a caravan repair shop.

In some instances, you will be able to use the original grill enclosure from the old kitchen which you've dismantled, together with the drop flap door. Ventilation vents may be required and you must conform strictly to any safety points made in the installation instructions.

Gas connection

As described in Chapter 10, connections should be made by a competent gas fitter. If the complete top has not been finally fixed, it may be easier to take this to a caravan specialist so that a length of copper gas pipe can be attached to the coupling on the hob and left as a short tail. This is likely to make it easier for the gas engineer to couple into the main supply when the work top has been finally screwed down.

Sealant

Even though neoprene rubber strips are fitted around the apertures to prevent spilt water

In order to give additional protection to prevent surface water from seeping underneath the units, silicone sealant was applied around the perimeters.

from seeping into the cupboards below, additional protection can be provided with silicone sealant. This can be applied around the perimeter of each unit; a cartridge gun and sealant can be purchased from a DIY Superstore. If it proves difficult to achieve a neat chamfered edge to the sealant, remember it can be smoothed with a finger dipped in methylated spirits before it's allowed to dry.

Glass lid

An attractive 'optional extra' in the Mini Kitchen range is a glass cover for the hob. However, this is **not** industrial glass and the lid

An optional glass cover gives a smart finish to the hob and protects the wall against spitting fat.

must not be lowered until the gas burners have cooled down.

In addition to its aesthetic merit, the raised lid is useful for giving protection from spitting fat, an important asset when fried egg and bacon is on the menu.

Waste water piping

An endearing feature of the Mini Kitchen design is the fact that both sink and drainer have a waste outlet. This is useful when

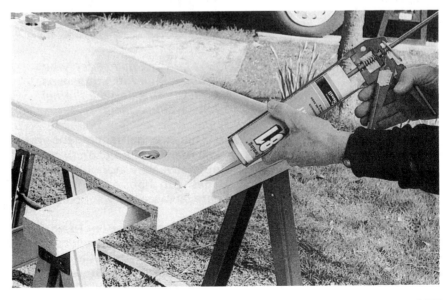

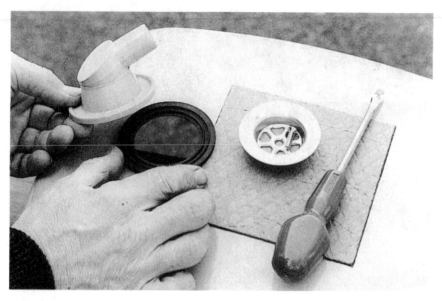

A large rubber washer provided with the units ensures that a water-tight seal is created around the waste water outlet.

dishes are left on a rack but it also provides a useful emptying point for half empty cups or saucepans when the sink has already been filled with clean washing-up water.

When the central screw is tightened, the waste outlet grille is firmly anchored to the plastic assembly on the underside.

A 'Y' junction is needed when fitting a Mini-Kitchen because both the sink and the drainer have waste outlets.

This arrangement means you will need a 'Y' junction to couple up the waste water outlet hoses. These junctions are stocked at a caravan accessory suppliers.

Mini-Kitchen – conclusion

Installing a Mini Kitchen may take the do-it-yourselfer two days to complete. But it looks notably attractive, with several colour options to suit different interiors.

There are other similar products on the market, some of which are designed so that the sink, hob and drainer are one single unit. Examples of this arrangement can be seen in the Primus Sievert brochures. Other types such as Cramer and Alde are also popular and you are advised to look closely at the various models before making a purchase. Their installation, however, is much the same.

Fitting a gas oven

Many caravans have a storage cupboard large enough to accommodate an oven and dealers will normally be able to supply a suitable appliance.

The accompanying photographs show an oven which was being fitted into an early 1970s caravan as part of a refurbishment scheme. Its glass front, easy-clean interior and flame failure device were important features. But like most ovens, it was fairly heavy (20 kg/44 lb) and a shelf had to be constructed using 9 mm ($^3/_8$ in) plywood.

The installation instructions also stressed that a non-combustible material is needed immediately *below* the appliance. Fire resistant boarding can be purchased from a builders' merchant; alternatively a caravan repairer might be able to supply an offcut of aluminium sheet. In some installations, a manufacturer might require that the entire enclosure is lined with a non-combustible material. Moreover, there is certain to be a specification concerning the air space needed around the appliance and this product included trim ventilators to hide the gaps left at the front.

A good feature of the oven illustrated here is the position of the gas connection. Its location below the door provides easy access for a gas engineer when

In this installation project, a glass fronted oven was installed in an early 1970s caravan.

A panel of fire resistant board (arrowed) has to be fixed below the oven as detailed in the installation leaflet.

Two vertical battens installed on either side of the water pump gave extra support to the shelf on which the oven was mounted.

The gas connection point for this oven is conveniently situated under the oven door and behind a narrow cover trim.

the appliance is finally coupled up to the supply system.

Overall, most ovens are fairly easy to install, although the loss of storage space is something to take into account. So, too, is their weight which will reduce the loading margin of the caravan. Apart from that, they open up new possibilities for caravan cuisine.

Microwave ovens in caravans

With more sites offering mains voltage hook-ups, microwave ovens are becoming increasingly popular. However, at the initial start-up, current demand is substantial and on those Continental sites which only provide a 3 amp supply, a microwave oven sometimes throws the site's emergency trip switches. Fortunately, most site hook-ups offer a 5 amp supply or more and provided there are not too many other appliances being used in the caravan at the same time, there's unlikely to be any problem. Using a generator supply is less straightforward and this was discussed in Chapter 8.

Weight is another consideration and the model shown being fitted in the next section weighed 17 kg (37 lb). It is also a problem that some models might sustain damage during towing. The Caravan Club checked this matter with eight manufacturers, publishing their responses in the members' magazine, *En Route* in April 1989. Some did **not** recommend their products for use in caravans and only Sanyo was completely supportive of the idea.

Obviously the suitability of a particular model needs checking before it is purchased. This is particularly true if it's going to be taken to countries offering a 220v mains supply instead of the 240v supply available in Britain.

In some cases, models are advertised which are specially recommended for use in boats or caravans. In addition the author has had several years of good service from a Sanyo model installed in a touring caravan and similar success with a Goldstar miniature microwave fitted in a motor caravan.

Fitting a microwave oven – general principles

There is obvious benefit if the microwave oven installed in a caravan can be easily transferred for use in the home. Both projects shown here were designed so that the oven could be easily removed.

When planning the installations, it was also acknowledged that when an oven is in use, it is more convenient if it is situated above waist height. But this leads to difficulties when towing; bulky items should be placed low down and as near to the axle as possible. In the case of the Sanyo project, the oven was always removed from its head height enclosure before hitching up and placed on the floor in the original box, complete with polystyrene packing.

Anyone who is a confident carpenter could construct the type of enclosure shown in the accompanying photographs. However, there **must** be adequate ventilation at the rear of a microwave oven. If a microwave gets too hot, it is likely to have an automatic cut-out which will interrupt operation until it has cooled down.

A 13 amp socket is also needed near the appliance and this means that the caravan must be wired up to IEE standards as described in Chapter 8.

Making and supporting an enclosure

To support the weight of the appliance, 9 mm ($^3/_8$ in) plywood was used. This was butt jointed at the edges and held both with screws and woodworking adhesive. Ply of this thickness is normally too heavy in a caravan, but this was an exceptional situation. When complete, the enclosure weighed $2^1/_2$ kg (5 lb), roughly the same as four large tins of baked beans.

Having formed a robust enclosure, this now had to be located so that its full weight would be properly supported. The point must be recognised that you could **not** achieve adequate strength if this was screwed into the wall alone. It was decided that at least one side of the enclosure would have its weight transmitted to the floor, either directly or via other furniture. In the caravan shown here, an existing vertical panel at the side of the sink units and cupboards fulfilled this requirement admirably.

Another method of transmitting the weight of a high level microwave oven to the floor would be to use some lengths of 19 mm ($^3/_4$ in) square section steel tubing. Dexion black or grey enamelled tubing is ideal.

Having taken the bulk of the weight in this way, it is then necessary to fix the enclosure to the wall. A recommended method has already been described in Chapter 11, in which a heavy instantaneous water heater had to be wall mounted.

Now a system is needed whereby the oven can be held securely in its enclosure. In this project, four recesses were cut to accommodate about 6 mm ($^1/_4$ in) of its rubber feet. This prevented the appliance from sliding around in the enclosure but left adequate space underneath for air circulation.

Two securing battens were then fitted across the front of the enclosure to prevent the appliance from sliding forwards out of its enclosure. These were positioned so they didn't

Fitting a Sanyo Microwave oven at head height.

a) A vertical support panel (arrowed) ensured that when a heavy microwave oven was installed at head height, much of the weight would be adequately supported.

b) A strong enclosure was made up using fillets glued in place to create sound joints.

c) The dimensions of the enclosure are carefully calculated to enclose and support the full weight of the appliance.

d) Space is needed at the rear of the enclosure to allow heat from the outlet (arrowed) to discharge quickly away from the appliance.

e) When the oven was placed within the enclosure, strips of decorative plywood were used to smarten the unfinished edges of the timber boarding.

f) Once the installation was completed, the benefit of having a microwave oven situated at head height was clearly evident.

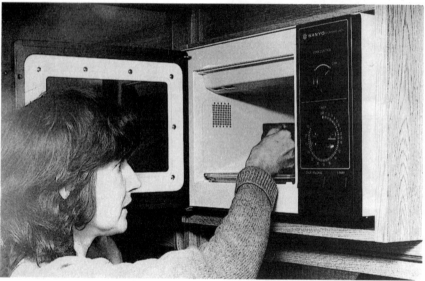

obstruct the door and were made with a dowel peg in one end which inserted into a hole in the plywood enclosure. At the opposite end, a small hole was drilled to receive a round wire nail. This is passed through the side of the enclosure and into the end of the batten thereby locking it in place. The nail was painted in black enamel paint so that it didn't rust.

The final task involved finishing the structure to match-in with the existing furniture. This was done by covering the enclosure with some matching 3 mm decorative plywood bought from a caravan supplier.

Repairing gas appliances
Whereas a competent do-it-yourselfer can do much of the work fitting kitchen appliances, repair work is quite different. In the event there is little to go wrong and routine maintenance work is minimal. However, as regards a gas hob, it is important to ensure that the burners are not blocked by residue from saucepans which have boiled over. Similarly any rust which has appeared during a long lay-up period should be removed. Cleaning work should not be limited to the surface of the hob alone.

Grills can similarly deteriorate

from rusting, especially the metal grid on either side of the central burner. It is this grid which glows red when the burner is alight, thereby helping the toast 'to brown'. But when it rusts badly it may start to disintegrate. There is no easy answer for this and it is usually a sign that a complete replacement is needed.

Another problem which occurs is sootiness around the burners on a hob. Saucepans start to become sooty, too, and sometimes the hob will become unpleasantly smelly. The reason for this is an incorrect balance between gas and air. Some appliances have an air adjuster, but others do not have this facility and the air/gas mix was set up and fixed by the manufacturer.

You should **not** attempt to cure this problem yourself. The appliance must be inspected by a qualified gas engineer who will know how to re-establish the appropriate balance. Whereas the owner is recommended to keep equipment clean, that is as far as it goes. Gas appliances must **not** be serviced by unqualified people.

Chapter 14

SPECIAL CARAVAN FITTINGS

There are many ways to improve the standard of equipment in a caravan. Provided the basic structure is sound, there's no reason why a practical owner shouldn't embark on a renovation scheme. A wide variety of products is available and in this last chapter, several projects are commended.

Fitting a shower
The caravanner who avoids large sites and prefers to stop in remote venues is likely to find a shower most useful. Few people, however, relish a cold shower and details about hot water systems are given in Chapter 11.

A toilet cubicle of suitable size is also needed, even though it *is* possible to purchase a wall fitting for erecting a shower nozzle on the *outside* of a caravan. This allows a curtained enclosure to be used outdoors, using hot water produced from inside the 'van. However, most caravans have an indoor cubicle which is obviously more convenient for conversion.

Principal items needed include a shower tray, a shower curtain, a mixer system with a shower rose and a waste water outlet. From the outset, it is also important to check that the position of the waste outlet isn't going to fall foul of a chassis member directly under the floor.

In the project shown here, a purpose-made tray was purchased from the manufacturer of the caravan and it had to be trimmed and prepared quite extensively before it would fit the cubicle. If you cannot get hold of a tray to match your van, an alternative is to purchase a standard tray from a caravan dealer. These are illustrated in Joy & King and Burdens wholesale catalogues and a dealer will be able to get delivery of any product listed in a matter of days. One example is an acrylic tray with a non-slip base measuring 570 x 570 x 100 mm ($22^1/_2$ x $22^1/_2$ x 4 in).

A caravan shower tray usually has minimal structural strength and needs to be supported by a timber framework. In this project a subframe was built from 9 mm

($^3/_8$ in) plywood and softwood. Then a support platform was fitted *underneath* a raised portion of the moulding to provide a plinth for a portable toilet.

Several tools were used to trim the acrylic tray and it was found that a sharp woodworking knife passed along a steel rule produced the cleanest cutting line. The waste water outlet also had to be formed and a drill attachment known as a 'hole saw' created a clean-edged cut-out through the timber and foam floor.

The tray was fixed using small countersunk brass screws; holes had to be drilled in the acrylic and countersunk so that the heads would finish flush with the surface. A silicone sealer was then used to waterproof all gaps around the tray. This was also applied along the corners of the cubicle walls to prevent water seeping into the rest of the caravan.

As regards the shower mixer, several models are manufactured under the Whale tradename. In addition, the

The shower base was purpose made to suit the toilet compartment.

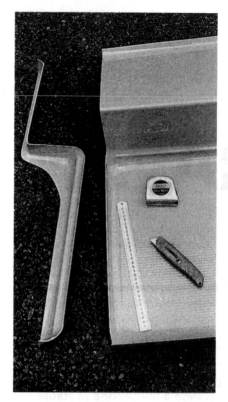

Trimming the excess material was done using a sharp cutting knife and a steel rule.

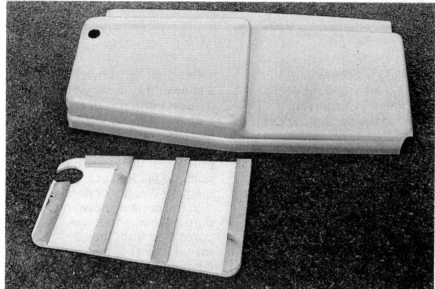

A sub frame was made in ply and deal strips to support the draining section of the tray.

A hole saw drill attachment is an ideal accessory for cutting the waste water hole in the floor.

When the waste water outlet has been fitted, convoluted hose is pushed and clipped into place.

A shower curtain, tubular rail and set of clips made by Croydex was purchased from a DIY superstore.

Whale catalogue shows details of modifications to a plumbing system to provide hot and cold water. As a general rule, the hot feed will have to be routed underneath the caravan from the water heater to the shower cubicle. In addition, the electrical switch on the shower tap will need to be wired up to the water pump.

Recognising that a cubicle will usually house a portable toilet, a bathroom cabinet and a wash basin as well, it is necessary to protect these items by fitting a shower curtain. This should also cover the door so that water isn't driven into the rest of the living area. In this installation it was found that shower curtains intended for the home were equally suitable in a caravan. For instance decorative fabric curtains are available in the Croydex range which are stocked in many DIY Superstores. In addition a matching Croydex mat with suction pads on the underside was purchased. This protects the acrylic base when the cubicle is used as a washroom or toilet.

Lastly, waste water has to be connected up to the shower outlet. This can either be linked with the main waste system via a 'Y' coupling or routed separately for discharge into an alternative waste water container.

Freschor Air Conditioner

Anyone who has taken a caravan to Mediterranean venues in the summer will know that it becomes a 'hot box' when parked on an unshaded site. The ideal answer would be to fit an Electrolux refrigerated air conditioner, but the weight of the appliance is more suitable for motor caravans with sturdier roof structures. However, the Freschor Air Conditioner is much lighter, although it will only operate on flat or nearly flat roof slopes. It cannot be fitted on a caravan with a pitched roof.

The Freschor uses a water evaporative principle rather than the absorption system used in leisure refrigerators. The principle of operation is like the phenomenon experienced if a wet handkerchief is placed over your mouth. When inhaling through the dampened fabric, the air is noticeably cooler and this continues until the handkerchief becomes dry.

Instead of a handkerchief, the Freschor has a special filter which is sprinkled periodically with water. A controlled delivery is induced by a float-operated switch which triggers a pump into action. Most types of caravan pump will fulfil the requirement to deliver water to the Freschor and a standard submersible pump and wall connector was purchased.

The Freschor is built with an electric fan which draws air through the wet filter and directs it into the caravan. This cools the interior. However, the appliance can also act as an extractor and when the control switch reverses the motor, it removes air from the interior.

The installation of a Freshor is straightforward in caravans fitted with a standard sized square rooflight. This is removed and the Freschor Air conditioner installed in its place. It would be more involved creating a new aperture in a caravan which is fitted with non-standard or smaller roof lights.

The work also involves creating a water feed to the Freschor and a narrow gauge plastic pipe is provided with the unit. The route taken by the pipe should also be used for the cable which connects the float switch in the Freschor to the wall connector for a submersible pump. Ingenuity and patience are needed to conceal the pipe and cable. In this project, the wall mounted connector to the pump was fitted in the lower section of a wardrobe. This meant that the plastic pipe and the wire could be led to the ceiling, but out of sight within the wardrobe. On reaching ceiling level, some probing with a length of thick wire in the ceiling void made it possible to pull the pipe and wire into the aperture left by the previous roof light. The link-up was thus

Access to the caravan roof was arranged using sections from an extending ladder, planks, and plenty of rope lashings.

Once the attachment screws were removed, the old roof light was easily detached.

The Freschor appliance must be unscrewed to produce its outer and inner sections.

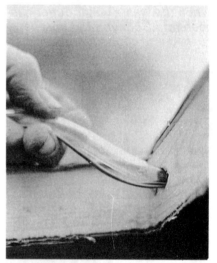

Both the water feed tube and the switching wire were fed through the void in the roof.

Mastic surrounding the aperture was carefully scraped away using an old wood chisel.

New W4 caravan sealant ribbon was carefully positioned around the original aperture.

The outer casing of the Freschor unit was bedded on to the new sealant, using access from the platform.

The panel with all the switching controls was mounted inside the caravan on the ceiling.

complete but without any untidiness on the surface.

Outside the caravan, a hose inlet and electrical connection were fitted for the additional submersible pump. The Freschor supply is normally kept separate from the drinking water system.

Mounting the unit on the roof poses an access problem, but the accompanying photographs show how an extension ladder was split into two sections and used to support a plank crossing over the roof. The sections and the plank were lashed together to create a safe working platform.

When dismantled, the Freschor is in two sections. Once the outer enclosure is located on the roof it is then bolted up to the switching panel which is mounted on the ceiling inside. The two sections are thus pulled together firmly. However, before carrying this out, a bedding of W4 Caravan mastic ribbon was laid on the aluminium roof around the aperture. The Freschor was then located, bolted-up and excess mastic was removed with a cutting knife. Finally, the join was weatherproofed on the outside using a silicone sealant. After five years in use, the join has remained completely rainproof.

In operation, the Freshor undoubtedly lowers the temperature in hot weather. However, it doesn't operate with the speed of a more expensive refrigeration system and it needs to be switched into operation before interior temperatures become unpleasant. But in very hot weather, it's a great asset, especially on unshaded sites.

Replacement rooflights

On a similar theme, there are a number of more sophisticated rooflights than the kind which caravan manufacturers fit as standard. For instance, Carafax rooflights are available with handle operated elevating mechanisms. These are especially robust and are manufactured in standard sizes so that direct replacement is easy.

Sequence photos showing installation of a Fiamma motorised roof ventilator in a glass fibre roof.

Prior to installation, the Fiamma roof vent must be separated into two sections.

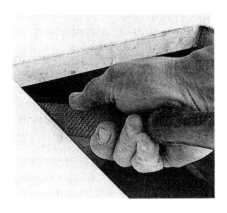

The rough edges of the fibre glass roof panel were tidied up using a wood rasp.

On the inside, the unit is tidied up with the addition of a perimeter frame.

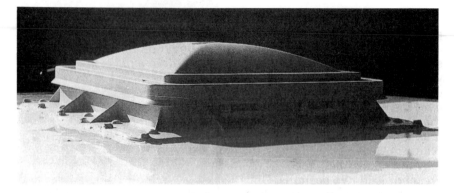

From the outside, the vent is neat and robust; silicone sealant was used around the perimeter.

Another type is a Fiamma rooflight which incorporates a motorised fan. This, too, is manufactured to the standard dimension, and can be fitted as a direct replacement. However, the installation necessitates the provision of a 12v feed to operate the integral fan. This is provided with a twin position switch which allows the fan to operate in either direction. Hence it can be used to extract cooking smells, or alternatively, to draw in air from outside.

The ventilator is provided with a mosquito net gauze to prevent the entry of unwanted insects. Fitting procedure is the same as that for the Freschor installation and bedding mastic **must** be used to produce a weatherproof seal.

Roof ventilators.
A rooflight is no help when a caravan is laid up for an

extended period and a permanently open vent like the Electrolux GY20 is more suitable. This has no moving parts and it's completely weatherproof.

Air extraction is based on aerofoil principles. As breezes pass across the specially shaped dome, suction is created so that air is pulled from the interior. The Electrolux GY20 is simple, effective and easy to fit.

The first job is to dismantle its three chief components. One part is an overlapping collar which allows the GY20 to be fitted to roofs of varying thicknesses. Where necessary

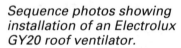

Sequence photos showing installation of an Electrolux GY20 roof ventilator.

On a caravan with a glassfibre roof, a circular hole was cut with an electric jigsaw.

A wooden spacer was cut in the shape of a collar for insertion into the roof void.

When the outer section had been bedded on mastic and screwed into place, the cover was finally added.

used as packing and several layers were cut with an electric jigsaw. The material acts as a spacer between the outer aluminium skin and the interior ceiling ply, but it also provides a solid fixing for the screws which hold the unit in place.

The Electrolux instructions are clear and if an installer has misgivings about cutting a hole in a caravan roof, it must be emphasised that the rubber seal provided with the kit undoubtedly keeps out the rain. However, it is still advisable to add some W4 bedding sealant as a further precaution.

A pleasing feature of the GY20

ventilator is the fact that its transluscent plastic admits light. If situated near a hob, it will be another product to help reduce condensation. It is inexpensive and requires no maintenance.

The Carver Carafan
The most obvious place for installing a Carafan from Carver is in a toilet compartment, especially if a shower has been fitted.

Most caravanners have house rules about the use of a toilet, and the fact that it is situated close to a kitchen underlines the benefit of having an extractor fan. Two Carafan units are available, both of which operate from a 12v low voltage supply. The standard version has a simple ON/OFF switch; the de-luxe model has time-lapse switching. This means that you can leave the fan in operation for a pre-selected time ranging from 60 seconds to 15 minutes. This can be an invaluable battery saver because you don't need to remember the fan is operating; the motor will switch off automatically.

Sequence photos showing installation of a Carafan 12v motorised extractor. Prior to installation, the two units of the Carafan must be separated.

The Electrolux GY20 ventilator is a neat unit which ensures that a caravan is kept constantly fresh inside.

this can be reduced in depth using a hacksaw. As regards location, the GY20 must be positioned **between** the struts which form the roof framework.

When fixed to a hollow caravan roof, you will also need to insert some timber packing pieces into the void between the interior ceiling ply and the exterior aluminium sheet. In the project illustrated here, waterproof Sterling board was

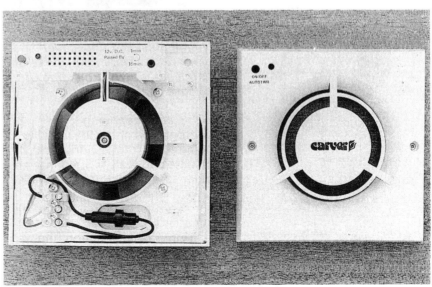

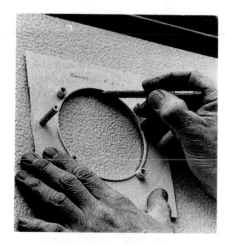

Part of the casing can be used to mark out the necessary aperture on the side wall of the caravan.

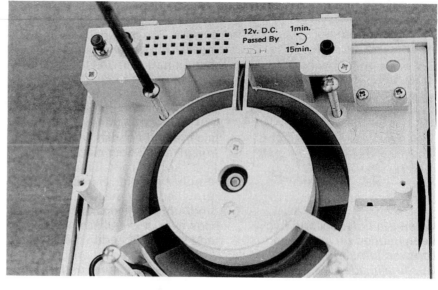

Working on a caravan with sandwich construction side walls, the aperture was carefully drilled around the perimeter.

By adding cuts with a sharp knife, the sandwich of aluminium, foam and inner ply was removed.

The inner part of the unit is bolted through to the outer panel, thus sandwiching itself on the wall panel.

On the outside a final cover piece is screwed into place prior to the addition of a beading of silicone sealant.

The accompanying photographs show the Carafan being fitted into a sandwich constructed wall. If fitted into an older caravan with hollow walls, it will be necessary to insert some pieces of wood around the cut aperture to act as spacers.

Prior to its installation, the two main pieces of the fan must be separated. In fact part of the outer face plate can be used for

marking the cutting line for the circular opening. Having done this, some installers might then form the cut-out with an electric jigsaw. In this project, however, only hand tools were used.

Using a hand drill, a series of very small holes were drilled around the pencilled aperture marked on the exterior aluminium. This was fifteen minutes well spent because when a sharp bladed woodworkers' knife was used next, it quickly broke through the aluminium portions left between each of the drill holes to produce a symmetrical circle. The polystyrene insulant could then be easily removed.

The inner and outer parts of the casing are held together by bolts, sandwiching the wall structure in the process. Again it is advisable to apply sealants as discussed earlier in this chapter.

As regards the feed cable to the fan itself, this must be derived from a suitable fused supply. The ideal would be to take the supply directly from an auxiliary accessory source on a 12v distribution unit. However, if a feed is drawn from a nearby lamp fitting, it is advisable to fit an in-line fuse holder near the fan. This should contain a 10 amp fuse.

As regards performance, the

Carafan has good pulling capacity. It is claimed to withdraw 29 cubic feet of air per minute and if you put your hand over the vent outside, the outflow is notable.

Rondo Cooker Hood
This type of extractor is designed for the kitchen. Steam from saucepans or a kettle will condense on cold surfaces and in a poorly ventilated caravan, the resulting build-up of damp can cause problems. The best answer is to remove steam at its source.

The Rondo Cooker Hood comprises a metal enclosure which houses a 12v fan and a fluorescent strip light. The motor is situated on the rear of the casing and its fan expells steam collected within the enclosure to the outside.

Sequence photos showing installation of a Rondo cooker extractor hood.

The Rondo cooker hood features one switch to activate the extractor fan and another to operate a fluorescent light.

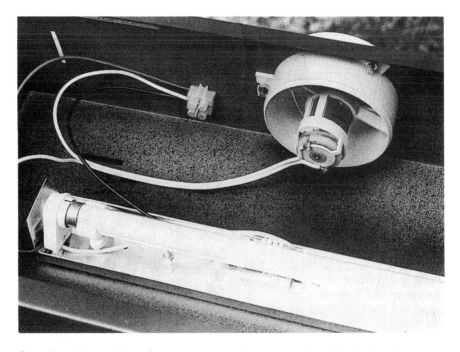

Opening the casing gives access to the connecting block for the 12v supply.

The extractor fan is located at the rear of the casing and a plastic vent is provided.

A special weatherproof cover bought from a caravan accessory supplier was screwed into position.

Unfortunately, a number of caravans lack a suitable position above a stove to mount this appliance. On the other hand it is something which is worth including in a complete kitchen re-vamp wherever possible. For instance the accompanying illustrations show how the Rondo cooker hood was fitted in a self-build motor caravan. This presented a particular problem on account of a sloping wall. However, by constructing a ply structure which created a vertical surface inside the 'van, and then by forming an enclosure directly behind the fan using glass fibre filler, the problem was overcome.

On the outside, a standard ventilator purchased from a caravan accessory shop was fitted. A hole was then cut through the side of the caravan to align with the position of the fan on the inside.

The electrical supply was taken back to a 12v fused distribution unit and connected up to the supply point intended for auxiliary appliances. In use, the hood is a useful addition. The integral light is not very strong and should only be considered as background illumination, but the small fan is powerful and removes steam effectively.

Fitting a radio cassette appliance

With a 12v supply on hand, it is surprising that few caravanners fit a radio in their caravan. A cassette radio is even better and suitable types are available from all auto stores. As a security measure it may be prudent to purchase a security coded model or one which is removable. On the other hand, it isn't difficult to create a false panel which hides the unit from view whenever the 'van is unoccupied.

To obtain radio reception, an external aerial is necessary because the aluminium exterior

A Panasonic security coded radio cassette player proved an ideal unit to install in a caravan.

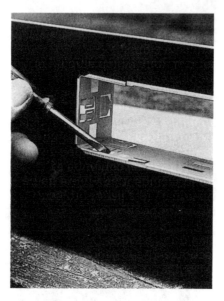

The unit is held within a metal case which is inserted into a cut-out and then secured with locking tabs.

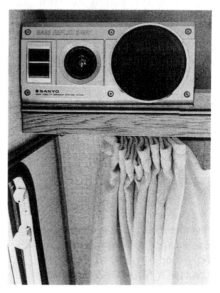

Speakers used on a car parcel shelf are equally at home in a caravan.

To couple up the wires tidily to a four speaker system and to the power supply, a connecting block was used.

Wall mounted speakers are often supplied with a cardboard template, making it easy to prepare cut-outs in the sides of a cupboard.

On a touring caravan, an aerial fitted high on a side wall can be in close proximity to the radio inside.

of a caravan creates a shield. In some cases fluorescent lights can cause interference to radio reception too, although audio tapes operate without problem. The cure is to fit a suppressing unit in the lamps nearest the radio. A suppressor made by LabCraft is available through caravan accessory shops and this is fitted within the lamp enclosure itself.

Fitting a cassette radio usually means forming a cut-out in the side of a cupboard, wardrobe or high level locker. The thin ply usually used for caravan furniture can easily be cut using a sharp woodworking knife which is passed several times across the surface using a steel rule for guidance. This produces a clean cut-out.

When comparing possible positions for the unit, remember that a number of wires will have to be connected at the rear of the radio casing. For this reason, access to the connecting strip is

an important requirement. Moreover, since it is best if the lead from the aerial is long enough and doesn't need an extension cable, the position for the radio has to be considered in conjunction with the mounting point for the aerial.

Thought must also be given to the location of speakers. Arguably the quality of stereo sound is not particularly memorable in a caravan, but in spite of this, it's appropriate to fit a *pair* of speakers. There's a choice of two types. Models designed to fit on the rear parcel shelf of a car are ideal for installing on a high level caravan shelf. Alternatively the types intended for fitting in a car door can be easily fitted in the side of a cupboard or high level locker. The accompanying photographs show these alternatives and are taken from two different caravan projects.

Once again, it is best if the 12v power supply is drawn via a 12v fused distribution unit. However, car radios are usually supplied with an in-line fuse holder so this is satisfactory if the 12v supply comes direct from the towcar battery or an interior feed.

Since the instructions with car audio products are usually very clear, the only work of significance in a caravan installation is the carpentry. As regards an external aerial, make sure that it is bedded on some proprietary sealant as described in the earlier sections in order to create a weatherproof installation. Both roof and wall-mounted aerials are available, although the latter is usually easier to fit neatly. This is because the incoming coaxial cable can be led directly into a high level locker and conveniently kept out of sight.

Fitting a caravan safe

Reports of caravan break-ins are not unusual and according to the caravan press, several

Continental venues have persistent problems. Items like cameras, passports, jewellery, travellers' cheques, credit cards and currency need to be satisfactorily secured. Curiously there are not many caravan safes on the market, and a few of the boxes intended for valuables are extremely easy to force open. The Bulldog Carasafe from Leisure Crafts is an exception.

In shape, the Carasafe is a cube measuring 200 x 200 x 200 mm (8 x 8 x 8 in). As the photograph shows, this is sufficient to provide space for an SLR camera, a wallet, passports and sundry small items. In thickness, the casing is manufactured of heavy gauge steel. For instance the door is 10 mm ($^3/_8$ in) thick and the remaining sections are 6 mm ($^1/_4$ in) thick. Add to this a seven lever lock with 12,000 different key combinations and a break-in will beat many burglars. However, the Carasafe must be thoughtfully installed so that a thief cannot simply lift it out to take it to a workshop with gas cutting equipment.

Perhaps the only disadvantage with a Carasafe is its weight. However, at 13.6 kg (30 lb), it is less heavy than a large Calor gas cylinder. It also scales less than a TP2 battery box, which complete with battery weighs around 19 kg (42 lb).

With weight in mind, a Carasafe should be installed as close to the axle as possible. Three models are available and these have fixing holes for attachment bolts in different faces of the cube. In the installation shown in the accompanying photographs, a model was chosen with holes in one of the sides to give a horizontal mounting position.

The idea is to bolt the Carasafe directly through the floor, with a metal plate acting like a large reinforcing washer on the underside. For security

Sequence photos showing installation of the Carasafe made by Leisure Crafts (Bridgnorth) Ltd

The robustly made Carasafe is large enough to hold items like passports, travel documents and an SLR camera.

The Carasafe is supplied with steel fixing straps, high tensile bolts and two keys.

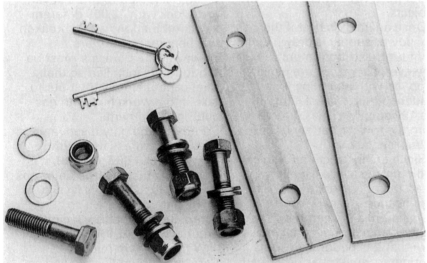

reasons, the bolt heads will be outside whereas the nuts will be hidden within the enclosure of the safe itself. In other words any attempt to unscrew the bolts from the outside would leave them freely revolving.

For additional protection, the Carasafe was also situated in a cupboard where its presence wouldn't be immediately obvious. Fixed underneath a sink, it can be hidden by the contents of the kitchen cabinet.

All you need to check before drilling holes is to ensure there are no chassis members underneath the floor to foul the position of the bolts.

Lastly, when coupling up the bolts, you are going to need someone to hold a spanner on the heads outside while you tighten-up the nuts on the inside. Overall this is a sturdy product which provides peace of mind and a safe home for valuables.

In this project, the Carasafe was fitted in a cupboard near the entrance and close to the axle.

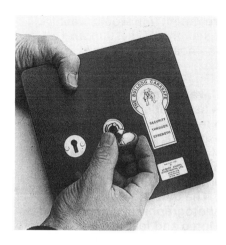

If not fitted flush to the floor and under a carpet, you'll need to fit the door knob first.

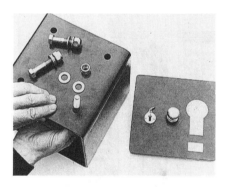

Models are available with holes drilled on several faces to suit different fitting situations.

With the Carasafe in position and the bolts inserted, the steel strips were located underneath the floor.

Water treatment

Water quality is an emotive subject. In some countries, tap water is only used for washing whereas bottled water is used for drinking. Water treatment takes different forms. For instance a simple paper filter will remove solid material, but it doesn't improve the taste of water or give any measure of sterilisation. On the other hand, a charcoal filter like the Whale unit described in Chapter 9 is able to improve taste which is useful when a supply contains unpalatable chemicals. But if a charcoal filter improves taste, it certainly doesn't play a sterilising role. To achieve this objective, you need to turn to a product like the IMI water treatment system.

The IMI unit shown in the photographs has to be installed somewhere in the pipe feed between the taps and the water source. To begin with, water is passed through a filter to remove solid matter. Then the unit deals with minute bacteria and viruses using short wave ultra violet light.

Sequence photos showing installation of the IMI water treatment unit from James Vale Water Treatment Ltd.

The unit can be positioned under a sink as long as there's access to replace the ultra violet lamp.

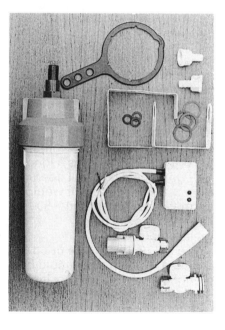

The kit comprises fixing brackets, a central control box and all the necessary hose unions.

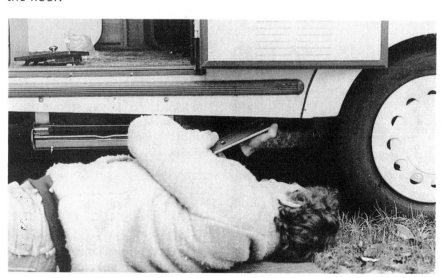

Since the unseen UV lamp is a vital component, a warning lamp on the main control panel verifies that it is working correctly.

The touring caravan model is fitted with push-on terminals for the water hoses.

One of the problems in water supply systems is the fact that certain viruses can somehow survive for considerable periods even when water has been chlorinated. With this in mind, the IMI purifier contains a long UV light tube which will operate from a 12v DC supply. It would normally last for around 7,500 hours before needing replacement.

The IMI unit has to be fitted **inside** a caravan and should be mounted in an upright position. A mounting bracket is contained within the kit and most caravanners would fit the unit under a sink. The complete assembly features a control box and the photographs show that components have to be assembled during installation.

As regards wiring, it is best if the lamp is connected up in conjunction with pump operation. The neon lamp only needs to operate when water flows through the system, so it is helpful if this is switched at the same time as the electric pump begins to deliver water as explained in the instructions.

The product is full of fail safe devices. For instance if a fault develops and the germicidal UV lamp fails to operate, a sensor detects the fault and triggers a warning buzzer. The only feature it fails to deal with is the matter of taste. In other words if you are seeking the ultimate in water treatment you would want to install the IMI system **and** a charcoal in-line filter.

Caravan step

A useful addition for a caravan is a fold-out step. This can be especially useful for short picnic stops, even if a larger portable platform is better once you've arrived on site.

The unit shown in the photographs is manufactured by Morco and features a neat slide-away action. The installation kit is provided with two heavy gauge mounting brackets and four bolts with Nylock shake-resistant nuts.

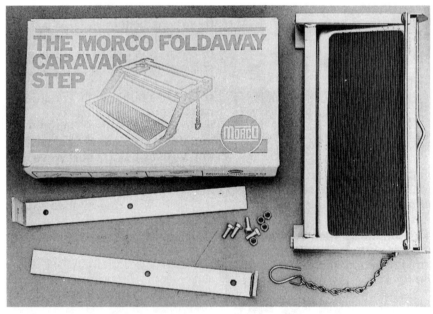

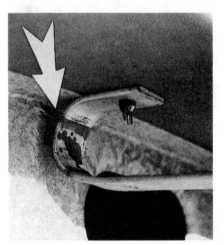

Sequence photos showing installation of a Morco Foldaway caravan step.

The Morco Foldaway step is a useful addition and can be fitted without needing to drill the chassis.

The fixing brackets were bent in a vice (arrowed) in order to give clearance from the chassis.

The front of the support brackets was bolted to the longitudinal timber batten forming the side skirt.

When ready for the road, you fold the step and slide it back along its side rails.

When fitting the step, it may be necessary to make small modifications to the mounting arrangement in accordance with the type of chassis and the amount of free space available. Obstructions like glass fibre side skirts, for instance, may need alterations.

The key point to remember is that a modern lightweight chassis must *not* be drilled for reasons given in Chapter 4. Even the heavier older chassis are best left undrilled as well. In other words, you will have to bolt the unit through the floor itself, making sure that any support plates inside the caravan will be hidden under the door mat.

The weight of an adult using a step can be quite considerable and you need to think carefully about the installation in respect of your particular caravan. Once the best means of attachment is established, the job itself is unlikely to take long.

Lastly it is important to keep the sliding sections of the step well greased. Even though it is

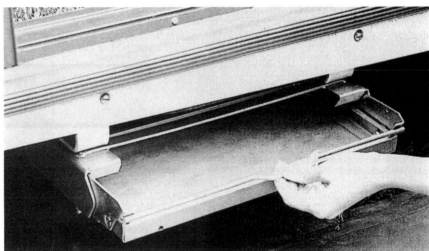

finished with a galvanised coating, exposure to road dirt can cause the moving parts to seize up. Provided this is recognised, the Morco step will give good service.

Other accessories
Obviously this list of projects could include many more items, but no manual can hope to include everything. When looking further, you will find there are a number of TV aerials on sale which can be permanently fitted. Some models even include in-line 12v control units which amplify or reduce a signal.

There are also solar and wind generators on the market. Perhaps it should be pointed out that these are mainly intended to provide a trickle charge for an inboard battery, thereby keeping it in sound condition. They are not able to provide a supply which is powerful enough, or sufficiently plentiful, to eliminate a battery altogether.

Lastly, there has been a justifiable interest in the Thetford Cassette toilet. These can be fitted by a competent do-it-yourselfer, but check its dimensions first. A number of older caravans lack the necessary space to

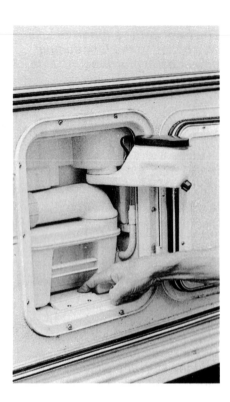

accommodate this sizeable unit.

As regards installation, a Thetford Cassette toilet involves a number of constructional tasks and the instruction manual explains everything clearly. In addition, a video programme has been made to show the fitting process. This is intended for caravan dealers, but it's likely that anyone supplying the appliance would be willing to lend the video to a customer. If your caravan has the space, this is undoubtedly another important contributor to caravan conveniences.

If a caravanner is anxious to receive good TV reception on holiday, there are many aerials for DIY installation.

The Cassette toilet from Thetford is sold with full instructions for owner installation.

Appendix A

The approximate age of a caravan can be gauged using the following details:

1960 Features
★ Late 1960s – Labcraft invented fluorescent lights for caravans using a 12v power source.
★ Gas cylinders carried on an open rack on the drawbar.
★ Water jugs became redundant as manual pumps appeared.
★ Trackway for an awning not often fitted.

1970 Features
★ Drawbar mounted locker boxes appeared in early 70s for the gas cylinders.
★ 1972 More caravans sold than ever before (67,000 tourers), due to the threat of purchase tax, forerunner of VAT.
★ Gas lamps continued alongside fluorescent lights until mid 70s.
★ Chassis like Peak, B&B and CI were heavy, needed painting and employed springs and shock absorbers.
★ Reversing on the over-ride mechanism required someone to engage a clip behind the coupling when reversing started.
★ Water pumps remained as manual units.

★ Body made around framework, clad in aluminium sheet and lined inside with ply.
★ Insulation modest. Floors usually uninsulated; wall voids filled with glass fibre quilt or polystyrene panels.
★ In 1978, use of non-safety glass became illegal. Aluminium frames went and acrylic double glazed windows appeared.
★ Post October 1979 all caravans had to have a rear fog lamp.
★ The need for a fog lamp feed led to the introduction of a double socket system with the towcar.

1980 Features
★ Bonded sandwich floors introduced at start of decade; bonded walls followed.
★ Lightweight galvanised chassis introduced, particularly from Al-Ko who took over B&B Chassis.
★ Automatic brake disengagement mechanisms fitted into drums.
★ Rubber suspension replaced coil springing on the lightweight chassis systems.
★ From early 1980s so many electrical items developed that fused distribution panels were introduced.
★ Separate inboard 12v batteries commonplace for the increase in low voltage appliances.

★ Electric water pumping became standard.
★ Wedge shaped designs arrived in mid 1980s for improving petrol economy.
★ From 1985, most caravans had an integral gas locker box rather than a drawbar 'add-on'.
★ In April 1989, auto reverse brakes made manadatory.
★ Mid 1980 saw many hot water systems installed.
★ The Cassette Toilet in late 1980s revolutionised the bathroom and emptying arrangements.

1990 Features
★ Fire retardant foams mandatory on all cushions
★ Fire alarms introduced.
★ Ripple finish used for most bonded sandwich walls lost favour with some manufacturers; smooth finishes returned.
★ Almost all caravans wired for mains as standard.
★ Low voltage fused distribution panels less like Concorde flight deck and more discrete.
★ Internal creature comforts reached unprecedented levels.

Appendix B

Contact Addresses

Please note:
Addresses change with disturbing frequency and the list below was correct in 1993. If there is any difficulty with the address for a manufacturer of a caravan product, check the advertisements in national caravan journals. As regards repair materials, information will often be found in DIY magazines.

Abbey Caravans Ltd, Swift Group, Dunswell Road, Cottingham, North Humberside, HU16 4JS (Caravan manufacturer)

ABI Caravans Ltd, Swinemoor Lane, Beverley, North Humberside, HU17 0LJ (Caravan manufacturer)

Adria Caravans, IMV Automotive International Ltd, Phoenix Chambers, 15-17 High Street, Bedford, Bedfordshire, MK40 1RN (Caravan importer)

AFS Rotel Ltd, Firsdale Industrial Estate, Nangreaves Street, Leigh, Lancashire, WN7 4TN (Manufacturers of the Scott stabiliser)

Alde International (UK) Ltd, Sandfield Close, Moulton Park, Northampton, NN3 1AB (Manufacturers of kitchen systems and central heating units)

Al-Ko Kober Ltd, Queensway, Royal Leamington Spa, Warwickshire, CV31 3JP (Manufacturers of caravan chassis, running gear and stabilisers)

Apollo Chemicals Ltd, Sandy Way, Amington Industrial Estate, Tamworth, Staffordshire, B77 4DS (Manufacturers of adhesives)

Automotive Products plc, Tachbrook Road, Leamington Spa, Warwickshire, CV31 3ER (Manufacturers of A.P. Lockheed brake assemblies)

Avondale Caravans, Avondale Coachcraft Ltd, Carlyon Road, Atherstone, Warwickshire, CV9 1JE (Caravan manufacturer)

Bailey Caravans Ltd, South Liberty Lane, Bristol, Avon, BS3 2SS (Caravan manufacturer)

BCA Leisure Ltd, Unit 7E, Westfield Mill, Mytholmroyd, Hebden Bridge, West Yorkshire, HX7 8SH (Manufacturers of Powerpart mains kits and Mobile Power unit)

Beauvale Furnishings Ltd, Hallam Fields Road, Ilkeston, Derbyshire, DE7 4BQ (Caravan cushion and mattress manufacturer)

Beckmann Stain Advisory Service, 94 Rickmansworth Road, Watford, Hertfordshire, WD1 7JJ (Manufacturers of Stain Devils)

Bessacar Caravans, Rowms Lane, Swinton, Mexborough, South Yorkshire, S64 8AD (Caravan manufacturer)

British Standards Institution, Linford Wood, Milton Keynes, Buckinghamshire, MK14 6LE (For information on BS requirements for touring caravans)

Buccaneer Caravans Ltd, The Airfield, Full Sutton, York, North Yorkshire, YO4 1HS (Caravan manufacturer)

H. Burden Ltd, Pytchley Lodge Road Industrial Estate, Kettering, Northamptonshire, NN15 6BR (Wholesale distributors of caravan accessories)

Burstner Caravans, Global Caravans Ltd, Roydon Mill Caravan Park, Roydon, Nr. Harlow, Essex, CM13 5EJ (Caravan importer)

Buzzard Caravans, BPH Designs Ltd, 109 Heath Road, Leighton Buzzard, Bedfordshire, LU7 8AD (Manufacturers of 'made-to-order' caravans)

Bumper to Bumper Ltd, 38 Melford Court, Hardwick Grange, Woolston, Warrington, Cheshire, WA1 4SD (Manufacturers of stabilisers)

Breckland Trading Co, Breckland House, Croxton, Thetford, Norfolk, IP24 1NQ (Manufacturers of Ranger Power pack)

Bruna Leisure Ltd, Mowbray Drive, Blackpool, Lancashire, FY3 7UN (Manufacturers of the Mowbray Stabiliser)

C.A.K. Ltd, 10 Princes Drive, Kenilworth, Warwickshire, CV8 2FD (Manufacturers of water systems including inboard water tanks)

Calor Gas Ltd, Appleton Park, Riding Court Road, Datchet, Slough, Berkshire, SL3 9JG (LPG supplies and appliances)

The Camping and Caravanning Club, Greenfields House, Westwood Way, Coventry, CV4 8JH

Camping Gaz (GB) Ltd, 9 Albert Street, Slough, Berkshire, SL1 2BH (LPG appliances: heaters, refrigerators, stoves, and Optimus Mini Kitchen)

Carafax Ltd, Rotterdam Road, Sutton Fields Industrial Estate, Hull, HU8 0XB (Manufacturers of caravan sealants)

Caralevel Ltd, Springhill Farm, Great Horwood Road, Little Horwood, Milton Keynes, MK17 0PE (Electrically operated automatic levelling system)

Caralux Upholstery, Amber Buildings, Meadow Lane, Alfreton, Derbyshire, DE55 7EZ, (Manufacturers of caravan upholstery)

Carlight Caravans Carlight Trailers Ltd, Church Lane, Sleaford, Lincolnshire, NG34 7DE (Caravan manufacturer)

The Caravan Club, East Grinstead House, East Grinstead, West Sussex, RH19 1UA

Caravan Life Magazine, Sanglier Publications Ltd, c/o Stuart Craig, Editor, 76 Gordon Road, Carshalton Beeches, Surrey, SM5 3RE

Caravan Magazine, Link House, Dingwall Avenue, Croydon, CR9 2TA

Caravan, Motorcaravan & Camping Mart, Aceville Publications Ltd, 89 East Hill, Colchester, Essex, CO1 2QN

Carver & Co. (Engineers) Ltd, Engine Lane, Coppice Side Industrial Estate, Brownhills, Walsall, Wesdt Midlands, WS8 7ES (Manufacturers of water and space heaters; Carafan extractor)

Castleton Caravans Ltd, Tinneys Lane, Sherbourne, Dorset, DT9 3EA (Caravan manufacturer)

CEC Plug-in-Systems, Willerby, Hull, North Humberside, HU10 6EQ (Manufacturers of Kestrel charger/distribution system)

Chamtek Adhesives Division, Newburn Bridge Road, Ryton Industrial Estate, Blaydon-on-Tyne, Tyne and Wear, NE21 4SQ (Manufacturers of Plusbond 140 and other adhesives)

Chateau Caravans (UK) Ltd, Alington Road Industrial Estate, St. Neots, Cambridgeshire, PE19 2SJ (Caravan importer)

Chronar Ltd, Unit 1, Waterton Industrial Estate, Bridgend, Mid Glamorgan, CF31 3YN (Manufacturers of solar power charging systems)

Coachman Caravans Co Ltd, Amsterdam Road Sutton Fields Industrial Estate, Hull, North Humberside, HU8 0XF (Caravan manufacturer)

Compass Caravans Ltd, Riverside Industrial Estate, Langley Park, Durham, DH7 6TY (Caravan manufacturer)

Cramer UK Sales Office, Marcus House, Park Hall, Stoke on Trent, Staffordshire, ST3 5XA (Manufacturers of gas cooking appliances)

The Croydex Co. Ltd, Central Way, Walworth Industrial Estate, Andover, Hampshire, SP10 5AW (Manufacturers of plastic accessories: shower curtains, rails, non slip mats)

Elddis Caravans (Consett) Ltd, Delves Lane, Consett, County Durham, DH8 7LG (Caravan manufacturer)

Electrolux Leisure Appliances, Oakley Road, Luton, Bedfordshire, LU4 9QQ (Manufacturers of refrigerators and caravan accessories)

Elsan Ltd, Buxted, Uckfield, Sussex, TN22 4LW (Manufacturers of caravan toilets and chemicals)

Eriba Caravans, Eriba Ltd, The Priory, A417 Faringdon Road, Lechlade-on-Thames, Gloucestershire, GL7 3EZ (Caravan importer)

Peter Everard Ltd, 83 Cashes Green Road, Cashes Green, Stroud, Gloucestershire, GL5 4RA (Manufacturers of Zig fused 12v distribution units; agent for PAG solar units)

Evode Ltd, Industrial Division, Common Road, Stafford, ST16 3EH (Manufacturers of Evo-Stik Adhesives)

Fiamma UK Sales, Evershed Wells and Hind, 10 Newhall Street, Birmingham, B3 3LX (Distributors of caravan accessories including diapraghm pumps)

Fleetwood Caravans Ltd, Hall Street, Long Melford, Sudbury, Suffolk, CO10 9JP (Caravan manufacturer)

Foam for Comfort, 401 Otley Old Road, Cookridge, Leeds, LS16 7DF (Suppliers of Dunlopillo and plastic foams for caravan upholstery)

Freedom Caravans, Silkmore Lane, Stafford, ST17 4JG (Caravan manufacturer)

Gimeg UK Ltd, 8 Sedling Road, Wear East Industrial Estate, Washington, Tyne & Wear, NE38 9BZ (Distributors of Riviera space heater, Rinnai water Heater, Rondo cooker hood, Freschor air conditioner)

Goldstar UK Sales Ltd, Goldstar House, 264 Bath Road, Slough, Berkshire, SL1 4DT (Manufacturers of compact microwave ovens)

Grade (UK) Ltd, 5 Factory Lane, Beeston, Nottingham, NG9 4AA (Manufacturers of Gaslow gauges and distributors of omnidirectional TV aerials)

G. & J. Hall Ltd, Burgess Road, Sheffield, S9 3WD (Manufacturers of Conecut HSS Sheet and tube drills)

Hawkins Electrical Ltd, Heath Road, Skegness, Lincolnshire, PE25 3SU (Specialists in site hook-up installations; former distributor of Carapart kits)

Hella Ltd, Wildmere Industrial Estate, Banbury, Oxon, OX16 7JU (Manufacturers of electrical towing accessories: relays, plugs, sockets)

Hobby Caravans (UK) Ltd, PO Box 114, Derby, DE2 7FE (Caravan Importer)

Hodgson Sealants, Belprin Road, Beverley, HU17 0LN (Manufacturers of caravan sealants)

H.C. Holifield (Oxford) Ltd, Nuffield Way, Abingdon, Oxfordshire, OX14 1RX (Manufacturers of the Handy Hitch)

Hunting Specialised Products (UK) Ltd, Acorn House, New Lane, Leeds, LS11 5DZ (Manufacturers of Finnigan's Hammerite Paint)

Holt Lloyd Ltd, Lloyds House, Alderlay Road, Wilmslow, Cheshire, SK9 1QT (Manufacturers of Holts Spraymatch paints)

Honda (UK) Ltd, Power Road, Chiswick, W4 5YT (Manufacturers of portable generators)

ICI Paints, Wexham Road, Slough, Berkshire, SL2 5DS (Manufacturers of Dulux wood colourisers)

International Concessionaires Ltd, T/A Gordon Lamb Caravans, Station Road, Lowdham, Nottinghamshire, NG14 7DU (Distributor of Westfalia SSK Stabiliser)

Joy & King Ltd, 6 Wooburn Industrial Park, Wooburn Green, High Wycombe, Buckinghamshire, HP10 0PF (Wholesale distributors of caravan accessories)

JV Water Treatment, Welsh Street, Chepstow, Gwent, NP6 5LL (Manufacturers of IMI combined water filter/ultra violet purifier)

Karcher (UK) Ltd, Karcher House, Beaumont Road, Banbury, Oxfordshire, OX16 7TB (Manufacturers of high pressure water cleaners)

Kawasaki Motors (UK) Ltd, 1 Dukes Meadow, Millboard Road, Bourne End, Buckinghamshire, SL8 5XF (Manufacturers of portable generators)

Knauss Caravans Concessionaires (UK) Ltd, 267-269 Kennington Lane, London, SE11 5QU (Caravan importers)

Knott (UK) Ltd, Europa House, Wharf Road, Burton on Trent, Staffordshire, DE14 1PZ (Distributors of brakes, hitches, and undergear)

Lab-Craft Ltd, Bilton Road, Waterhouse Lane, Chelmsford, Essex, CM1 2UP (Manufacturers of lamp units, TP2 battery box and other accessories)

Lamplas (Durham) Ltd, Pont Factory, Leadgate, Consett, County Durham, DH8 6LA (Manufacturers of Lamplas GRP locker boxes)

Leisure Accessories Ltd, Britannia Works, Hurricane Way, Airport Industrial Estate, Norwich, NR6 6EY (Distributors of Shurflo diaphragm water pumps and Qest rigid tube plumbing)

Leisure Crafts Ltd, Much Wenlock, Shropshire, TF13 6DH (Manufacturers of Bulldog Stabilisers, Carasafe and Security Locks)

Lucas Electrical Ltd, Parts & Service Division, Great Hampton Street, Birmingham, B18 6AU (Manufacturers of electrical towing accessories: relays, lamps)

Lunar Caravans Ltd, 6 Sherdley Road, Lostock Hall, Preston, Lancashire PR5 5JF (Caravan manufacturer)

LV Motors Ltd, 1, Royston Road, Baldock, Hertfordshire, SG7 6NT (Manufacturers of Aerogen windchargers)

Mardon Caravans, Riding Caravans Ltd, The Workshops, Forkerleys, Burstwick, Hull, HU12 9HA (Caravan manufacturer)

Marlec Engineering Co. Ltd, Unit K, Cavendish Courtyard, Sallow Road, Corby, Northamptonshire, NN17 1DZ (Manufacturers of Rutland Windcharger)

Maxview Aerials Ltd, Setchey, Kings Lynn, Norfolk, PE33 0AT (Manufacturers of omnidirectional TV aerials)

Monroe Auto Equipment (UK) Ltd, Rosemary House, Lanwades Business Park, Kennett, Newmarket, Suffolk, CB8 7PW (Distributors of Load leveller and Ride leveller shock absorbers)

Morco Products Ltd, Morco House, 59, Beverley Road, Hull, North Humberside, HU3 1XW (Manufacturers of water heaters, caravan step and accessories)

Munster Simms Engineering Ltd, Old Belfast Road, Bangor, County Down, Northern Ireland, BT19 1LT (Manufacturers of pumps, showers, taps and water systems)

The National Caravan Council, Catherine House, Victoria Road, Aldershot, Hants, GU11 1SS

National Inspection Council for Electrical Installation Contracting, (NICEIC) Vintage House, 36-37 Albert Embankment, London, SE1 7UJ (Certification to confirm a caravan is correctly wired for mains electricity)

Panasonic UK Ltd, Panasonic House, Willoughby Road, Bracknell, Berkshire, RG12 8FP (Manufacturers of cassette radios suitable for caravan operation)

PGR Products, 16 Crofton Road, Lincoln, LN3 4NL (Manufacturer of Winterwheels and other accessories)

Practical Caravan, Haymarket Publishing Ltd, 42 Hampton Road, Teddington, Middlesex, TW11 0JE

Primus Sievert UK Ltd, 9-11 Gleneldon Road, London, SW16 2AU (Distributors of Primus gas appliances, leak detectors, kitchen units)

Proctor and Gamble Ltd, (Health and Beauty Care), Egham, Surrey (Manufacturers of Milton Sterilising fluid)

Rabone Chesterman Ltd, Summer Hill Works, Camden Street, Birmingham, B1 3DB (Manufacturer of measuring and cutting scale for cutting carpet and veneer)

Remis UK, 1 Manor Close, Great Harrowden, Wellingborough, Northamptonshire, NN9 5AG (Distributor of Remis blinds)

Saltofix Ltd, 22 Mile Oak Industrial Estate, Maesbury Road, Oswestry, Shropshire, SY10 8HA (Manufacturers of hydraulic corner steadies)

Sanyo Marubeni (UK) Ltd, Sanyo House, Otterspool Way, Watford, WD2 8JX (Manufacturers of microwave ovens suitable for caravan use)

Shock Tactics Ltd, Unit 1, Livingstone House, Howard Street, Batley, West Yorkshire, WF14 6AA (Suppliers of M.A.D. and OSRAV auxillary coil spring kits)

Sprite Caravans, Sprite Leisure Group Ltd, The Oaks Business Park, Oaks Drive Fordham Road, Newmarket, Suffolk, CB8 7SX (Caravan manufacturer)

Sterling Roncraft Consumer Services Department, 15 Churchfield Court, Churchfield, Barnsley, S70 2LJ (Manufacturers of Colron wood dye and Ronseal varnishes)

Swift Caravans, Swift Group Ltd, Dunswell Road, Cottingham, Hull North Humberside, HU16 4JS (Caravan manufacturer)

Sypsal Holdings Ltd, Cockshutt Lane, Broseley, Shropshire, TF12 5JA (Manufacturers of aluminium chassis)

Tabbert Caravans, Tabbert (UK) Ltd, PO Box 668, Denbigh, Clwyd, LL16 4AQ (Caravan importer)

Thetford Ltd, Unit 6, Centrovell Estate, Caldwell Road, Nuneaton, Warwickshire, CV11 4UD (Manufacturers of caravan toilets and chemicals)

Tornado Power Systems, Yew Tree House, Main Street, Tingewick, Buckinghamshire, MK18 4NL (Manufacturers of mains inverters)

Triflow Lubricant is now available from any branch of Wyko-EWB, whose head office is: Queens Cross, Dudley, West Midlands, DY1 1QW

Trophy Caravans, Orchard Mill, Westhead Road, Croston, Nr. Preston, Lancashire, PR5 7R (Caravan manufacturer)

Trylon Ltd, Thrift Street, Wollaston, Northamptonshire, NN9 7QJ (Suppliers of polyster resins and fibre glass materials)

Tyron UK Ltd, PO Box 38, Thame, Oxfordshire, OX9 2PH (Distributor of the Tyron Safety band)

U-POL Polyester Repair Paste, Denington Industrial Estate, Wellingborough, Northamptonshire, NN8 2QS (Manufacturers of U-POL Repair Paste)

Vanroyce Caravans Ltd, Gillibrands Road, Gillibrands Industrial Estate, Skelmersdale, Lancashire, WN8 9TR (Caravan manufacturer)

W4 Ltd, Unit B, Ford Lane Industrial Estate, Arundel, West Sussex, BN18 0DF (Distributor of mastic sealing strip and caravan accessories)

Witter Towbars, Chester, CH1 3LL (Manufacturers of towbars and accessories)

Wolfcraft UK, Sales & Marketing, 39 Walnut Tree Lane, Sudbury, Suffolk, CO10 6BD (Distributor of tools and accessories)

Woodfit Ltd, Kem Mill, Whittle le Woods, Chorley, Lancashire, PR6 7EA (Distributors of kitchen accessories, hinges and woodworking ironmongery)